Advance praise for *Wome*

"Virginia Woolf once declared that women need to develop the habit of freedom. We are not in the habit of making the connection between self-esteem and dignity, activism, or personal freedom. For that, we need the fire of inspiration. But it's right there, in the common experiences we share, in our common desire to act as if everything we do matters. And it's right here in the pages of *Women of Spirit.* Maybe you'll recognize the woman you are, maybe you'll find the woman you want to be. Either way, these stories will inspire you."

— Anita Roddick OBE, founder, The Body Shop

"Katherine Martin weaves together a bounty of soulful stories from women whose lives beautifully demonstrate having heeded that 'still small voice' within. By entering into these pages, men, too, will be transformed by the power and the courage of the feminine spirit."

— Ayman Sawaf, executive EQ,
Emotional Intelligence in Leadership Organizations

"Encouraging and enlightening. A book every woman should make time for."

— Lata Ryan, executive producer of feature films and television programs, including *Grosse Pointe Blank, The Proposition, The X-Files, Monkeybone,* and *The One*

"*Women of Spirit* inspires us to take a stand and make a difference in the world around us. Katherine Martin also helps us bravely face those daily, less spectacular, challenges in our personal lives, difficulties which can be the hardest, and most important, to surmount. This book's personal stories of women who reached for the stars shows us that we can do the same!"

— Francesca De Grandis, author of *Be a Goddess!*

"*Women of Spirit* makes me proud to be a woman. I absolutely love it. I wish it was required reading for all children so that they would allow their own inner inspirations to come forward. By following the guidance from our inner voice, we can change the world."

— Echo Bodine, author of *Echoes of the Soul* and *A Still, Small Voice*

"To continue our personal work to make this a better world, we must on occasion be re-energized and re-charged. We need to be reminded that our actions matter... that as individuals we have the power within us to transform others and society. That's what *Women of Spirit* did for me."

— Mike Lindberg, chair, Oregon Arts Commission

"*Women of Spirit* shows us what is possible when we face and move through our fears. What we, as women, can achieve. These stories made me stop and think about my own courage and about the courage of my mother and of other women who came before her. I am proud of us all. This book will shine a light on your own courage and your own beauty."

— Simone Angel, MTV Europe veejay

"Once again, Katherine has struck gold in her quest to find nuggets of wisdom and inspiration to share. Each story is personal, nearly private, and unearths experiences that brought both smiles and tears to this reader. This book left me to ponder and plan on how I might contribute more effectively to the healing of humanity."

— Rev. George McLaird, author of *Marriage Maze* and *Transformation Is an Inside Job*

"Katherine Martin's new book, *Women of Spirit,* is a rich and unprecedented compilation of true-life stories of courage and hope. Guided by spirit, these remarkable women took risks and persevered in the face of tremendous obstacles — personal challenges, fear, criticism, hatred, and social injustices — in order to stay true to their hearts' wisdom and offer their authentic selves and gifts to the world. Their triumphs not only brought about great personal peace and fulfillment, but also introduced positive changes that have impacted the lives of many others. A 'must read' for the courageous spirit residing within us all!"

— Valerie Rickel, founder, SoulfulLiving.com

MAY 2005

Mom -
This book reminded me of you!
You are such a beautiful,
courageous woman.
Hope you enjoy it!

WOMEN OF SPIRIT

I love you,
Ang

Women of Spirit

Stories of Courage from the Women Who Lived Them

Katherine Martin

Book II in Katherine Martin's *People Who Dare*™ Series

New World Library
Novato, California

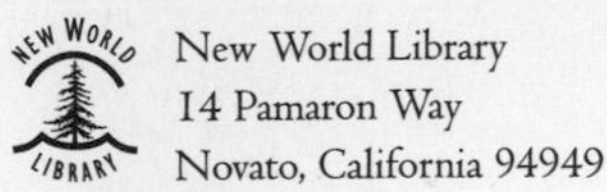
New World Library
14 Pamaron Way
Novato, California 94949

Cover design: Mary Ann Casler
Cover illustration: Roxanna Villa
Text design: Mary Ann Casler

Grateful acknowledgment is made for the use of the following: Reprinted with the permission of Scribner, a Division of Simon and Schuster, Inc., from *The Same River Twice: Honoring the Difficult* by Alice Walker. Copyright © 1996 by Alice Walker. Dai Qing's story was translated by Nancy Hearst (librarian at the John King Fairbank Center for East Asian Research, Harvard University), Nancy Liu (professional translator and writer and doctoral student at Columbia University), Peter Rand (author of *China Hands,* Simon & Schuster, 1996), and Professor Lawrence R. Sullivan (associate professor at Adelphi University, New York, and research associate, East Asian Institute, Columbia University). It is adapted from the story that first appeared in the journal "Chinese Studies in Philosophy" 27, no. 2 (winter 1995–1996): 50–60, from publisher M. E. Sharpe. Gabrielle Strong's poem first appeared in *Strawberry Songs,* an anthology of Native American poetry, put together by the Red School House.

Library of Congress Cataloging-in-Publication Data
Women of spirit : stories of courage from the women who lived them / [edited by] Katherine Martin.
p. cm. — (People who dare series ; bk. 2)
ISBN 1-57731-149-3 (pbk. : alk. paper)
1. Women social reformers—United States—Biography. 2. Women—United States—Biography. I. Martin, Katherine. II. Series.
HQ1412 .W657 2001
305.4'092'273—dc21 2001003011

First printing, October 2001
ISBN 1-57731-149-3
Printed in the Canada on acid-free, recycled paper
Distributed to the trade by Publishers Group West

10 9 8 7 6 5 4 3 2 1

To my mother-in-law
Joan Hixon Martin,
explorer

I've often felt that to my family, I have sometimes been a curious, even miraculous, stranger. Forging ahead, insisting this is wonderful, that is okay, love is the main thing, freedom is great, while they have waited for me to trip over my optimism and fall on my face in disillusionment. This could still happen, of course. But it will have to happen as a consequence of my being who I truly am. For that great gift, that I am me: with this spirit, this hair, this skin, this fluid, whole sexuality, this vision and this heart, I dare not apologize. I am too grateful. One of the last things my mother said coherently to me before she died, while looking at me as if seeing me for the first time (also a possibility), was "You a little mess, ain't you." Meaning someone selfish enough to fully express her being. We looked deep into each other's eyes. I said, "Yes."

Alice Walker, *The Same River Twice*

TABLE *of* CONTENTS

Inspired to Take a STAND

Inspired to Be YOU

Inspired to CHALLENGE

Inspired to PERSIST

Acknowledgments

In speaking of spirit and courage, I honor with bone-deep gratitude:

My husband and partner, Franc Sloan, whose deep work on the courage projects is mostly apparent to me and who, with my son, Benjamin Martin, have shown me the courage to love and be loved more deeply than I ever thought possible. They continue to teach and thrill me with who they are and who they are becoming.

My parents, Virginia and Stuart Lane, whose constant love and support has always been the wind at my back and whose love and happiness together is the stuff of sweet inspiration.

My sister, Nancy, who has always been my hero, a courageous woman whose integrity, wisdom, and compassion stand out and whose gifts arise in the things that matter most deeply.

To the women of this book, who so generously and openly told their stories. Thank you for daring to make maps, for challenging injustice, for speaking your truth, for doing the unexpected, for being authentic. In your presence, I am honored and drawn to be more. Although most of these stories I've written from interviews, several women sent me their own: thanks to Anne Firth Murray, Joanne Spencer, Carrie Barefoot Dickerson,

Susan Sweetser, Paula Brisker, Rayla Allison, Elaine Suranie, Candice Slaughter Warmke, Heffa Shücking, Dai Qing, Jean Griswold, Susan Vanderveen, and Gwendolyn Endicott.

To you, dear reader, whose courage and spirit I celebrate.

To my friend Judith Orloff, who championed this work from day one, who guided me along the way and is an ongoing source of inspiration and courage, whose words in the foreword to this book made me cry, and whose riveting story is in *Women of Courage.*

To Lisa Schneiderman, Joanne McCall, and Ken Sherman, who believed in this work and gave it wings.

To editorial director Georgia Hughes for sharing the vision and clarifying it with such keen insight. To Munro Magruder for his marketing wizardry. Also to Marjorie Conte and Monique Muhlenkamp in publicity. And to Marc Allen for publishing works that matter. To everyone at New World Library who worked on this book in some capacity.

To Ellen Pack, Lisa Stone, Lisa Kinne, and all the crew at women.com who saw the vision and created a dynamic cauldron of courage online: Marcia Whyte, Shari Noland, Audie Marks, WebbieGirl, Arnetta, Marcia McIntosh, Melinda Vasil, Melinda Iverson, Naomi Mendelshon, Ruth Cox, Kate Hoepke.

To A.T. Birmingham, who, through two books, has generously connected me with daring women, "longnecks" of the Giraffe Project in Langley, Washington, which honors people who stick their necks out for the common good. And likewise to the Goldman Environmental Fund, the world's largest prize program honoring grassroots environmentalists.

To my friend Kelly Stone for her loving and generous support of this work. To Herb Hamsher for his clarity and deep insight. To Paul Bassis for watching after Julia Butterfly and getting me 180 feet up Luna via portable phone. To Joanne Astrow for connecting me with Margaret Ensley.

And to my pal Shari Walker: the braces are off!

To Louanne Moldovan, theater director and founder of Cygnet Theatre, for bringing *Women of Courage* to the stage in a way that continues to move audiences to the bone. To the actresses who embody the women of courage: Wendy Westerwelle, Vana O'Brien, Luisa Sermol, Kate Hawkes, Dawn Leonetti, and Victoria Parker. And to the women whose lives they portray: Fanchon Blake, Dr. Elizabeth Newhall, Becky Black, Jennifer Jako, and Patty Rosen. And to my friend Amy Archer for her beautiful passion for the material and for her generosity in bringing it to the attention of the right people. To Alan Nause of Artists Repertory Theatre, Lark Palma of the Catlin Gabel School, Deborah Evind of Portland Community College, and others who have brought *Women of Courage* to their theaters and schools.

To Debra Evans of Whole Life Expo, for her faith in me and for her tireless work in creating *Women of Courage* events. And to Rowan Gabrielle and Nick Hart-Williams and Halla Ayla and Ayman Sawaf for bringing a grand vision to Whole Life Expo.

To Deepak Chopra for bringing *Women of Courage* to the Chopra Center.

To Harvey Kahn for connecting me to Judy Collins. To Vicky Davies and her folks Dorothy and Julian for courage sleuthing that led me to Susan Point.

To graphic designer John Burton and Kurt Lammers and the advertising genius of Loren Weeks and Dave Bronson at their firm, BLW & Associates in Portland, Oregon.

And to the following people who helped in one way or another with individual stories: Alex Morgan, executive assistant to Iyanla Vanzant and Bernadette Griggs, her personal assistant; Lutzie Mason, assistant to Joan Borysenko; Katherine DePaul, president of Judy Collins's company, Rocky Mountain Productions, and to Bridget Maybury; Geraldine Ferraro's assistant, Mary; Ginger Hendricks, executive assistant to Mary Manin

Morrissey; SARK's business partner, Adrienne Steele; and Professor Lawrence Sullivan for his patience and attention to detail in bridging me to Dai Qing.

To Jill Lawrence, Nancy Lee, and Donna Wick and to all the radio and television hosts who have spread women of courage stories during the past year. To Kim Ode of the *Minneapolis Tribune,* Chris Cunningham, Jan Mitchell, and others who have captured this work in articles and reviews. To Drew Marchman, Kay DeMartini, Barbara Kelly, and other events coordinators who have hosted *Women of Courage* at bookstores around the country. And to the women at Mills, Lewis & Clark, and Augustana Colleges, whose exuberance, confidence, and commitment to live lives that matter created lively and meaningful dialogues and gave me a new hope for the future.

And to everyone at Publisher's Group West who champions this work.

Thank you.

Foreword

"When spirit knocks on your door, you don't have to be 100 percent there — if you open the door just a crack, then spirit will flood in. You don't have to be totally enamored with spirit or totally believe in what's happening. If your heart is just a little bit open and you're just a little bit willing, spirit begins to work on you."

The spirit of the feminine is being reborn. As women, our voices are growing strong. Our intuition is astute, our resolve powerful. Courage is at our core. This book is a tribute to the inspiring, courageous acts of the women in these pages. But this book is not only about them — it's also about us. As we celebrate their courage, we must also claim it for ourselves.

In our culture, we have come to equate courage with acts of bravery involving great physical risk. Typically, courage is portrayed as larger than life — which makes it hard to relate to and intimidating. We neglect to acknowledge how each day, in large and small ways, we are all courageous: when we take a stand for our beliefs, follow our hearts, treat someone with compassion, refuse to tolerate abuse or mistreatment. *Women of Spirit* is our wake-up call to become empowered and to take responsibility for the light we all shine so brightly.

As a psychiatrist and an intuitive, I work with patients every day to help them summon the courage to find and live by their authentic inner voices. This work is especially important to me because, as a child, my intuitive voice was not honored by my physician parents. Though my parents were deeply loving people, they revered science and the intellect — not intuition. It took me years to gain the courage to speak out, to allow my intuition full creative expression in my medical practice and personal life. As a result, I received the greatest gift of my life. From my own experience, I realize that courage isn't always easy. But when we fight for what is most true in ourselves, we set our spirits free. Everyone deserves such freedom. The stories of the women you will read about can show you how.

These women are my heroes. They exemplify dramatic, public kinds of courage, as well as the private, internal, and spiritual kinds. It takes courage for a Harvard professor to leave her secure faculty position and listen to an inner calling to pioneer the new mind-body-spirit field. It takes courage to leave an abusive relationship. To expose sexual harassment. It takes courage to make public the slave conditions in garment sweatshops and demand accountability from manufacturers and retailers. To fight for gun legislation when your son is murdered at his school. It takes courage to leave a fast-track glamorous job in search of the soul. Katherine Martin, the brilliant, loving author and editor of this book, is also my hero. For years, she's devoted her time and passion to disseminating the powerful stories of women in a still largely patriarchal world. I want to acknowledge her courage and the worth of her unswerving mission.

Courage rises up to meet us when we attend to something deep inside of us. It is within our reach if we just listen.

In the quiet moments of our lives lies courage.
In the everyday steps we take is courage.
In love is courage.
In being different dwells courage.
In the cry against injustice lives courage.
In stepping up to responsibility lies courage.
In reaching out to others is courage.

If I've learned anything about courage and intuition it is that they demand that we live in the moment without preconceptions of how life should be. Doing so may mean that we go against what the majority opinion says and follow our hearts. Or it may mean taking the road less traveled. Relatives, friends, and colleagues may try to talk us out of our convictions. This was my experience. They may criticize, dismiss, or mock us. Our challenge — and it is a worthy one! — is to stay true to our beliefs and to fiercely lead our lives according to our inner truth. I am a strong proponent of nonconformity; it liberates us from peer or societal pressure so we may be free to live an authentic and uniquely self-styled life.

There is something magical about starting a new book. You are about to embark on an amazing journey. Relish the stories you will read and take them to heart. Allow them to dazzle and move you. Then apply what you've learned to your own lives. Take risks. Make changes. Be everything you were meant to be. Don't let anyone keep you small. Embrace your own courage and soar!

Judith Orloff, M.D.
Author of *Dr. Judith Orloff's Guide to Intuitive Healing* and *Second Sight*
Los Angeles, California

Prelude

Claiming Courage, Breathing Spirit

"You gain strength, courage, and confidence by every experience in which you really stop to look fear in the face. You must do the thing which you think you cannot do."

— Eleanor Roosevelt

This is a book about courageous women, women of spirit.

Are they any different from me or you? As people are naturally, uniquely different, of course. But do they have some courage gene that you and I do not possess? No. Courage is in us all, waiting to be claimed, to be stepped into, to be lived. We need but answer the call. That call often comes from deep within the recesses of our soul, a stirring of our spirit. *Step up. Be heard. Be seen. Your life matters.*

We may not listen to that calling, we may not want to hear it. Sometimes we deny our courage when we're afraid of being afraid. When we wince at making mistakes, at being wrong. When we guard ourselves so carefully that we avoid being seen, really seen, outside a preconceived notion of who we're supposed to be or what we're supposed to do. The women in this book are seen for who they are. They stand out. They have the capacity to let life get messy, knowing the power of chaos and trusting that out of chaos comes order, often divine order, and I use that word *divine* in the broadest sense to mean the sacred beyond us. They have developed keen intuition and listen to it carefully, even if it appears to make no sense. They can live with the irrational, the illogical. They pay attention to synchronicities.

These women also have opinions and don't mind letting you know about them, sometimes very publicly, as in the case of Penny Harrington, the first female chief of police in a major city. Other times those opinions come from deeply private experiences, as in the case of SARK, who created a mini-empire with books like *Living Juicy* and *Succulent Wild Woman.* "I can't imagine not living authentically and speaking my mind," she says as we talk about the great risk, the great fear, of exposing sexual abuse in her family, and of revealing it in this book when her public image is so steeped in the "magic cottage with fairy dust and snails and a little trail of cats following her."

These women have strong principles and values, and they'll risk much to stand by them. They have great character and integrity. Some of them risk their lives to break down prejudice, racism, and hate and do so selflessly.

At times, spirit runs through us with a kind of graced innocence. Julia Butterfly Hill climbed 180 feet up a thousand-year-old redwood as part of what began as an Earth First! tree-sit. Was she afraid? You bet. But she had had a spiritual awakening in an ancient-growth forest, and she was following a call, a passion. Her commitment to that calling kept her up in Luna during some of the worst winter storms along the northern California coast, being whipped around for sixteen hours in ninety-mile-an-hour winds and fearing for her life, until she began to hear the voice of Luna. For two years, she stayed in Luna, creating an indomitable environmental legacy. She told me her story by portable phone while she was still 180 feet up, getting thrashed by the wind but also enchanted by nature. "Oh, wow, beautiful, hold on for a sec," she said during our interview, "I haven't seen a bird that like, ever."

I started this study of courage seven years ago while working on what would become, for me, a surprisingly intimate book, *Women of Courage.* In the beginning, my focus was on the obvious: those larger-than-life kinds of courage. It took a Polar explorer telling me that leading the first all-women's expedition to the South pole wasn't courageous to rattle my mind-set. I was interviewing her precisely because she fit my definition of courage, which was the one held predominantly in our culture: doing something against all odds at great physical risk. Climbing the highest mountain. Crossing the unfordable river. Ann Bancroft had been to both poles and was a legend in her own time.

"To be honest, Katherine, that wasn't courageous for me," she said at what I thought was the end of our interview but turned out to be just the beginning.

What on earth?

"In those wild, open places is where I find myself," she went on, "that's where I'm at home, where I'm at peace."

But . . .

"Let me tell you about being dyslexic at a time when there wasn't much known about it." Ann had a dream of being an elementary school teacher. When her college counselor said to her, "Give it up, your grades stink, get a B.A. and go on with your life," Ann was stunned. Standing up to this intimidating authority figure and saying, "You don't understand, that B.A. means nothing to me if I can't teach" was Ann's defining moment of courage. When her advisor tried to get her to buckle down, give up her sports, hit the books — thinking Ann was just a jock — she stood her ground. Sometimes our greatest courage is knowing who we are and being true to that. Ann did just that: "Sports is where I get the confidence to face the difficulty of the academics. I won't give it up."

It took Isabel Allende answering all my questions about that dangerous, terrifying time in Chile after the bloody coup in which her uncle was brutally murdered, a time when though at great risk she went on missions to take to safe houses and embassies people who otherwise would have been tortured and killed as political prisoners...answering all those questions and then getting up from the couch on which we sat in her Bay Area studio, crossing the room, and saying, "Yes, but that wasn't courageous for me. The time that required the most strength and courage was the illness and death of my daughter, Paula."

I have been humbled time and again during these last seven years, as I see and hear and feel the profound power of quiet courage. It's found in the exhalation of love. In forgiving. In caring with an intensity of compassion that makes the impossible possible. Quiet courage is traveling to the edge of reality as we know it to peer on the divine. It's in facing truth when what we see makes us shudder.

Quiet courage is often unwitnessed, with no bells and whistles, no fanfare. Instead, it is startlingly intimate and vulnerable. Joan Borysenko talks about the final hours with her mother in the hospital. "I asked her something that I normally wouldn't have had the guts to bring up, something that was completely out of character for me...for just the briefest moment, I got bold, perhaps because we had had a touching moment of forgiveness." Sitting at her mother's bedside, she said, "Mom, I'd like to exchange a soul quality with you. When I look at you, the quality I see more than anything else is courage. And I feel that I'm totally lacking in courage. Would you make me a gift of your courage?" Her mother, not one to share her inner life, turned to her and said, "Well, the soul quality that I see the most in you is compassion. And when I look at my life, I feel that's what I've lacked."

Shortly after, her mother slipped into a coma. In the middle of the night, meditating at her bedside, Joan had a vision of going into the light with her as she died. "I saw everything about the meaning of our lives together. It was the most extraordinary experience. With clarity, I saw the great circularity of the moment, that she had given birth to me physically and now I was helping to birth her soul back to another realm. It was perfectly divine how we had helped and aided each other."

In the deepest spiritual breaths we take comes courage. A far cry from bravado, it derives from the French word *coeur,* meaning heart. And, yes, courage is always a matter of the heart. Courage is a matter of people claiming themselves, bone deep. It's about people demanding that freedom for others as well. It is loud and noisy and messy and mouthy. It is also quiet and intimate and vulnerable and fragile. What a paradox. Courage takes us far and wide into the very meaning of life.

In her book *Anything We Love Can Be Saved: A Writer's Activism,* Alice Walker writes, "There is always a moment in any kind of struggle when one feels in full bloom. Vivid. Alive. One might be blown to bits in such a moment and still be at peace.... To be such a person or to witness anyone at this moment of transcendent presence is to know that what is human is linked, by a daring compassion, to what is divine. During my years being close to people engaged in changing the world, I have seen fear turn into courage. Sorrow into joy. Funerals into celebrations. Because whatever the consequences, people, standing side by side, have expressed who they really are, and that ultimately they believe in the love of the world and each other enough *to be that.*"

One of our great myths about courageous people is that they're fearless. To the contrary, from what I've seen and heard, courageous people are filled with fear. The difference is what they do with their fear, how they use it to get where they're going. Rather than letting fear numb, paralyze, or hold them back, they look it square in the eye, asking, What is this fear made of? Am I bigger than it? Can I walk through it or around it? Can I use it to motivate me? Fear turns into courage.

Seven years after that first book, my understanding of courage has changed significantly. I've learned these truths, and more: Courage is doing that which you think you cannot do but know you must. Courage is being true to who you are. Courage is being willing to be wrong, to fail, to make mistakes, in the pursuit of what's right. Courage is living a life that does not compromise who you are and what you believe.

The women in these pages will captivate you. Some of their stories will make your hair stand on end. Some will cause you to weep. Some will fire passion in you. Most of all, let them change you. Let them get under your skin so that courage and spirit begin to breathe in the very fiber of your being.

The Hazel Wolf Story
A Courageous Life Lived

"I decided I'd had enough of this supposed monster. I could and would not put up with it any longer."

Hazel Wolf was born in Victoria, Canada, in 1898. In her twenties, she came to the United States and began a life of activism that would earn her a plethora of environmental and humanitarian awards. At age 101, she was still going strong. Only a broken hip kept her from joining street demonstrations in the fall of 1999 during the World Trade Organization meetings in Seattle, where she lived.

Hazel laid the groundwork for Native American tribes and environmental groups to talk with one another, share concerns, and find common ground on issues affecting the environment. She coordinated actions of Northwest environmentalists and Native American tribal leaders, traveling through the Pacific Northwest logging region and urging environmentalists and forest workers to lobby together for funds to retrain workers. She also took medical supplies to Nicaragua and used her ninetieth birthday as an opportunity to hold a fundraiser for medical equipment for that country.

My father wrote on the back of a photograph of me standing inside my crib: "Sow the wind and reap the whirlwind." I must have been a handful.

The traditional ways to discipline children in those days were to spank them, not to draw blood, but more or less gently with a slipper applied to the bottom; and to scare the wits out of the young culprits by threatening them with a bogeyman if they don't shape up.

My parents used these traditional methods, which were not frowned on in those less kind and gentle times. I was about five years old. I don't recall in what way I had annoyed my mother, but she resorted to the second option. It was night, and a stormy one, and she told me that the bogeyman was outside on the porch with a big sack to take me away if I didn't mind her. It was then that I decided I'd had enough of this supposed monster. I could and would not put up with it any longer, big sack or no big sack. I went to the door and opened it, and the bogeyman wasn't there! *Now that took courage.* I'll never forget that night.

I learned something important that night, and I've been guided by it through the 101 years of my life, especially in my civil liberties work, which preceded my becoming an environmentalist. Life can be dangerous for even the most sheltered of women, and it's good to have that sense of freedom that comes with knowing, as early as possible, that the bogeyman isn't there — well, hardly ever.

Hazel was awarded the State of Washington Environmental Excellence Award in 1978 and was named Conservationist of the Year by the National Audubon Society in 1985. She received a citation for environmental work from the Washington State Legislature in 1988 and was named "environmental angel of the first order" in 1992 by the Washington Environmental Council. In 1995, she won the Washington Physicians for Social Responsibility's Paul Beeson Peace Award "for her lifelong dedication to peace and preservation of the environment" and was

made an honorary vice president of the Sierra Club, which she "treasures." She helped to found twenty-one of the twenty-six Audubon Society chapters in the Pacific Northwest. Washington's governor proclaimed March 10 as Hazel Wolf Day and, on June 15, 1997, Seattle University paid tribute to her with an honorary doctorate degree. Shortly thereafter, a 116-acre marsh was set aside in perpetuity and named the Hazel Wolf Wildlife Preserve.

When Hazel turned one hundred, seven hundred people celebrated with her, as the "Kids for the Environment" Fund was established, honoring her life-long advocacy for children and the natural world. She was still secretary of the Seattle chapter of the Audubon Society, a post she had held for thirty-seven years. In January of 2000, with her family by her side, Hazel passed away, having lived another of her dreams, to see the twenty-first century. In their obituary, the Sierra Club noted that Hazel had touched many people with lessons such as: 1) Live simply and with purpose. 2) Have courage, have fun, and find common ground. 3) Open doors for young people. 4) Challenge complacency. 5) VOTE!

Inspired to Do the UNEXPECTED

Joan Borysenko

"My children were suffering, my marriage was suffering. And, once again, my inside wasn't matching my outside. . . . Yet I couldn't get myself to leave. If I jumped ship at age forty-two, that was it for me. I'd never get back into an academic environment. And I'd have given up over twenty years of fussing and scraping and competing in order to do what I wanted. . . . If I left [Harvard], no one would ever listen to me again. I'd wither up in the suburbs, all alone and with nobody listening."

Joan Borysenko, Ph.D., is one of the most prominent figures on the mind-body landscape, blending science, medicine, psychology, and spirituality in the service of healing. At one time a cancer researcher, she holds three postdoctoral fellowships from Harvard and cofounded the mind-body clinical program at Beth Israel/Deaconess Medical Center in Boston.

It's hard for me to look though the threads of my life for a courageous moment. What on earth would that be?

I was a pathologically shy child, practically crippled with fear. I had to rehearse speaking to people, going over and over a simple statement before I could make it. I never ate in front of people — that would have been much too embarrassing. And I've always feared doing the wrong thing, making the wrong choice, disappointing people. My life has been marked by things that I felt called to do, even though I was in some terrible state of fear. So mine is a wimpy story. To this day, I am painfully introverted, a rather odd thing for a person who travels the world two hundred days a year lecturing to thousands of people, looking for ways to build bridges and to inspire people to reach deep inside themselves for what is meaningful and kind and good in their lives. I'm a much better candidate for what I did in the earlier part of my career, which was being locked up in a laboratory with my microscope.

I started on the path to that microscope when I was ten.

In the fifth grade, I had a terrifying nightmare in which my family and I were in a jungle with headhunters chasing us and booby traps, snakes, and scorpions all around. When I awoke, I was literally in a psychotic state; I couldn't tell the dream from real life. I was absolutely sure that headhunters were chasing my family and would kill us all. I shook out my shoes, thinking scorpions were in them. Within days, I developed a second mental illness as a way of trying to cope with the first: obsessive-compulsive disorder. Excessive hand washing was just the beginning. During the next few months, I developed a dozen different ritual behaviors, such as reading upside down, backwards, and three times in a row. If I were interrupted in any of my rituals, I had to start over, because the rituals kept my family safe from horrors that only I could see, horrors that existed behind a thin veil in the unmanifest world. This was pretty potent stuff. I can't even begin to access the terror that I lived with during that time.

My parents were so distressed that they would cry themselves to sleep at night. I could hear them and began trying to hide my behavior, because now I needed to protect them not only from the headhunters, snakes, and scorpions but also from the pain of not being able to help me. In spite of my efforts, I'd often get sent home from school — like the time I hallucinated that headhunters were running down the hall, throwing poison darts at me, which, through the extraordinary power of the mind, actually produced red marks on my arms. Believe me, when you go to the school nurse with red marks on your arms and say, "I've been hit by poison darts," they send you home fast!

My parents took me to a psychiatrist who ran tests, but he didn't really know how to treat me. The odd thing about my behavior was that it seemed random. I had a beautiful childhood in Brookline, Massachusetts. My parents were very loving. I wasn't traumatized, molested, or bothered by anything in particular. I had it easy. The only upsetting thing in my very normal childhood was that we'd moved across town; that tells you something about how fragile I was in those days.

Inside the illness, however, was a gift: it drove me to do something I might never have done. I sat to pray. I did not come from a prayerful family. I came from an agnostic, culturally Jewish family. But when push comes to shove, it's a human tendency to pray, and those prayers are focused and deep. They gave me a definite sense that I could recover but that it would take an enormous act of will: I could never, ever do another one of those ritual behaviors, like reading upside down. And I knew, as surely as I knew my name, that if I ever did, I would stay stuck in that mental illness forever. As I prayed, a state of peace came over me, and a poem went through my head. In a funny way, it was a poem about courage. If I repeated the poem, instead of doing the rituals, maybe I'd be okay:

> Somewhere in the darkest night
> There always shines a little light
> This light up in the heavens shines
> To help our God watch over us

When a small child is born
The light, her soul, does adorn
But when our only human eyes
Look up in the lightless skies
We always know
Even though we can't quite see
That a little light burns far into the night
To help our God watch over us.

It was only a matter of days before I came back into my right mind. The nightmares stopped. The hallucinations stopped. I simply returned to normal. And nobody ever asked, "What happened?" I'm sure they were too terrified and thought, "My God, she seems okay, let's not rock the boat." My illness remained one of those deep, dark family secrets.

Throughout my life, when I feel overwhelmed, I repeat that poem. And it calms me.

Three things became clear to me as a result of that childhood experience: I wanted to understand the human mind and psychology; I wanted to understand the physical functions of the human brain, to know how it was possible that somebody could become crazy instantly and recover instantly; and I wanted to know more about God, spirituality, and inner knowing. I felt that my recovery was an answer to a prayer and that, somehow, I'd seen the face of God. My whole life would become a braid of these three strands: psychology, biology, and spirituality. That's where it started.

I thought I was on course when I went to Bryn Mawr College, to Harvard Medical School for a Ph.D. in medical sciences, followed by a postdoctoral fellowship there, and then to Tufts Medical School, climbing the academic ladder, starting as an assistant professor of anatomy and cell biology and eventually doing cancer research. I was bringing together the biology and the psychology. It was intellectually interesting. But the spark was missing — and that spark was spirituality.

I'd married at twenty-one, right out of college. I'd had a child in the second year of medical school. Now my marriage was failing. Stress was everywhere. I turned to meditation and yoga, and I began a spiritual search, which seemed so disparate from the cancer research.

My external life wasn't reflecting my internal life.

At that time, Herbert Benson was doing some of the first research that looked at the autonomic nervous system, at how behavior could regulate blood pressure. I had worked with him over the summer following my graduation from Bryn Mawr. Eventually, he would research meditation and what he called the "relaxation response" and I suddenly realized — *Aha! this is the kind of research I want to do.*

People thought I was absolutely nuts to consider working with Benson. I was about to be tenured at Tufts. I was doing important cancer research. I had lots of grant money and a great teaching record. I'd be leaving all this for a soft-money position, meaning that I'd have to write my own grants, I'd have no guarantee of a position beyond the one-year hire, and I'd be demoted to instructor rather than promoted to professor. It would be my second postdoctoral fellowship. Just to study meditation.

As I was contemplating this irrational decision, my father developed chronic lymphocytic leukemia. His case was virulent, and they put him on high doses of cortisone. Unfortunately, he was one of the unlucky few who suffer a side effect known as "manic psychosis." Having been the world's most patient, loving, listening, compassionate person, he became like a stranger inhabiting his own body with pressure of speech and flights of ideas, making it impossible to talk to him. It was excruciating to watch this drug disappear him. His body was alive, but his soul was dead.

My mother and I kept speaking to the doctors, trying to find an alternative way to deal with the cancer. They'd say, "Look, if we take him off the drug, the cancer cells will proliferate, and he'll die." So we became stuck in that bind of quality of life versus quantity of life. When someone isn't in their right mind, the family has to choose for them. And that's a terrible burden, a terrible responsibility.

While we were dealing with this decision, my father had to have surgery to remove his spleen and was taken off the cortisone. Briefly, he came into his right mind. By this time, my parents had made the migration that Jews make from Boston to Florida, and I flew down for his spleenectomy. I found my father lucid and loving and thought, *Thank God, he has some good time left.* Two days after I returned home, I got a call at 6:00 in the morning. The following evening, my father had waited for my mother to fall asleep, put a chair underneath the window, and jumped. They were some thirty floors up. Apparently, it was his way of saving the family from further suffering.

Because I was the medical one in the family, I felt responsible for his death. I was a cancer-cell biologist and yet I had been of no use whatsoever. This haunted me, and I decided that doing research with cancer cells wasn't my calling. More important to me were the *people* with the cancer. If I could help even one family, then I would find some meaning in my father's terrible death.

As good fortune would have it, Benson had gotten his very first grant in a brand-new field called behavioral medicine. And I left my painfully secure tenure track at Tufts. By now I had divorced and remarried and had had another child. Going from a professor's salary to postdoctoral status was difficult. But it put me on track with my vision.

I was at Harvard from 1978 to 1988, and during that time, I won the Medical Foundation Fellowship for what amounted to a third postdoctoral fellowship in a field called psychoneuroimmunology. I also managed to get licensed as a clinical psychologist and, by 1980, to start a mind-body clinic with Benson and an Israeli psychiatrist named Ilan Kutz. This practice became the biggest part of my personal growth. Every week, I worked with three or four different groups of people with various illnesses, starting with cancer but eventually including AIDS and other stress-related disorders.

Talk about courage. The people in those groups had it big time. Like the twenty-seven-year-old woman with stage-four Hodgkin's disease who had two young children and was so sick with chemotherapy that the only way she could manage was to put the two kids in the bathtub so she'd be next to the toilet to vomit. From these people, I learned a lot — how people make meaning out of their lives, how they find good things in bad circumstances, and how important we are to one another. What one person can't do alone can be done when several people come together, just from the goodness of their hearts and their desire to help.

People with serious illnesses tend to reflect on the big questions, the existential ones. "Am I just this body or, when I die, will there be something else?" And "If there's something else, what am I doing here on planet earth anyhow? What's the point of this? Is it to learn, is it a test, is there a heaven, is there a hell?" People start to wonder, "Was my life a success? Are there any loose ends?" Forgiveness becomes critical, not only of yourself but of other people, to making peace. In a certain way, I became, de facto, a pastoral counselor. Being with those groups was a blessed part of my life.

The other side of the story, however, was that I worked excessively and commuted an hour or two each way from the south shore into the center of the city. As associate director of the division of Behavioral Medicine, I was doing research, seeing individual patients, and running as many as five groups a week, sometimes into the evening. Each group was made up of twenty patients, and I had to know them all intimately, be keenly aware of their progress, and listen to their stories.

I was absolutely exhausted.

I had no life of my own, none whatsoever. My children were suffering. My marriage was suffering. And, once again, my inside wasn't matching my outside, because what interested me the most was the spiritual dimension of the work and for me to be explicit about that dimension wasn't appropriate in that medical environment.

Yet I couldn't get myself to leave. If I jumped ship at age forty-two, that was it for me. I'd never get back into an academic environment. And I'd have given up more than twenty years of fussing and scraping and competing to do what I wanted. How many people would have loved to be in my position at Harvard, even though I was only a lowly instructor in medicine? I could have stayed in that position indefinitely, gotten grants, run clinics. Who was I to throw it all up in the air saying, "Well it's not quite what I want to do; I'd rather be talking with people about meditation and spirituality"? My brother was flabbergasted: "You'd give up a real career to do that? How flaky! What a terrible risk!" And the egotistical, narcissistic part of my fear warned, "The only reason people listen to you is because you're at Harvard." I'd written a book, *Minding the Body, Mending the Mind,* which was based on our clinical program at Harvard. Unexpectedly, it became a best-seller and I was sure that it sold so well only because I was at Harvard. If I left, no one would ever listen to me again. I'd wither up in the suburbs, all alone and with nobody listening.

That was my state of mind when, one night during an evening program for AIDS patients, I said, "This might seem like a cheap shot, because you have something from which you could die soon and I'm healthy, but the truth is, none of us knows the moment of our death. It's one of those mysteries and surprises. We need to live every moment as if it could be our last and not be lulled into a sense of complacency that we have forever." By way of example, I said, "I could be in an accident on my way home tonight and die before you."

On my way home that night, I was in a head-on collision.

Fortunately, it wasn't at high speed and the other person suffered very minor injuries. I would have been fine, but the shoulder harness on my seat-belt didn't catch and my face slammed against the steering wheel. My nose opened up like the hood of a car and just about lifted off my face. I ended up in the hospital for five days for reconstructive surgery, and as I was lying there with my nose in a sling, I reflected on the fact that I'd just been given one big, fat cosmic punch in the nose — literally. If God had appeared in a burning bush, it couldn't have been more obvious. I could listen to my fear and perish — because I would surely die early doing my Harvard job. Or I could jump into the abyss, even though I had no other job lined up, even though I didn't know what would happen next.

I called from the hospital and gave my resignation.

Later, when I was researching *A Woman's Book of Life,* I discovered that what I went through was right on target for a woman in her forties. It's a time when we experience a movement toward integrity, toward authenticity. We're not young anymore, but we're not old either. And we start looking backward and looking forward, trying to make meaning out of where we've been and putting into perspective where we want to go. By then we know our weak points and our strengths, we know what gives us joy and what makes us dry up. And we know something about what we've been given to do in terms of service. I believe strongly that we all have some unique gift that we give to the world. It may not be a big thing. It may be the most ordinary thing. This is a time when we begin to reflect on how we give life to the world. What are our dreams and visions? What does life look like now? If we find that life is smaller than our vision, if the way we've arranged our lives blocks us from offering our gift, then we suffer enormous stress. I've heard it time and again from women who say things like, "I just knew if I didn't leave this job, I was going to die!" Or "If I stayed in this relationship, it would kill me!" It's remarkably visceral for women. "If I continue down this path, I'm going to lose tissue." And that's what was alive in me.

I have never been graceful about these kinds of changes. I have never said, "It's really clear that this is what I need to do next." I go kicking and screaming, which is another thing I discovered to be common among women. I often ask groups of women, "How many of you have stayed in a situation much longer than you should have because you were afraid? You knew it was time to leave, you were called to do something else, but you just couldn't mobilize." Almost every hand goes up. We stay too long. We stay out of compassion. We stay out of fear. We stay out of a hundred different motivations. We don't follow our hearts. And, in a way, you can say that courage — from the French root *coeur,* which means "heart" — is in following our hearts.

As it turned out, my transition to the work I'm doing now was much easier than I thought it was going to be. In reality, I had nothing to fear. I was already getting requests to lecture or give workshops, and the book was a best-seller, regardless of the reason. But fear blinds, and it kept me from seeing that I already had another career.

Going forward, the challenges I faced weren't about being credible or finding work, but about lifestyle. I travel half the year, and I have to get on an airplane no matter how I feel, whether I am sick, whether I'm well, whether I'm anxious, whether I'm peaceful. I have to meet a whole bunch of new people and stand up in front of thousands and say something. No matter what. Every time, I have to trust that what needs to be said is going to come out of my mouth, that I haven't been led all this way to simply fall on my face, that I can be of some use. And yet, every time I go on a trip, I think, *This time, I'm going to get up on stage, and I'm going to open my mouth and nothing is going to come out.*

Shortly after I left Harvard, my mother's health deteriorated. In what would be her last hour before slipping into a coma, I asked her something that I normally wouldn't have had the guts to bring up, something that was completely out of character for me. People often speak of things not normally spoken about when death is lingering, and, for just the briefest moment, I got bold, perhaps because we had had a touching moment of forgiveness. I said, "Mom, I'd like to exchange a soul quality with you. When I look at you, the quality I see more than anything else is courage. And I feel that I'm totally lacking in courage. Would you make me a gift of your courage?"

My mother, who was not an emotionally demonstrative person or someone who shared her inner life, turned to me and said, "Well, the soul quality that I see the most in you is compassion. And when I look at my life, I feel that's what I've lacked."

And so we had a moment in which we quietly exchanged these qualities with each other.

Shortly thereafter, she slipped into a coma. In the middle of that night, I was sitting at her bedside with my son, who was twenty. We were meditating, and simultaneously we had a vision of going into the light with mother as she died. In my vision, I saw everything about the meaning of our lives together. It was the most extraordinary experience. With clarity, I saw the great circularity of the moment, that she had given birth to me physically and now I was helping to birth her soul back to another realm. It was perfectly divine how we had helped and aided each other.

When I opened my eyes, nothing in the room was solid. Everything was made of light, and everything was interconnected. I looked across the bed at my son, and he was weeping. He looked at me and said, "Everything is made of light. The room is filled with light. Can you see it?"

"Yes."

"It's Grandma's last gift. She's holding open the door to eternity so that we can have a glimpse." He told me what had happened for him and then he said, "You must be so grateful to her."

"Yes," I said, "and in a way that I never was when she was alive."

"Your mother was a great being," he said, "because she played a part in life much smaller than who she really was. And she did it for you, so that you would have to resist her in order to develop the gifts that you have to give to other people."

The few days after a person dies are often filled with special gifts. I started to dream about my mother, and one dream stood out: I was in the mountains of Colorado, which is interesting because, at the time, I lived in the suburbs of Boston and hadn't yet moved to Colorado. In the dream, I was hiking and came across a door in a mountain, which looked liked the entrance to a café. I went in and found a group of older women, who told me it was a school for spies, that the meaning of *spy* was "to seek clearly," and that when you see things clearly, you have courage.

"This is what I need," I said. "I want to be part of your school for spies. I want to sign up."

So I signed up and took all the classes. The day of our final exam, I got separated from my class, because I'd stopped to play with a group of children. I went outside and saw a tree with a big hollow under it. What on earth was that? I had the feeling that it had something to do with the final exam, and I simply jumped into the abyss, not knowing where it would take me. Underneath me, a raft inflated, a yellow raft. Yellow was my mother's favorite color; the cover on her pillow when she died was all yellow roses. The raft inflated under me, and I zoomed through underground space, coming out, once again, into divine light.

When I awoke from the dream, my first instinct was that I had just gathered courage from my mother. I went into the kitchen to make my morning coffee. Oddly, a decal was stuck on the coffee machine. It looked like the Coca-Cola™ logo, swirly white letters on red. What a funny thing. I looked at it more closely. It wasn't the Coca-Cola™ logo at all. It said, "Courage."

I asked everyone in the house if they'd put it there, if they'd seen it before. No one had. It had just miraculously appeared. Years later, I heard someone talk about "apports from the Spirit World," through which things can manifest from another realm.

I called that decal my "red badge of courage." I wanted it to signal my permanent standing in the ranks of the courageous, meaning that life would be forever easy after that and I wouldn't struggle with the same old things with which I'd always struggled. But the fact is, life didn't magically get better. And I've come to appreciate that no magic moment will suddenly rid me of fear. That it takes courage every day to get up and live.

When people say to me, "Gee, Joan, you're so peaceful to be around. I'd like to be like you," I always say, "No you wouldn't. My inner life is not one of total peace. I've got all my difficulties and all my problems, and they're no different from yours." I know now that I'll never come to a moment of enlightenment in which the wisdom, the knowing, the love, the mercy, the compassion, are guaranteed to me. Maybe I'll get a glimpse of it or have the grace of an experience of it . . . but then life goes on. It's not the destination that matters but the joy you make along the way. And that was the gift of collecting my mother's courage, to see that this is what life is all about, that it simply takes courage to get up and live every day the very best that you can live it.

Joan has written eleven books, including the best-selling Minding the Body, Mending the Mind *as well as* A Woman's Book of Life *and* A Woman's Journey to God.

Mary Manin Morrissey

"Holding the energy of believing when nothing in the world confirms your belief is daunting. . . . I had to carve a deeper faith in myself than in the results."

Mary Manin Morrissey is founder and senior minister of Living Enrichment Center in Wilsonville, Oregon, serving almost four thousand people weekly. Her message is spread to more than a hundred countries through radio outreach as well as a nationally broadcast TV program that reaches eighteen million homes. Her latest book, No Less Than Greatness: Finding Perfect Love in Imperfect Relationships, *offers spiritual principles that help bring us closer to God, to ourselves, and to others. Her popular book* Building Your Field of Dreams *became a PBS documentary and has been used in churches across the country. Mary is a renowned humanitarian who has addressed the United Nations on non-violence and has worked with the Dalai Lama.*

My life was shaped by a moment in my youth that infused me with the knowledge of something greater than me, a recognition of the presence of life energy that's everywhere, always. I would draw on it not only to live but also to live bigger and truer to myself than I could ever have imagined.

I grew up in a *Leave It to Beaver* town, in a split-level home in the heart of middle-class America with doting parents and a shaggy dog. My junior year of high school started out predictably with my being elected class vice president, making the dance team, and being crowned homecoming princess. Perfect.

But then it all started to crumble when I missed my period.

Ten days after a doctor told me I was pregnant, I was sitting on a hard bench in a courtroom waiting for a judge to sign a marriage license. Abortion was out of the question. And unwed mothers lived in other peoples' towns, not ours. Nine months later, I gave birth to a baby boy. My young husband became a milkman to support us, and at night I finished school in the segregated high school for juveniles. Both of us had had dreams. Now I carried mine in my pocket in the form of a tattered piece of paper on which I'd written the single word *teacher* to remind myself of it.

Less than a year later, I collapsed with kidney failure and was given six months to live. My right kidney was gone, and the left one was failing quickly. The night before my surgery, a minister came to see me, Dr. Mila Warn. My mother-in-law had heard her preach and had asked her to visit me in the hospital. "You know, Mary," she said sitting at my bedside, "everything's created twice. First as a thought and then as a thing. When you're embarrassed, your face gets red. When you're scared, your hearts beats faster. And when you think toxic thoughts, your body gets toxic. Right now, your body is full of toxic energy. So what's been bothering you?"

Who was this woman? Toxic thoughts, toxic body? Never mind, it was the question, "What's been bothering you," that caught my attention. I told her about getting pregnant, about shaming myself, my family, my school. I hated myself for that, hated my body.

"Can you imagine that both your kidneys are healthy?" she asked after I'd unloaded.

I told her of course not. My right kidney was gone, I'd been told so, by the doctors.

"Okay. Then let's work with the possibility that, when they remove your right kidney tomorrow, everything that is toxic in you goes with it and that your body gets well, instead of getting worse."

During the next several hours that night, she and I imagined all my shame and guilt and diseased thoughts being swept into my right kidney. And then we focused on my left kidney being perfectly healthy. More important, we began to envision what my future would be.

That night, I chose life.

As the surgeons worked on me the next day, they were baffled. My left kidney had not a trace of disease.

My spiritual awakening had begun.

Before this experience, my gods had been the guys in the white coats with "M.D." following their names. The Minor Deities. Their word was *the* Word. They ran tests and assessed results. Now I recognized that a Higher Word was available and that, by accepting the diagnosis but not the prognosis, I had healed.

Very few people know when they're in their last week, their last day. We operate as if life is going to go on forever: "Someday, I'll do this" or "When I fill-in-the-blank, then I'll do that." But right now is the some day. Everything that makes life worthwhile is available today. Over time, I came to recognize that the people I admire because they seem to have such great lives are no less insecure than I. They have all the same challenges and difficulties. They don't go forward in the absence of fear, they go forward in its very presence.

Having been on a very short leash, I now wanted to know more: What am I a part of? What makes life meaningful? I didn't want to live a mediocre, skim-the-surface life. I wanted to go deep. And the place I started was

Christianity. I wanted to know everything I could about it. Eventually, I would also want to know about mysticism and ancient philosophy and psychology and the world's religions. In Aldous Huxley's *The Perennial Philosophy,* I began to see that one truth surfaces in all religions and philosophies: Life is good, and it's all about love. Loving your life, loving what you do, loving the people around you is what gives life meaning. From Lipke, I learned the difference between life happening to you and life happening *through* you; I learned that life is the projection of our own thinking.

Up to this point, my way of thinking had led me dangerously down a path toward death. Clearly, I needed a new way of thinking and people who would support me in a new way of living. I wanted to stop being someone who thought life was happening to her and start being someone through whom life was happening. No longer would I be the victim of my circumstances. I would choose the life I wanted to live, set my intention there, and with God working through me, bring it to fruition. But I couldn't ask God to do it all. It was up to me to choose, to make the commitment. To live on the growing edge, which meant always looking for what's most truthful, right, and life giving. That took courage. If I was stuck and unwilling, my dreams would be stuck. Even God can't steer a parked car.

I was on my way to becoming a minister.

After getting a degree in psychology, I followed my husband, Haven, into the seminary. I wanted to be a minister. In my last year, I received offers from three churches. It hadn't occurred to me to do anything other than work for a church. I wanted to be around people with whom I could practice the craft. I also wanted the support of being within a church system and, practically, I needed the security of a paycheck to help support our growing family.

A few months before graduation, I started getting this nudge to pioneer a work. I had never even thought about pioneering a work. It just sort of dropped in as an idea. I didn't know where it came from, but it shifted my thinking, even though I had not a clue how to do it.

Our lives are defined by the decisions we make and the direction we take. Where I went for guidance on this issue was critical. If I went only to the intellectual, factual, and rational, then circumstances would always define my decisions. If I went to the intuitive while also honoring the facts, then what I decided would be right, life giving, and truthful. In the end, the important questions were, "What seems most true? Most life giving? Most right?" Even though the church felt right in terms of economic responsibility, I had to follow the bigger vision of my ministry or I'd forever be operating out of compromise. And I just couldn't do that. I was too committed to a life connected to spirit and partnered with God.

We moved our family back to Oregon, to a family farm. With Haven's brothers joining us, we had great romantic notions of living off the land, of a life that would bring us closer to God. Never mind that none of us had ever farmed. We worked like dogs and lost ten thousand dollars the first year. On Sundays, we held services that no one attended. Even our closest friends began to think we were fooling ourselves.

Four years later, we had a congregation of fifty. The hall we rented cost twenty-five dollars; we paid for it by washing the floors and scrubbing the toilets. We set up an office and waited for somebody to call. Holding the energy of believing when nothing in the world confirms your belief is daunting. Was I really meant to pioneer a work? It certainly wasn't happening the way I had imagined. Tenaciously, I clung to the belief that I was on the right track, even though I didn't have any evidence in the world to substantiate it. During that time, I had to carve a deeper faith in myself than in the results.

Then suddenly, the church began to grow. For a good six years, it grew rapidly, until the congregation numbered about 1,800 people. We called ourselves the Living Enrichment Center, and, for Sunday service, we rented a movie theater in a mall in Beaverton, Oregon, where I grew up and lived that *Leave It to Beaver* life. To accommodate classrooms and offices, we rented twenty thousand feet of office space in the building next door.

On the church's ten-year anniversary in 1991, we held a visioning process in which each member wrote down his or her dream for the church on a card that we put in a time capsule to be opened in 2001. As I read the statements in the privacy of my office, it became very clear to me that the church wanted its own home. We no longer wanted our sanctuary to be a dark, dirty, sticky-floored theater smelling of popcorn.

And so the board and I began to envision building our own church in ten years. According to the architects, it would cost about fifteen million dollars. We had about forty thousand dollars — enough to make a down payment on bare land, which we could pay off over a period of three years while at the same time raising money. Once the land was paid for, we'd have equity to get the loans to build our church. It seemed possible. And it seemed doable in ten years.

As we worked, the board and I would imagine actually living our vision statement, which read, "We have a global headquarters. It's a beautiful home, a campus with landscaping that reflects God's beauty: trees, flowers, meditation gardens with benches, resting places, statues of holy people. Our home is large enough to meet the needs of our community, with room for expansion. Our sanctuary is simple, yet an elegant place in which to worship. We enjoy natural light streaming in to bless all in attendance. As our church's children are of high priority, we invest in lavish youth facilities and children's play areas. We have a kitchen, large enough to meet the needs of our congregation, where we have lunches, brunches, and Wednesday night dinners. Our facilities are ecologically sound and environmentally pleasing."

One day, a board member said, "If we had a symbol of celebration to signify that we'd made it, what would that be?" At just that moment, I was opening my desk drawer and inside was a deflated green balloon. I held it up. "This." I blew up the balloon and taped it to the wall and we all huddled underneath it and said, "We made it!" When we delivered the collective vision statement to the congregation, we shared this symbol of celebration. And that's how the entire congregation began using the visual cue of a green balloon to remind them of our new home.

Around this time, a mentor of mine, Jack Boland, came to town to speak at our church. He was then senior minister of the Church of Today in Warren, Michigan. And he was dying of cancer. Although I knew he was sick, I didn't know that he had only six weeks to live. Jack was a major figure in my life. He had believed in me and my ministry, and felt I had a great calling. He helped me to believe in myself.

Over breakfast, he said, "Okay, so, enough about me. I want to hear about you. What's happening, what's your dream for the church this year?"

Telling him about our collective dream, I said, "This year we're going to acquire our land, and then we'll spend about three years raising the money to pay it off. Then, we'll use that as an equity base to build our first building." I was very excited and continued to paint the picture of what we would accomplish in ten years.

Jack looked at me and said, "Why don't you just have the whole church this year?"

"It's a fifteen-million-dollar dream," I said, "and we have only forty thousand dollars in our building fund."

"Do you believe you can have your church this year?"

"Not this year, but eventually."

Back and forth we went and finally, he said, "Mary, do you believe that I believe you can do it this year?"

Now, I knew the faith of Jack Boland was great. He believed outrageous things all the time and saw them manifest.

I smiled. "Yes, I believe you believe I can do it."

And he said, "Well, believe in my belief. Let my belief carry you now."

With that comment, I saw how I had closed off avenues of support from the universe by deciding that the dream would happen in a very linear and logical way. Buy land. Pay off land. Use land as equity to borrow money. Build. Ten years. Certainly, it might happen that way, but I had left no room for miracles. I had it all figured out.

"Be transformed by the renewing of your mind," say the Scriptures.

It wasn't likely that we would have a fifteen-million-dollar building that year, but it was a possibility. I left that breakfast transformed. A corner of my mind had been opened by Jack Boland.

Six months later, in July, we received our eviction notice from the movie theater. They were going to remodel and make smaller theaters, none of which would hold our congregation, which was now at 2,500. We had thirty days to move. The eviction couldn't have come at a worse time, since Haven and I were struggling with our marriage, which was coming to an end.

As the thirty-day countdown began, the church board and I considered the possibility of moving into a giant tent outside the mall, but it would last only a few months before mother nature froze us out. We found a beautiful facility to rent, but I worried that this temporary move was going to eat into our precious building fund.

Recalling this moment in my book *Building Your Field of Dreams,* I wrote, "As we move toward our dream, at times we may find ourselves faltering, tempted to scale back our plans. We may doubt our own abilities. Here, our partners in believing help propel us forward. They tell us that we do not have to limit ourselves to the confined world of practicality. Our greatest dreams require that we learn to practice outrageous thinking, and our partners keep us attuned to the outrageous by constantly asking, 'If you didn't believe it was impossible, what would you do?'"

At our church, we became outrageous thinkers.

I wanted a church just off the freeway, the right location for a business, according to everything I read. Location, location, location. When we heard about forty-five acres in the country for sale by the state of Oregon, I knew it was wrong for us. I went out to look at it anyway. The main building on the property was 95,000 square feet. At one time a rehabilitation center, it had sat empty for years and was badly run down. It cost three million dollars. It would take another three million just to renovate it and another four million a year to run. That year, the church would bring in about two million dollars. Financially, it made no sense. But I felt I had to let the congregation make the decision.

We gave tours of both the beautiful rental facility and the forty-five acres in Wilsonville. We had a core group of about four hundred congregants who were strongly committed and contributing, people we knew would be there for the church long-term. We made sure they were included in this decision. Personally, I had no sense about where we should go. The rental space was safe. The forty-five acres had great potential, but the drawbacks were big.

The vote from the congregation was exactly fifty-fifty. It was up to me. "You're the spiritual leader of this community," said my board. "You're going to have to make the decision."

I went home that night and said, "Dear God, I need help." In my meditation room, I prayed. "I felt the nudge from You that said, 'Start this church and pioneer a work that genuinely honors all paths to God.' What do You want for this church now?" I heard nothing.

The next morning, I was awakened at 6:30 by a call from a consultant who had worked with us on envisioning our dream. He said, "I woke up in the middle of the night with a voice telling me to make sure you go back to Wilsonville with an open mind."

"I've pretty much decided against it, because it's three miles off the freeway, down a two-lane road, and there's no light at night. Nobody will come out there."

"Well," said the consultant, "the voice said to tell you to go with an open mind."

So I drove back out by myself. The main building had been empty for eight years. It smelled bad. The pond was completely covered over like a swamp. Animals had been on the property, and it stank of them. I looked out over the dilapidated property. "What's the right thing to do?" I asked.

In the quiet of the moment, it was as if a veil lifted. I could see into the future. Kids on the lawns having Easter egg hunts. People in different garb doing ceremonies outside. It was startling. It scared me to my bones. If I said "yes" to this and it flopped, it would flop big. It would be a huge failure. But I had to choose what gave life, not what was safe.

When I told the board, some of the business people said, "There's really no way we can do that." But a couple of people believed along with me. One was my board chairman and the other was a consultant for the church. They both said, "We don't know how, but we believe it's doable."

Ten months from the time the congregation had created a collective vision of a new home for the church, we moved into our permanent facility in Wilsonville. Ten months. Not ten years.

The courage to make that decision to go forward in the absence of knowing how we were going to do it was huge. It came from asking, down deep, "What's the truth?" When we get to the bedrock truth, we can tap an energy that leads us to live a life that's greater than the life we've known before, free from the limitations of the past. It comes from the *coeur* of courage, living from the heart.

Bringing the dream of the Living Enrichment Center into reality took the steady, unshakable faith of a few. Jack Boland taught me that we need other people to believe with us. And those two other people who steadfastly believed with me carried us through; we hung onto one another. We called and supported one another. There was never a moment when all of us gave up believing, so we could lean into one another's believing. It was very, very powerful. And that's what I think Jesus meant when he said, "whenever two or more of you are gathered in my name." The dream happens in the presence of like-mindedness, beyond circumstances. The result is transformation.

I could have spent ten years safely growing my ministry by renting a facility that would never make me look bad. Or I could take a giant leap into the abyss believing that I had been guided, even though I didn't have any concrete evidence to prove it. With this leap, the risk of looking bad was huge. And I felt a tremendous responsibility to the people who contributed money. At every level, I was scared, both for myself and for the people who believed in me.

How does divine power get transmitted through a human being? If you want divine power in your life, how do you get it? It doesn't happen *to* you, it can only happen *through* you. It's in the action. Move in faith, move in your believing, move in unison with others who support that believing — and then, the energy of divine power can move to manifest what you believe. A lot of people want the power first, and then they'll take the step. But it doesn't work that way.

Living in courage means you're always on your growing edge asking, "Where is aliveness leading me?" It's the border between the reality we've known and the reality we could live in if we step into a bigger picture. We need to move vigorously in the direction of our dreams while remaining pliable so that God can guide us to our true destination. Be restless. Don't settle for a little life.

Last Easter, we had a thousand kids hunting for eggs on the beautifully manicured lawns of the Living Enrichment Center. Not long ago, we had a group of Sufis here, wearing their turbans and white garb, doing a ceremony outside. Seeing them was a déjà vu, a remembering of that vision I had while standing outside a dilapidated, dank, wretched-smelling building. As I looked out over their ceremony, I wept and said, "Dear God, You are so good."

Last year, Mary was invited to be a part of a group of fifty people who spent four days in conversation with the Dalai Lama. Shortly after, she was part of a small gathering with Nelson Mandela, discussing nonviolence. She's currently working on a project with the United Nations, which has designated the first ten years of the new millennium as the Decade for Nonviolence. "The challenges now," she says, "are about accepting our greatness and being willing to play bigger, to stand up taller. It takes tremendous courage to do that."

Anne Firth Murray

"I was risking credibility, and I was risking relationships. In the end, however, following my heart and sticking to my principles was the path to empowerment."

Founding President Anne Firth Murray created the Global Fund for Women, which has contributed more than ten million dollars to some 11,000 women's rights groups in more than one hundred countries during the last twelve years.

About a decade ago, I decided to leave my well-paying job running an international population program at a foundation and lecturing on women's health at the University of California in San Francisco, to start the Global Fund for Women.

The Global Fund for Women grew from a vision — a vision of a changed world, of empowerment for women, and of an organization that would "put its money where its mouth is." The Global Fund is the concrete expression of an idea I had for an organization that would raise money and give it away to women's groups around the world — groups of women working on difficult and controversial issues such as sex trafficking, genital mutilation, and women's right to participate in political processes, as well as many other issues that I didn't even imagine at the time. This organization began with just an idea. But what if it had not materialized?

When I was putting together the Global Fund, lots of people — even some who had worked in foundations and in international development agencies — said that it couldn't be done. They said people wouldn't give money to an international women's organization. They said I wouldn't be able to create an organization that could give away money worldwide with any real accountability. They said I wouldn't be able to do it without the central involvement of one or two very wealthy women. What if they had been right? What if I had left the security of my university and foundation work and failed?

Was it a risk to start an organization from scratch, without any idea of where the money was going to come from? Maybe. On the other hand, in my work in international philanthropy, I had seen that women were unfairly treated with regard to financial and other resources, and I knew many people cared about such inequality and would support my endeavor. I cared deeply myself, having experienced discrimination that ranged from not being able to get a credit card in my own name after I was divorced to being inequitably paid for work that was equal to that of the men I worked with to often feeling it was "my fault" when I was harassed.

For such personal reasons, and because it simply seemed unjust that women in all societies carried such heavy burdens and yet were undervalued, I felt driven to make the Global Fund a reality. Nothing seemed more worthwhile than to create an organization that would not only help women but would help them in ways that engendered respect, trust, and even love.

Every day that I worked at the Global Fund, I read letters from women wanting to connect with us.

These women gave new meaning to the word *courage.* A woman in South India named Vasantha started an organization called GUIDE (Gandhian

Unit for Information, Development, and Education) that works with very poor women in small villages. Among other things, GUIDE organizes demonstrations against "bride burnings," events in which brides are "accidentally" burned to death to make way for another bride who will bring a dowry. Their organizing and protesting is truly brave. In Chile, the Colectivo Mujer, Salud y Medicina Social, focuses its work on women's health and reproductive rights, gives workshops on sex education and domestic violence and conducts research on AIDS, abortion, teenage pregnancy, and rape. Such issues are difficult to raise in some countries, let alone to address directly. A group of women in Mexico has begun a campaign to legalize abortion there. Being outspoken about reproductive rights and legalized abortion in Latin America is truly gutsy. Examples from around the world abound: women in Eastern Europe protesting violence, lesbians in Asian countries speaking out about sexual orientation, women in South Africa demanding political rights, women who dare to be feminists in countries governed by Islamic law or women in Catholic countries who persist in demanding reproductive rights.

After my years at the Global Fund, my perspective on risk taking has changed. Taking a financial risk to do what I felt compelled to do pales in comparison to the work of these women. Still, leaving a secure situation to take on an absolute unknown like the creation of the Global Fund was a big jump. Indeed, it would not have been possible had my daughter not already finished law school and my friends not encouraged me to follow this desire to make a difference to women in the world.

Once I had been struck with the idea of creating the Global Fund, the process was very much like creating a work of art: I wanted to finish it, to see it complete according to my vision. I worked like a crazy person for four or five years, involving friends and family, raising money from foundations and individuals, organizing people who wanted to volunteer to make the vision real. The idea proved to be infectious.

I had moments of daring along the way. More risky than financial loss, for example, was my insistence on certain principles — such as evenhandedness and complete openness with all staff and board, such as treating all donors equally rather than according to a hierarchy of giving. My methods did not conform to standard models of organization and fund-raising that were more comfortable for some donors and some board members, models that pit the more powerful against the less powerful. Some board members resented my giving real responsibility to very young staff people. Some donors wanted special recognition for their gifts. Some wanted us to use their funds in ways that limited our freedom or did not focus directly on the mission of the organization. Daring to stand up to such pressures was tiring. I was risking credibility, and I was risking relationships. In the end, however, following my heart and sticking to my principles was the path to empowerment, as I adhered to what in my heart made sense, even if some others disagreed.

Twelve years after the Global Fund was founded, thousands of people have become involved as donors, grantees, advisors, staff, volunteers, and friends. Hundreds of women's groups working on tough issues have been assisted not only with financial aid but also by being connected with others who care. What we were able to do was important, but the way the work was carried out may have been even more important, as this greeting from a grantee group working on reproductive rights attests: "Thank you for leading the Global Fund for Women in such a way that we always felt 'you are one of us.' That moral support, to know somewhere in the USA there are women, you especially, who do, think, and work like we do has been very, very important."

In 1996, I again followed my heart down another road. Seeing that the vision I had in 1987 was now a reality, I decided to leave the administrative leadership of the Global Fund while at the same time continuing as a donor and volunteer, in order to have time to read, think, and write about how organizations can be created with greater consciousness and more heart. While many have wondered why I would "dare" to leave this successful, respected organization to face the unknown, my heart told me that the time was right. Following one's heart is risky at times, but it is also the path to freedom.

Over the years, I have come to value a few lines from James Stephens, the Irish poet, who mirrors my views when he says, "I have learned that the head does not hear anything until the heart has listened and what the heart knows today, the head will understand tomorrow.... If you listen to your heart, you will learn every good thing, for the heart is the fountain of wisdom."

The challenge for me has been to listen to my heart. This may seem like a small risk, but it is one that is often difficult to take.

A native New Zealander, Anne worked at the United Nations as a writer, taught in Hong Kong and Singapore, and spent several years as an editor with Oxford, Stanford, and Yale University presses. For the past twenty-five years, she has worked in the field of philanthropy, serving as a staff member and consultant to many foundations. From 1978 to the end of 1987, she directed the environment and international population programs of the Hewlett Foundation in California. From 1994 through 1998, she was a consulting professor of Health Research and Policy at Stanford University. She is currently a scholar-practitioner at the Union Institute, supported by the Mott Foundation, and a consulting professor in Human Biology at Stanford University. On the side, she is a gardener and beekeeper.

Lynne Franks

"Talking with thousands of women all around the world, I began to see that what holds women back is women themselves. Nothing can stop us, except our own lack of esteem and confidence, our own fears of failure, our own fears of doing our businesses on our own. We have an illusion of not being capable. But it is only an illusion."

Futurist and P.R. guru Lynne Franks worked in her father's butcher shop at the age of twelve, left school at sixteen, and started her own public relations firm at her kitchen table at age twenty-one. Lynne Franks P.R. grew into one of the largest public relations firms in the United Kingdom, helping to launch Tommy Hilfiger, the Spice Girls, and Swatch. Her trendy, high-stress life became the inspiration for the British cult-TV series, Absolutely Fabulous! *No one, least of all her, could have anticipated that she'd leave the fast-track and the glamour.*

I spent twenty years building up what was the most successful and high-profile public relations company in the U.K.

I achieved everything I always thought I wanted, which was to be at the top of my industry. It was glamorous, exciting, fast paced. I mixed with all sorts of famous people. I had lots of material benefits, a wonderful big house, a personal staff both at home and at work. I had two children and what had started out as a great marriage. But after twenty years, I began to feel a hollowness inside. Something was missing. My marriage began to suffer, because I was too busy being the great communicator in public to talk meaningfully with my husband at home. I didn't have enough time for my children. I didn't have enough time for myself. I'd forgotten what it was like to be a human *being,* because I was too busy being a human *doing.*

All the things I thought I was building my business for, the real core values of what I wanted to do with my life, were being neglected. That was brought home to me with sudden clarity when my two best women friends, also in the public relations business and, like me, passionate about their work, got very sick with cancer within a fairly short time and passed away. They both had children the same ages as mine. Their deaths were a watershed for me and woke me up to my own mortality and to the importance of following my heart. I was certain that if I didn't make changes in my life, I would get sick too. It literally felt like a matter of life and death for me to get out of what I was doing and to have a more balanced life.

I wasn't sure what I wanted to do, only what I *didn't* want to do any longer. Having practiced Buddhism for a number of years, I was drawn to be more service oriented rather than singularly focused on business. Although business is a necessary part of life, and it certainly has given me the financial package that has kept me going, I no longer needed the big house. I no longer needed all the trappings. I wanted to go back to doing my own shopping and cooking meals for my children, who were already in their teens. I wanted to live life based on reality, not hype.

Making the change at the time I did was particularly odd because of a series that had been running on British television. I'd done P.R. for the writer of *Absolutely Fabulous,* who would become defensive when the media recognized that her series was drawn from my life. The lead character was named

Edina, which coincidentally was the name of a girlfriend of mine. Every week on television, I'd see this crazy character, knowing she was taken from my life and that all of London knew it. So at the same time that I was going through my own transformation, there was Edina staring at me from the tele every week. The show became a national obsession and put me in the interesting position of questioning a lot of the aspects and details of my life whilst at the same time seeing them parodied on national television. It was quite bizarre.

Having decided to make a huge shift, I began to snoop around the edges of the New Age movement, metaphorically wearing sunglasses and hoping no one would recognize me. Several weeks later, Edina went off to find herself at a New Age center. Seeing things I value and take seriously spoofed to such a degree was hard. My children swore that our life was actually far more bizarre than the series.

Edina had another effect on my life, which was a mixed blessing in a way. People began to think of me as Edina. How peculiar to lose my own identity to a sitcom character. But the upside was that she stirred a lot of interest in me. People were fascinated to meet the person behind the character and, as a result, I had opportunities to talk with them about things that mattered to me. Edina gave me a platform, and that platform would eventually carry S.E.E.D., an acronym for Sustainable Enterprise and Empowerment Dynamics.

Determined to create a more balanced life, I sold my business. And promptly took to bed for three days with sedatives. Having birthed it, I grieved the loss of my company and all the excitement and fun it generated. The British press ran the story as front-page news, shocked that a woman at the height of her success would choose to step off the merry-go-round.

Little did they know.

Letting go was huge, absolutely huge. I had had a very large support team, a lot of people working for me in my house, in my personal life, in my business. The Lynne Franks P.R. staff numbered fifty. Every detail of my life was cared for: I had a chauffeur, a cook, a gardener, a maid. I lived in a very rarified and unrealistic way. And I was controlling it all, the conductor of the orchestra. Letting it go was very, very scary.

And I didn't need to do it.

I didn't need to do it.

The same week that I gave up a career that had become my entire identity, my marriage of twenty years — which I thought would last forever — came to an end. And because of nodules on my vocal chords, I was forced to give up my Buddhist chanting, which I'd done, albeit a bit on the run, for ten years. It was like jumping out of an airplane without a parachute, knowing that if I stayed on board, the plane was going to burst into flames. Who was this woman hurling through the air?

I was a forty-four-year-old woman with two children whom I loved deeply. I had a whole life ahead of me, with my feet back on the ground. Whatever I did, I was determined to make time for my children and to do meaningful work that would matter. I got out of bed and threw myself into changing my lifestyle. The choice was mine. I went full force and got involved in all sorts of things, starting with women's issues.

The Beijing-United Nations Conference was coming up, and the U.K. seemed to have no awareness of it whatsoever. I decided it was time for the voices of English women to be heard. What if I put on an event just for women? I knew how to create live events, I had done it regularly and glamorously in my public relations business. *What Women Want* began to take form in my mind. With the support of Anita Roddick, founder of The Body Shop, and a few other women who shared my vision, I started putting the event together. When I'm passionate about something, little stands in my way. In this case, I felt, everything was possible.

What Women Want was the first conference for women in the U.K., and nothing quite like it has been done since. A cultural and musical festival, it featured talks and seminars on all aspects of English women's lives, including domestic violence, health, education, children, and sexuality. We had Germaine Greer. We had blessings from nuns. And on the last day, we had a big concert with Sinead O'Connor and Chrissie Hynde and other artists. The English newspapers headlined it, "Sex, Nuns, and Rock 'n Roll at Women's Festival." The event was highly reported and a great success. The concept of S.E.E.D. was born and along with it a vision of a Global Women's Network.

Having been a writer early in my career, I went to Beijing as a journalist to cover the conference. When I returned, I talked to senior editors of newspapers in the U.K. and realized how little they knew about the shift that was going on for women, that we were starting to have a voice and living differently, not trying to parody men's ways. It was time for me to dedicate myself to this change. I'm a communicator, that's what I do. And so I decided that I would put my experience and talents into things in which I believed. I helped to launch the first women's radio station in England, hosting a weekly show that allowed me to interview powerful women who were making a difference in the world.

Whilst working to create a grassroots revolution in women's businesses, I traveled the world on a spiritual journey that would take me to sacred sites and religious people from Ireland to India to China to Hawaii to California. It was a journey that would also take me to socially responsible, humanitarian entrepreneurs, from rural businesses in India to large corporations in the States. What I learnt during that time coalesced in me as a passion for sustainable businesses run by empowered women. To create a global network of support, I designed S.E.E.D. programs, which are not only about economics but also about personal growth, creating value, developing relationships, and being financially empowered. Whether in rural Africa or Eastern

Europe or England, women want to create value in every aspect of their lives, including their business lives.

Talking with thousands of women all around the world, I began to see that what holds women back is women themselves. Nothing can stop us, except our own lack of esteem and confidence, our own fears of failure, our own fears of doing our businesses on our own. We have an illusion of not being capable. But it is only an illusion.

To help women break through that illusion, I started writing *The S.E.E.D. Handbook,* which opens with a manifesto stating that each of us will plant seeds as well as pick the blooms, make the time to stay in tune with our higher selves, and never let go of the big vision. That we will put our values, including integrity, compassion, and love, at the center of our enterprises. That we will remember the "three "R's": respect for others, respect for ourselves, and responsibility for all our actions. That we will include humor and laughter as part of our business plans. That we will not neglect friends or loved ones in any way. And that when we lose, we won't lose the lesson.

Still working on *The S.E.E.D. Handbook,* I moved to California to get a different perspective on my work. This move was very scary for me because, although I'd been visiting the States for years, I'd never lived anywhere outside England. I had to learn what it was like to start over in a new country and leave my family behind, even though I would go back regularly and still had a home there. To finance myself, I started a public relations business called Global Fusion, going back into the very thing I'd left, but in a much smaller way. I never expected that I'd do P.R. again, and I constantly look at myself and wonder, Where does this entrepreneurial drive come from?

I go back at least four generations to women who had families and husbands who were either sick or not available and so had to take responsibility for the family and became entrepreneurial themselves or took over family businesses. My grandfather was a peasant who came over from Russia at a very young age and started a business that he grew to a respectable size. Sadly, he died of alcoholism. To keep her family, my grandmother started a boarding house. My father had several businesses, including a family butcher shop, which became quite successful. Yet having been in the war and affected by his alcoholic father, he became manic-depressive. During my childhood, he would erupt with great ideas and then fall sick and disappear into the bedroom for months at a time. My mother, a very grounded and tenacious woman, would step forward to run his businesses. When I was young, I worked in the butcher shop, and she always encouraged me that if I wanted to earn money, it was up to me to do it. *"You can do anything,"* she said.

Believing her, I started Lynne Franks P.R. at my kitchen table with a lot of passion, naïveté, an answering phone, and an old car. My greatest asset was my enthusiasm. Katharine Hamnett, who is now internationally famous, became my first client for twenty pounds a week. The business grew quickly and put me on the cutting edge of what was glamorous and hip in London. I was young and alive and caught up in it all. I didn't so much do P.R. as live it.

By the time I left, I'd been dubbed the "P.R. guru" by the London press. The scariest part of my transition from P.R. guru to me was being on my own. It was hard to be single. It wasn't supposed to happen that way. I was supposed to be married forever, have a family, get a house, then a bigger house, and everything would just carry on. I totally bought into the English version of the American Dream. Only quite recently have I come to realize that the only thing we can depend on is change. Nothing is forever. And that was the hardest thing for me to face. I like to feel that I'm in control of everything, that everything will go on nicely. In fact, nothing will go on nicely except my relationship with the divine. And staying in that center, with God in the center of my being, is one of the easiest things for me to lose. If I don't have enough meditation time or if I don't make that space for myself, I lose it very easily, and then I start looking outside to other people for some kind of reassurance.

Which never works. I need to create that reassurance for myself, from inside.

My transition continues to be rocky. Just when I think I've got everything flowing beautifully in my professional life, in my personal life, the 5:00 A.M. call comes from London and, whoops, something's changed again. It's a constant two steps forward and one step back. If I let go of control, if I trust and do what I should be doing, everything goes fine. The minute my personality gets involved, I start trying to take over and, in a natural way, that's when things go wrong. It's a paradox in a way, because as an entrepreneur, I must be constantly making plans, starting with a business plan. But the truth is, with Global Fusion and with S.E.E.D., I've had about twelve business plans, because the businesses keep developing and evolving and changing. That's the thing about vision: you have your vision, but you must be flexible to see how things are in the moment and adjust.

My travels around the world have shown me that an enormous shift in consciousness is under way. Old structures don't work anymore and are giving way to new truths that arise from our soul, our spirit, our intuition. Within those new truths is the hope for our future, a sustainable future. It is a time to be present, to be attentive, to be true to ourselves as we make this revolutionary shift, to create a positive future, a world we'll be proud to be a part of. It's time to grow ourselves and to grow a future for the world.

Last May, Lynne produced the first S.E.E.D. Expo in London, combining the concepts of S.E.E.D. with What Women Want. *Her workshops have been held at Bloomingdale's, which dedicated an entire window to S.E.E.D, and her presence on iVillage.com in the entrepreneurial business channel gives her contact with a global network.*

Regina Ballinger

"I am aware now of life as a process of learning,
and I am becoming more comfortable with the idea
of not needing to know the 'right' answer right now."

Regina Ballinger was controller of a large New England law firm when she began to suspect that something critical was missing in her life.

In 1992, I was working as a controller of a three-hundred-attorney law firm.

I had been there seven years and had recently completed my M.B.A. by attending evening classes. My life was a success: I had my own home, a new car, a comfortable paycheck. But something wasn't right. I felt a gnawing sense of something being awry, something intangible, and it persisted even as I tried to ignore it.

I had been working for about sixteen years as a woman in a man's world. I enjoyed it. I have three brothers, so I was used to being around the "guys." My undergraduate training was in accounting, at the time a very male-dominated field, and, in addition to enjoying the intellectual stimulation and competition of the male world, I liked the challenge of being a women pioneer of sorts on the frontier of the male corporate world. While pursuing my career in the eighties, I even quite comfortably wore those gray pin-striped suits accompanied by a little silk tie.

When I joined the law firm in 1985, the culture I encountered was so extreme that I guess it was inevitable that I would eventually become aware that something was amiss, and, although it took a while, that subliminal discomfort eventually became impossible to ignore. The organization I worked for was male dominated, nothing new there. The hierarchy was more overt than any I had encountered: In their scheme of things, there were the lawyers, and then there was everyone else. A lone-wolf mentality was encouraged, with bottom-line orientation: The partners shared profits based on their individual financial contribution. Here, more than anywhere else I had worked, I had a sharp sense of being compensated for my skill set — period, end of sentence. I felt a complete compartmentalization of my role in interacting with attorneys. I learned and accepted the idea of doing my work without "personality leakage." Another lesson quickly reinforced was to never let the words "I don't know" cross my lips, something that, in other competitive experiences, I had already been trained to do. To be quick, decisive, and action oriented were the attributes rewarded, and so I was all three. If evening hours and weekends were required to get the job done, I was happy to oblige. It was part of what I needed to do to be successful.

But that nagging, percolating discomfort was not to be assuaged and, eventually, I decided to look for a position with another organization. I began networking to jump-start the process. As I contacted resources, one woman's name kept emerging as a mover and shaker. She was the chief financial officer of a local high-tech company, and she graciously agreed to meet with me early one morning. After some brief introductions, this woman proudly related to me the story of her first child's birth: The child was born on a Thursday night, and she was back to work on Monday morning. As she told this story, something inside me was screaming.

That gnawing feeling got worse.

Something considerable, yet unknown, within me had been unleashed. After reviewing my financial situation and confident of my future, I decided to leave my job without having secured another one. My plan was to take the summer off and be back at work in a financial capacity in the fall. The decision to leave was definitely scary — I had no idea where I was going to land, but something inside me knew it was the right move for me to make. I was surprised by how many men in the firm, once my letter of resignation was submitted, came into my office, shut the door, and shared that they would love to be doing what I was doing.

Something interesting and unexpected happened after I left the firm. I started to become inexplicably happier and happier. I spent my days working in the garden, cooking, reading (often books on leadership, organizational development, and spirituality). I did whatever my heart desired and, when autumn rolled around, I didn't feel ready to return to the workplace yet. I talked with my husband, John. He, too, was aware of how much happier I had become and was totally supportive of me taking more time off.

That more time off kept becoming longer and longer until now, several years later, I am still on "sabbatical" and treasuring it. No one is more surprised than I am that I still haven't returned to the workforce. Not knowing where I'll wind up professionally and financially is not always easy to cope with. But I have learned much about what was percolating in me back at that law firm. A fair amount of it had to do with me not liking the person I had become, with how far away from my values I had grown in order to fit into a highly competitive business culture. I had unflinchingly, unquestioningly, and unconsciously signed up for a system that rewarded only my masculine characteristics. Don't get me wrong, I love those parts of me. But this same system didn't value or reward my feminine characteristics, and it became apparent to me that I wasn't valuing those parts of myself either.

I now have words to put to that uneasy feeling: It was the feminine part of me — call it yin, call it right brain, call it emotional intelligence — that would not be denied and wanted acknowledgment and life breathed into it. That was what I heard screaming inside me that early morning as I listened to the female CFO talk about her firstborn.

Today, I am in touch with and love those long overlooked and undervalued feminine parts of me that are reflective, collaborative, nonlinear, intuitive, and creative. I try to honor *all* of who I am and who others are. I feel more whole and balanced. All those wonderful activities like gardening, cooking, reading, or simply being still that I engaged in so hungrily when I first left work are meaningful to me. I had overlooked them for too long. I hope never to forget how important it is to make space for those nourishing components of my life. The word that has found a home in my awareness is *both.* Both the masculine and the feminine principles are vital to creating a satisfying sense of wholeness in my life.

Where I will go professionally and how I will incorporate this awareness, I don't know. I think of going back into an organization in a leadership capacity, perhaps financial, perhaps operational — helping to model a kind of leadership that creates a more effective organization by honoring the whole person — or perhaps as a consultant, coaching industry leaders about the value of and honoring of the feminine qualities of the men and the women in their workplaces. I am aware now of life as a process of learning, and I am becoming more comfortable with the idea of not needing to know the "right" answer right now. The biggest lesson for me so far is about consciously choosing a balanced definition of success that reflects my internal musings, as opposed to the externals of house, car, salary, and an awareness of what I now value in myself and others, both the masculine and feminine qualities. And I am forever grateful for that persistent gnawing that didn't go away until I paid attention.

Regina works for a consulting firm in Boston.

Marcy Basel

"Achieving something that I thought was impossible gave me a new feeling about who I am. I have a different kind of faith in myself. I don't get as easily discouraged, because I know that with persistence, the right idea will unfold. Nothing seems beyond my reach. I know that, with courage, I can follow my heart no matter what."

Marcy Basel is a doctor of Oriental medicine.

"What are you doing?"

He was a small man, glaring at me, mean looking.

What's his problem, already, I thought. I was standing at the counter of the pharmacy at the Emperor's College of Oriental Medicine in Santa Monica, California. I felt like crap. The last thing I needed was this Korean guy and his who-are-you-and-what's-in-that-paper-bag attitude.

"Come over here! Let me look at your tongue."

I was sick. I didn't need him to tell me that. I'd simply come in to get some herbs. I stuck out my tongue, which was coated sickly white.

He didn't like the looks of it. "Let me feel your pulse. I'll give you the herbs you need."

Any other day, I probably would have squared off with him: "Look, I don't know who you think you are, but this is none of your business." Today I didn't have it in me. I held out my wrist. He felt my pulse and scurried behind the counter. *Oy, I just want to go home and crawl into bed.* Setting three herbs next to my small paper bag, he brusquely said, "Take those out." I spilled out the herbs I'd just picked from the shelves of roots and herbs and medicinal potions to treat whatever it was that was making me feel horrible. They were the same herbs he'd just set on the counter.

"How did you do that?" He was really upset.

"I don't know, I just looked at the shelves and picked them." *Who is this guy?*

"I'm Dr. Kim, this is my college," he said, seeming to read my mind, his tone softening. "Would you come with me, please." I followed him into his office. "Please sit," he said, indicating a chair as he eased down behind his desk. "I'd like you to meditate with me."

Talk about strange. He closed his eyes. Because I'd been on a spiritual path most of my life, meditating wasn't foreign to me. Don't ask me why; I closed my eyes and sank into meditation. The thought that disturbed the stillness in my mind was, *Why is he so familiar?*

When we finished, Dr. Kim looked at me with a startling clarity and said, "You've been coming back for two thousand years to be a healer. I'm here to facilitate that. I will pay for your studies for a year. If you see that it's right, you can stay and continue the program."

The program? Me? Oriental medicine? *What's he talking about?* I'm an artist! I couldn't make it through a medical textbook if you paid me.

I left his office shaken. How weird.

Later that night, at home, I startled myself by remembering the most profound meditation I had had a year earlier during a spiritual seminar. In the meditation, I was in a huge place of worship two thousand years ago. High stained-glass windows were everywhere, letting in warm colors. It was very sweet. Standing by a fountain in the center of this sacred place, I saw two very old people. They had those brown eyes that turn blue with wisdom. They were healers. "We're ready, now, to leave our bodies," they said to me. "May we give you our healing practice?" They wanted me to carry on their tradition. I said no, I wasn't qualified, I couldn't heal the way they did, which was primarily with light and color and water. I don't remember what they said in response, if anything, but they gave me a small stained-glass window on a little stand.

As I thought about that meditation and about picking out those herbs at the college pharmacy and about the meditation in Dr. Kim's office, I began to consider the possibility that, maybe, possibly, perhaps, I should think about his suggestion and not dismiss it. Listening to something that has absolutely no reason or logic, letting myself be guided by, I'm not even sure what, I began to think about the idea of studying Oriental medicine. *Oy, not only am I right brain, I'm forty. That is hardly the right mix for medical school.*

Nevertheless, I couldn't get the idea out of my mind. It was so different that, quite possibly, it was right. As I went about my day, teaching my private art classes, I'd find myself thinking about it. I even said something about it to my teenage son. "Whatever," he shrugged.

I began to feel drawn to the idea as though someone had hooked it behind my heart and was gently pulling. Finally, I went back to the college and talked to Dr. Kim. "Okay, I'll try."

Fear came rushing in. *I'm not smart enough. I'll fail. I'll make a fool of myself. I'll be humiliated. I'll never make it through four years.* In fact, the stress would be tremendous. I'd hear horror stories about the state boards, which ate people up and spat them out, forcing them to reconsider or sit again for the exams. To think about what was in front of me was daunting.

My first day of class is burned into my memory. The "History of Oriental Medicine" was taught by Dr. Kim. I felt awful, out of place. I was totally claustrophobic in a room with closed doors and thirty people sitting stiffly at their desks, taking notes. *No way am I going to be able to do this for four years.* Toward the end of class, Dr. Kim said, "I'm going to call three people to the front, and I want you to come up, take a look inside my body, and tell me what you see." He must have noticed that I was tormented. "We'll start with Marcy Basel."

I went up to the front of the class and looked him over, head to toe. Believe me, I surprised no one more than myself when I told him about a problem on his left side and, in particular, the left part of his lung. He called two other people, who came up and surveyed him and gave their assessments. When we were done, he looked at me and said, "When I was a child, I had a problem with the left part of my lung, and it has never healed quite right. How did you know that?"

I felt an odd sense of calm come over me. This was right. I'd be okay once I was working with people, if I could just get through the books.

That first year was the year from hell. I was living in Malibu, a coastal town just north of Santa Monica. Three months into my studies, Malibu went up in flames during the worst fires in decades. It started while I was in school. My son was at his school in Malibu. When I heard the news, I panicked. That feeling of separation was unlike anything I'd ever experienced. Frantically, I called friends who had kids in my son's school. The children had been vacated and sent to a safe place north of Malibu. I was beside myself, racing north on the Pacific Coast Highway. Police blockades were up. No one was getting through; it was a mess. I went back to the school, where I was supposed to take a midterm that day. "I can't take the test," I said to Dr. Kim, "I can't do this; my son's just been caught in the Malibu fire."

"Is he safe?"

"Yes."

"Then, take the test, it will be good for you to use your mental focus."

I took the test. And barely passed.

Not long after, Malibu was hit with some of the worst floods in decades. All we needed now was an earthquake. It wasn't far behind. And it was big.

That was my first year of medical school. Full of natural disasters, which is how my inner landscape felt. I couldn't get my brain to work. I couldn't remember data, and we had floods of information to memorize, a plethora of herbs and roots and how they affected the human body, acupuncture points and what they stimulated and healed, on and on, ad nauseum. I tried all kinds of tricks, copying study habits of other people in class. Nothing worked. Either I was an idiot for thinking I could do this or something else was going on that I clearly wasn't aware of yet. It was breakdown or breakthrough time.

That I didn't quit still surprises me. The last thing I needed was a big challenge. Raising my son alone was challenging enough. I didn't want to be bothered with difficult things. Looking back, though, I think I was worried that, if I dropped out, it would be one more thing I didn't complete. So staying was a big lesson in persistence and in the meaning of progress. I came to appreciate that I didn't necessarily have to get great results or even do so well. Progress could be measured in teeny-weeny steps, which, put together, became an evolution.

At one point, maybe a year and a half into school, I realized that since I was by nature an artist, I would probably be able to remember facts better with a visual or physical sensation. I started making charts, gluing herbs on boards next to information about their properties. I'd set these around my apartment, so that I'd see them frequently as I walked from room to room.

Everybody digests information differently. It was key for me to recognize this, to stop hitting my head against the proverbial wall trying to learn in a way that didn't work for me and to develop my own way. On my daily morning walks, I took flash cards and pictorial information and studied while I walked. I took books into nature and read in between gazing up at a tree or turning my face into a breeze. I took long hikes in the mountains and thought and pondered, and if something didn't make sense to me, when I got home, I researched until it did. I needed to know *why* something existed in a certain way, rather than simply that it existed. I became a voracious reader and researcher. In time, I reached a level of understanding much deeper than memorization. And this understanding kept deepening into the levels of the emotional and psychic and of how those aspects of a person affect the disease and the diagnosis. It reached the point where if somebody gave me a physical complaint, I would hear the different things they were saying and tune into the problem on an intuitive level. At times, before even asking the patient what was wrong, I'd touch a place on her body and she'd say, "I can't believe you touched me there. That's exactly where I have a problem." It made me think of the moment when Dr. Kim said to me, right after our first fortuitous meditation, "All you need to do is pass the boards, because you have a gift, a level of intuition, and you can heal people using your intuition."

That's when it all came together, and I started excelling.

I went from barely passing to getting an A in physics and then straight A's across the board. By the time I got to a lab and actually saw inside a cadaver, I was in heaven. Everybody in class was saying, "It stinks in here, it's disgusting." But for me, it was art.

What it took to get me here was the courage to step up to a challenge that was greater than I had ever humanly felt capable of. We all have our ideas about who we should be, what we should do, and how we should do it, ideas about what our past says about us, what we're capable of, what friends and family say about us. I had mine about this idea of becoming a doctor of Oriental medicine. But somewhere deep inside me, I knew I was in that college for a reason, I knew on some profound level that it was going to work. I put aside my interpretation of myself to achieve something greater, something more than I'd ever envisioned for myself. And that's where the real transformation took place. Having the courage to let go of all the stuff that had tied me up in a small identity. So that no matter what happened to discourage me — fires, floods, earthquakes, the fear of being dumb, the failing of tests — I could still hold the idea as right and continue to move through barriers and, eventually, it was as though I came to a critical mass. An opening. A place where I was in the flow and everything made sense.

Achieving something that I thought was impossible gave me a new feeling about who I am. I have a different kind of faith in myself. I don't get as easily discouraged, because I know that with persistence, the right idea will unfold. Nothing seems beyond my reach. I know that, with courage, I can follow my heart no matter what.

One of the most rewarding things I've done since passing my state boards and being certified a doctor of Oriental medicine is to treat my mother. She called saying she had terrible lower back pain. It was sciatica. I flew home to Philadelphia and worked on her. She was scheduled for surgery in May. She never went. And I think it was this experience that began to change my entire dynamic with my parents. In fact, my whole family structure changed. They never thought I'd finish medical school. The Jewish acupuncturist from an East Coast upper-middle-class family. *Oy vey.* You just don't do that. Now they call me if anything is wrong. My mother recently phoned, saying her tongue was funny and she didn't feel good. She had thrush, which shows itself with a white coating on the tongue and aching in the joints. For two months, I told her what to do, changed her diet, got her treatments with an acupuncturist, and after two months, the thrush cleared up.

Every time I walk into my office, I am reminded of the power of inner knowing, guidance, our higher selves. When we take the time to be quiet, to listen to ourselves deep within, a whole sea of answers can be found. But it's hard to hear when we're running around like mad. My first whisper about working in the healing profession came from a deeply spiritual place, that meditation in the sacred place with the two healers asking me to take their practice. Although I didn't follow it right away, it was a clue that, fortunately, was buried close enough to the surface for me to see it again. Following it is my most tremendous accomplishment so far.

Marcy is an acupuncturist and herbalist in California. She has worked with an oncologist to treat cancer patients and is developing a stained-glass prototype for healing through the use of light and color.

Inspired to Face TRUTH

Iyanla Vanzant

"Facing the truth was one of the bravest things I have ever done. I was addicted. Not to drugs. Not to alcohol. But to unconsciously creating situations from which I needed to be rescued, situations that would allow me to feel bad for myself, that I could wallow in, that I could whine about, that gave me juicy stories to tell. Looking that square in the eye was awful."

Iyanla Vanzant burst into celebrity with her best-selling book, Acts of Faith *and her appearance on* Oprah, *where she has become a regular guest. She's been called "an empowerment specialist," a "spiritual bounty hunter," and "a spiritual goddess." Where she came from to where she is now is an arc of inspiring proportions. Born in the back of a taxi in New York City, she lived in the projects and was passed from one relative to another after her mother's death when she was two. Then there were the rape by an uncle when she was nine, the pregnancy when she was sixteen, the abusive husband who once beat her so badly she was hospitalized, the attempted suicide. Iyanla speaks from experience, and she speaks deeply from her heart and soul. For Iyanla, life is all about spiritual lessons to be learned, internal landscapes to be explored, responsibilities to be taken, and beliefs that shape one's life.*

My most courageous moment is not a moment at all but a series of moments strung together around a singular theme: telling myself the truth, the truth about who I am, about what I want, about what I'm doing. That takes an incredible amount of guts, faith, and strength. For me, it's most challenging in relationships. Some people do their learning in careers. Some people do their learning alone. Me, I do my greatest learning in relationships.

"Iyanla, you've had such a hard life, with an abusive husband and three kids." I hear that all the time. But from where I sit now, looking back, I say, "No, I've had a blessed life," because the level of learning I experienced in that relationship was deep. In moments of weakness and darkness, I was forced to face the truth about myself. And in those moments, nobody was there for me to argue with, nobody was there to blame. What was there was a tiny voice that knew the truth for me, about me. It was the voice of my spirit, and it would come when I was crying because I had no money or food for my children. It would come after I'd been beaten. And it would say something so outlandish, so frightening, that at first I refused to listen:

Get out of this relationship. It was a little whisper, but it sent a shudder through my body. It made me cry.

Having been abused as a child, I had no sense of self. All I knew about me was what other people said, and that wasn't too nifty. When I got married and had children, I recreated the dysfunctional patterns of my childhood. I had a very abusive, codependent, dysfunctional relationship. Of course, I didn't know any of those words back then — these are all eighties and nineties terms. This was the seventies, and I was young and convinced that whatever my husband did was okay, that the sun rose and set on his behind.

And so I argued with that little voice. "If I leave him, I'll have nobody. If I don't have this relationship, I'll be alone." I was angry. Not at my husband, but at God, at the Goddess, and for that tiny little voice telling me that I needed to give up something I had convinced myself I needed so badly.

Then, one day, I don't know if I was crying or bitching, but damn, I needed help. I had done all I could do to make things work with my husband, to make things right for my kids. But I'd been beaten one time too many. I'd been hospitalized. I'd even tried to take my own life. I couldn't figure out what to do next. I just sat down and said, "Help." Over the years, I've learned that "help" is the most powerful prayer you can utter. If you sit quietly and ask, help will come. It may not be the help you want, you may not like what you hear, but it will come.

Get out of this relationship.

Once again, that's not what I wanted to hear. "Is there anybody else up there? Can You give me something else?" I was terribly unenlightened. I had no clue.

In the end, I finally had to admit that I was staying because I was afraid. I was staying because I didn't believe I could do any better. Because I was addicted to being abused. The truth was painful. Facing it was one of the bravest things I have ever done. I was addicted. Not to drugs. Not to alcohol. But to unconsciously creating situations from which I needed to be rescued, situations that would allow me to feel bad for myself, that I could wallow in, that I could whine about, that gave me juicy stories to tell. Looking that square in the eye was awful. I was face-to-face with my own demons. Alone. I confided in no one, certain that if my friends knew this horrible thing about me, they'd take their love away.

I packed up my three kids, Damon, Gemmia, and Nisa, who were five, three, and a year and a half. Quietly, we left the apartment in Brooklyn. At 5:00 in the morning. With no money and nowhere to go. I had a kid on each hip and was trying to hold onto the five-year-old, who was miserable because it was so early. He was carrying his plastic bag of clothes, and I had the other two bags. The train station was only a block and a half away, but we had to hurry, to get away before my husband woke up and realized we were gone.

At the station, I sat Damon and Gemmia on the stairs. "Oh, my God." I suddenly panicked. "What am I gonna do now?" The first step is always the hardest. The first step is where we need the most courage, not only in taking it, but also in understanding why we're taking it. If I hadn't understood why, eventually, I would have gone back.

It was quiet. No train coming into the station. No train leaving. And yet out of nowhere came a man, a young white guy, which was unusual because I lived in a predominantly black neighborhood. He stopped right on the stair above my children and looked at me. "Do you need something?" he asked. Not "Do you need help?" Not "Can I help you?" But "Do you need something?"

"Yeah, I need a cigarette." He reached into his pocket and drew out a cigarette... and a token. Now, I didn't have a token, but I also hadn't asked him for one. Without another word, he stepped around the kids and went off down the street. How did this guy know I needed a token? I was so taken aback that I forgot to thank him. I turned to shout, "Hey, thanks." Only seconds had passed. To the right was a long city block. He couldn't have gone left because the train tracks were there. Straight ahead was another long block. He was gone. Simply vanished. And in that moment, I knew that he was an angel. I had a very spiritual response to that: "Oh s—." Typical. "No, no, it couldn't have been an angel. No, no, no."

With that token, I got away from a man I was sexually addicted to and began to acknowledge some very ugly things about myself, no way around it. I was addicted to being abused. I was addicted to the dysfunction in our relationship. And I use the word *addicted,* because anything you do that creates a physical reaction once it's withdrawn is an addiction, whether it's drugs, alcohol, cigarettes, food, dysfunction, sex, or abuse.

And so that's how I learned that I could trust the voice. That it wouldn't lie to me. Usually, when people tell me things I don't want to hear, I think they're lying. Or I get mad at them. But you can't get mad at your gut. You can't get mad at your soul.

With a little ingenuity, I eventually got back into my apartment. I went to the neighborhood hardware store and said to the gentleman there, "I need to change the lock on my door."

"Do you need to change the lock or the tumbler?"

"I don't know the difference." I knew so little about taking care of myself in the world. I had no woman training. No life skills. I learned how to write a check when I went to the bank and asked the woman at the desk to teach me. She sat with me for forty-five minutes explaining the whole process of banking and paying bills.

"To buy a lock is to buy the whole thing," said the gentleman at the hardware store. "To buy a tumbler is to buy the part you put the key in."

"I just need the part you put the key in."

Very patiently, he showed me how to change the lock. And it was as though Someone was watching over me.

I went back to my apartment building. Using the phone in the booth on the corner, I called my husband at work to make sure he was there, because I knew it would take him at least an hour to get home. When he came to the phone, I dropped it, ran to the apartment, and in less than twenty minutes changed the tumbler in the door, raced across the street to the daycare center, got my kids, hurried back up to the apartment, locked the door, and pulled down all the shades. I was back home with my kids.

It took several years to get free of this man, during which he stalked me, shoved me around, and humiliated me. One day, he beat me up in the street and ran off with the children. My stepmother said, "Good, let him have them, you need a rest." Eventually, I got a court order to protect us.

For eleven years, I was on welfare. One day, while I was still with her, an African American caseworker at the welfare office said something to her colleague that shocked me into getting not one, but two jobs. She said, "These welfare mothers make me sick. We should take them all out to the field, put them on their knees, and shoot them like cows."

Not only did that shock me into getting off welfare, but it also motivated me to go to college. I was in Medgar Evers College, planning to go to law school, when I met my next challenge in the form of a younger man who was just divine, an absolutely phenomenal human being. From the moment our relationship became serious and intimate, he said to me, "I do not want a ready-made family. I will never marry you." I heard what he said, but how it translated in my brain was, "I don't want you, something's wrong with you." So for five years, I tried to be right for him and to change his mind.

October 18. I'll never forget the date. I was in my first year of law school. That night, we got all dressed up and went to a Stevie Wonder concert at Radio City Music Hall. When we came back to my apartment, we sat down together and he said to me, "I'm done with this. I'm through." Just like that.

"What does that mean?"

"I'm leaving. I'm ready to settle down and get married."

"What are you talking about?" Instant dumbness: what do you mean, what are you saying, I don't understand, how could you say that?

"I told you I didn't want a ready-made family. I want my own children, with a woman I'm married to for the rest of my life. And I'm ready for that now." With that, he walked out the door.

I sat there stunned. I couldn't move. I couldn't do anything.

So here comes the voice: *You can't change people. You have to accept people as they are. Why would you spend five years in a relationship with a man who wanted something other than what you wanted?*

To which I responded, as any normal, red-blooded female would, "Shut the hell up, that's not what I want to hear." I got into bed and pulled the covers over my head. I didn't eat, I didn't sleep. I cried, I vomited, and three weeks later, a friend came to my apartment and banged and banged on the door until, finally, I went to see who it was and let her in.

"Okay, that's it," she said. "Mourning's over. You knew from day one that he was gonna leave you. Why are you acting like you didn't know?"

It took everything in me to hear her instead of arguing, to get out of bed and cut the drama and the P.M.S. — the Poor Me Syndrome — to stop making him wrong and bad and to admit, "I did this to myself. I have to stop giving myself over to people." It was a pivotal moment. Every challenging, difficult, nasty situation I had experienced from the time I was sixteen years old, I had done to myself. It took a great deal to acknowledge that, to forgive myself and to make better choices.

When the truth falls upon you, it works you to the core. I knew I had to investigate why I had done these things to myself.

The first thing I had to get over was thinking there was something wrong with me. For a single, black mother living in the projects with three kids, going to law school, and presenting an image to the world that I could do it all, that was real hard. I didn't have a clue why I was doing what I was doing, or what to do next. I was in over my head. I had to sit down, shut up, and listen. Nothing else to do. I'm very lucky, and blessed, that my inner guidance is strong and tenacious. It persisted even when I was rebellious and, eventually, it won out.

You see, the Goddess always has a plan. God will meet you where you are. My connection to God and the Holy Spirit and the Goddess are what I held onto, and I learned that They didn't love me any less because I was making myself crazy. I didn't lose any Brownie points because it took me so long to see the truth and change.

Discovering who I was and what made me tick also required that I listen to people's criticisms. You can imagine how easy that was for me. Normally, when someone criticized me, I'd feel bad and run around trying to get people to see things my way. In the process, I didn't always tell the truth about what the person said in the first place, which eventually got back to that person and then I'd be in a whole great big mess. When I was afraid that someone wasn't going to like me or was going to be mad at me or leave me, I'd lie. I'd say whatever I thought I needed to say to keep someone from being angry with me or from leaving me. I didn't know it then, but now I understand that I did these things out of fear.

It was the divine essence of God and the spirit of Goddess that moved me to pay attention, to not run away and to not lie. Now when people criticized me or said things about me, instead of getting hurt and angry and mad, I'd take it in and ask to be shown any kernel of truth in it. And when the truth was revealed, oh, my God, it was horrible, absolutely horrible by our usual standards. Things like, "You have a tendency to draw negative attention to yourself because negative attention is the only kind of attention you ever got."

Not surprisingly, a common theme in my life was betrayal — close friends, family members, or people I really trusted would betray me, embarrass me publicly. My spirit had something to say about that: *People lie to you because you lie to people and to yourself. People lie about you because you lie about people.* Jesus, I thought my teeth were going to fall out. That was ugly. It was much more comfortable to be "poor me" than to face the truth that I'd lie to impress people, to make them think I knew more than I did or had more than I had, that I'd been places I hadn't been. All because I didn't know who I was. And I didn't know that who I was, just as I was, was good enough. That it was okay. What I'd grown up with, all I'd ever known was, "There's something wrong with you... because you can't keep still, because you can't stay clean, because your mother's dead and you're being raised by a grandmother who doesn't really like you, because your hair won't grow, because you're black, because you're female." That was the template, those were the threads that were woven into my quilt: There has to be something wrong with you for people to treat you the way they do.

My greatest courage was pulling those threads out of the quilt, dismantling it when I didn't know how to make another one.

My challenges today are very different. As a self-empowerment guru of sorts, it's particularly hard to be faced with situations, experiences... *opportunities* to know myself a little better and a little deeper, when at any moment the *National Enquirer* might be out in my backyard waiting to catch me in a raw moment. When my second book, *Acts of Faith,* became a best-seller and my son Damon, who was then twenty, went to jail for selling drugs, I thought, "Oh, my God." It was very, very difficult dismantling that, looking at it and working through my guilt and fear, working through my self-condemnation, my judgment of him, my judgment of myself, my anger with white America... all of it, in less than twenty-four hours. Once I understood what was really going on, I told the world. I wasn't going to let anybody use it against me.

Exposing myself publicly was risky, but I've learned that there's a healing in it, for me and for others. Truthfully, I saw it coming with my son and I didn't listen, because I was afraid to acknowledge that maybe I hadn't given him what he needed. Today I understand that I gave him what I had and if he needed more, I just didn't have it. To be able to say that was huge: "I've made mistakes. If I had it to do all over again, I'd probably do it a lot differently. But at the time, it was my best." To not beat myself up about it or hold myself guilty about it, but just to be aware of what I'd done and forgive what needed to be forgiven.

Damon went to jail for three and a half years. In retrospect, it was the best thing that could have happened. Had he not gone to prison at that time, he would be dead. He was hanging out with the kind of people you see in Cine-Max smut. Interstate trafficking of stolen cars and drugs. Stuff I can't even spell. The minute he was old enough to think for himself, he did everything he could do to prove that he was independent, out from under my control. And he made some poor choices. Now, at twenty-nine, his emotional development is somewhat lagging because he missed critical years being in prison. But he also learned a lot. And I learned to stop being a mother and how to be a friend.

After all these years, one of the things I've had to acknowledge to my children, and to myself, is that everything they needed from me I learned after they needed it. I asked them to forgive me for not being present emotionally, which I couldn't do until I'd forgiven myself. My children are such divine beings. "Forgive for what?" they said. "We always knew where you were, we always had a home and food." But I know that what I didn't give them emotionally still affects their lives. They have challenges because of the steps we missed together. And I can't change that. I can only be available to support them when they feel the need for growth. When I learn something new, I tell them. When I find a good book, I get one for them. When I hear of somebody who has some insight or enlightenment, I let them know. I share with them. And I let them know I'm still growing, I'm still learning. So far, all of them are appreciative. Except my youngest daughter, who, at twenty-six with two kids and a dysfunctional relationship of her own, is me all over again, which is difficult to watch. Every now and then, I offer her a gem of wisdom. Usually, she throws it back at me. I pick it up and go on about my business.

Some people expect me to be a finished product, some expect me to walk on water. But I'm gonna take a boat anyway. When things show up in my life, I stop and question, "What part of me is this?" At times, I don't know if I have the courage to do what's being asked of me. It happened when I was on *Oprah.* I found a pocket of unworthiness in me that I didn't know still existed.

The first time I was on *Oprah,* I thought, "This is great. This is a wonderful opportunity to share my work with the world." I was focused on sharing the work, helping people, guiding, supporting, offering another perspective. After about the sixth show, that kind of faded away, and I said, "Oh s—, the most powerful woman in TV is asking me — again — to be on her show." I almost lost my mind. Who the hell did I think I was that I could come out of an incestuous, dysfunctional family into promiscuity and more dysfunction only to cross my legs on TV with Oprah Winfrey — again? I had to be outta my mind.

To deal with that, I had to open a pocket of unworthiness where I had put, "I am unworthy because I didn't come from the house in the suburbs with the picket fence, and because all three of my children have different fathers, and because I've been in a number of dysfunctional relationships, and because I was addicted to abuse, to men and sex, to drama and crisis and being a victim, to needing to be rescued." Of course, nowhere in that pocket was the fact that I had worked my ass off to not only transform myself and my life but also to transmute the energy I was accustomed to living in — and that's why Oprah Winfrey wanted me on her show again. It wasn't about me. It was about the same everlasting love and divine presence that's available to everybody. It was about serving God.

A Course in Miracles calls it the Holy Instant when you recognize and realize your oneness with God. If I were to string together my moments of courage, they probably wouldn't amount to an hour. My whole life: one hour. Because it only takes ten seconds to get the insight and then, the moment you hear it, it only takes two seconds to accept it and acknowledge it. Sometimes, you acknowledge it but you don't accept it. Sometimes, you hear it and you don't even acknowledge it. So those courageous moments probably don't even add up to an hour in all my forty-eight years. But they have been the most profound, life-altering experiences that I have ever had.

And it has nothing to do with being on the best-seller list, it has nothing to do with being on *Oprah,* it has nothing to do with having two cars in the garage. It has only to do with the courage to be vulnerable to God, to myself, to those around me. It has only to do with the courage to trust that right where I am, God is, and She speaks to me.

Iyanla graduated summa cum laude from Medgar Evers College in Brooklyn and got her law degree from City University of New York Law School. She practiced law in the Manhattan district attorney's office and later was a public defender in Philadelphia. She has written ten books, produced a CD inspired by gospel, and created a line of inspirational greeting cards for Hallmark. Founder of Inner Visions Worldwide, a personal-growth organization based in Maryland, she also operates a prison ministry, reaching some three thousand people in 150 institutions. She has sold more than five million books dealing with self-empowerment and self-healing.

At home in Maryland, Iyanla lives with her husband, Adeyemi Bandeli, former director of Atlanta's African-American Panoramic Experience museum. Her daughter, Gemmia, son-in-law Alex, and their two-year-old daughter also live with her, as well as daughter Nisa's five-year-old son, Oluwa, age five.

A woman with a big and infectious laugh, Iyanla's letting herself have fun these days in ways a child on welfare never could. "When I was twelve, I never got a pair of heels, I never got to go to a hairdresser or to a department store," she told the Dallas Morning News *a few years ago. "When I should have been experimenting with how I wanted to look, I was sixteen and raising a baby. Now that I'm forty-six, I get to try myself on. Next year, I may be bald, I may go back to braids, I may 'lock my hair again. I don't know. But the message doesn't change. God loves you. So stop looking at me."*

Gabrielle Strong

"A very small circle of people would be willing to back me up if I wanted to address such a hot issue as abuse. Standing up on behalf of young women and girls was painful. I felt very isolated. At times, it was so hard I would cry. But I kept at it."

At the age of twenty-four, Gabrielle Strong became executive director of Ain Dah Yung — which means "Our Home" in Ojibway — the only shelter for American Indian children in Minnesota's Twin Cities and one of only a few in the country. She was young to take on such a daunting job and couldn't have guessed how deeply it would take her into her community.

My greatest challenge, and greatest gift, has been working within my Native American community to expose and heal one of our best-kept secrets: abuse. This work is personal for me, having been a high-risk child myself and having witnessed domestic violence in my home growing up.

I am mixed blood: Dakota Indian and Italian. I was born in New York, the daughter of an Italian father from Brooklyn and a mother from the Sioux-Dakota tribe of the Sisseton-Wahpeton Reservation in South Dakota.

By the time I was twelve, my parents had separated, my mother had moved us to Sisseton and later, with her sisters, to Morris, Minnesota, where they attended the University of Minnesota. After a hard time at an Indian boarding school in Oklahoma, I returned home and, in my senior year at an Indian alternative school called the Red School House, a woman named Lavon Lee came to talk to the four graduating seniors about Macalester College. Back then, the college had a significant Indian population and program, including a Native American cultural center. Lavon helped us fill out applications. I was the only one who followed through, and I was accepted.

That I would go to college wasn't a surprise. My parents and my community expected it of me. Because I had potential, they said, "Go, get educated. We need help in our community, for our people. Do whatever you need to do, and come back to help."

Ironically, the other side of this story was my addiction to drugs and alcohol, an early pregnancy at nineteen, and a dysfunctional relationship. When my partner became abusive and violent, I stayed because he was the father of my child and I thought I should try, at all costs, to make our relationship work. Where I got that crazy idea I don't know, but I tried to the point where it damn near killed me. That was my learning.

I had witnessed domestic violence as a child and had been on the wrong end of discipline that my parents never would have called abuse. What they doled out to me was corporal punishment. I don't begrudge them for the way I was treated and am very close to my mother to this day. Rather, I try to understand and examine what brings us to these points in our lives. What was the healing that my mother, and her mother too, had to go through in their lives? I know what our legacy is, I understand it. The violence inflicted on us goes back deep into our heritage. Suicide and depression as well. How do we heal that? How do we not pass that on to our children and our children's children? How do we change?

I myself wasn't the best parent, being young and out drinking and partying and engaging in behavior that put my baby and me at risk. My recovery started with an invitation to a Sundance Ceremony on the Standing Rock Reservation in South Dakota. The Sundance Ceremony is one of the most important in our Dakota tradition. It's hard to describe, because it's so sacred yet not like a church. Our church is everywhere, it's a way of life. During the Sundance Ceremony, for four days we fast and pray for the things we're grateful for, the things we need, for healing for ourselves and others. We dance all day in the hot sun and sacrifice by having no food or water. It's a very powerful experience.

The Sundance Ceremony at Standing Rock transformed me. It touched not my mind, but my heart and soul. In the transcendence of the ceremony, I met my spirit and saw that I wasn't taking care of it. The revelation was stunning. Yes, I'd had religion in my life. I grew up with it, but it was a practice. Spirituality I rejected. That comes with adolescence. As teenagers, we go out and try to find ourselves. In my case, I did the searching in a rough way, in a self-compromising, self-destructive way.

Being at the Sundance Ceremony, seeing it and taking part in it, was all I needed to change. And it stuck.

I was still a student at Macalester, but with two children now and on my own. Were it not for Lavon Lee, I don't think I would have made it to graduation. Coping with campus life while going through all that I was going through was a struggle. Hearing Lavon say, "It's going to be okay, you can do it" made all the difference. It's that simple sometimes; we don't need to be in therapy for years, we just need good friends, good helpers. Lavon Lee was one of those helpers for me.

I graduated from Macalester in 1986. At first, I wanted to be a teacher. But because of my past addiction and healing, I decided to go into human services instead. Part of my own therapy was using my experiences to help other women and taking part in the creation of the first American Indian shelter, Women of Nations, in the Twin Cities. And then I went to work at Ain Dah Yung, one of only a handful of shelters for American Indian kids in the country.

Ain Dah Yung is critical to helping American Indian kids and their families get legal, educational, and social services, including counseling for parents and kids in crises. We bus our kids to their schools, regardless of the district, so they feel a sense of continuity and have a better chance of succeeding. If a kid is in trouble with the law, we work with probation and social welfare officers. We're a very activist organization with a staff of thirty helping ten kids, ages five to seventeen. Some are runaways, some are homeless, some are sent to us by Ramsey County Social Services or juvenile court. They come because of abuse, neglect, family conflict, social problems. They show up at our door, and we take them in and help.

I started at Ain Dah Yung as a youth counselor when I was twenty-two years old. Maybe it was my age that gave young women the courage to talk about the sexual exploitation and abuse. Maybe it occurred at the hands of respected men in the community. The important thing is that young women came to Ain Dah Yung to find not just solace but help and refuge. I would not turn my back on them.

Within our community, little support or resources existed to deal with abuse. Only a very small circle of people would be willing to back me up if I wanted to address such a hot issue. Standing up on behalf of young women and girls was painful. I felt very isolated. At times, it was so hard I would cry. But I kept at it, and, over the years, I've been part of a growing circle of people who address these kinds of difficult issues.

Because I was so young, confronting leaders who were mostly male and mostly older was a big challenge. The climate when I started was very different from what it is today. Maybe it was the issues I was trying to address that made it hard to be heard. People didn't want to touch abuse. I wasn't going to back down. Some people called me the "Little Shit."

Within two years, I was made director of Ain Dah Yung. Twenty-four is pretty young to be taking on the leadership of a shelter. In the beginning, I got caught up in whether people liked me and what I was doing. As I matured in the job, I realized that it didn't matter if people liked me. What was important was their respect. And I think people respect me. Some of them may not like me, but they respect my work and now I feel supported by the community and our leaders.

When I started as director, we had a budget of less than one hundred thousand dollars and one small shelter site. Now we have a budget of close to 1.3 million dollars, three different sites, and a wide array of supportive services and initiatives. I'm proud that I've been a part of that growth and that I've blazed a trail in some ways for young women and men to have a place where they can come to talk about things they haven't been able to talk about or to confront things they haven't been able to confront because of fear or stigma.

Abuse was one of our best-kept secrets. Domestic violence and sexual abuse go on in our families, they happen to our children, they're a reality in our community. And I hope to be able to continue to talk about these and other kinds of things that are a detriment to our well-being. In doing so, we all better understand the historical legacy that we walk with, the generations and generations of violence against us, and we reach out to teach that legacy within our community and to the non-Indian community.

Recently, that legacy came home to me in the worst way for a mother. I live in an urban setting in St. Paul. It's an intertribal community, an indigenous homeland to several of our tribes. Dakota people. Ojibway people. Ho-Chunk, Winnebago. I made a conscious decision to live here instead of running off to the suburbs. Because this is where our families live, this is where I wanted to raise my children. I choose my particular neighborhood because it's home to a very diverse lot of Indian and Hispanic families. I feel fortunate that we have one of the largest urban Indian communities in the country. But with that comes all kinds of issues.

Two and a half weeks ago, my fourteen-year-old son was outside, on the street in our neighborhood, when a car full of kids drove by and started shooting. By the grace of God, he moved in such a way that none of those bullets hit him except in his legs. Earlier in the day, he'd seen a dispute, and, even though he didn't participate in it, just by virtue of being with the kids who were arguing and fighting, kids he's known all his life, he was shot three times. He was the only one hit.

We're still in a hypervigilant state, getting the guidance and the direction that we need to deal with this. And I keep asking: Why do youth feel that they have to resort to guns to solve their disputes? Back in my day, it was a big deal to get beaten up. These days, guns get in the mix too easily; I'm stunned by how available they are to kids.

I've had to call on every ounce of my strength and energy, spiritually as well as physically. The prayers and energy that people send sustain me, my husband, my other children and have helped my son to heal. At first, the doctors thought they would have to put a rod in his leg because the bone was shattered so badly. But, held together by pins, the bone is growing back.

My son has a long road of recovery ahead, not only physically but also emotionally and spiritually. We're strong in our Native American belief and faith, and we try to understand what happened and not hold onto the anger. At the same time, I don't want to see this happen to other people's children, and I want to see justice for my son, I want to know who did this. They still haven't found the shooter. We've gathered as a family and prayed for him and for the other youth who were in the car. We know that they may not have people gathering for them. The kids in the car were non-Indian; the overwhelming majority of violence against Indian people is committed by non-Indians.

In the past, I was the one whom other parents came to with stories about violence. Now it's struck my own son. Some days at work I question how much more I can I face, because I'm dealing with his healing and my own.

This is tough work. Maybe I'm just stubborn. Maybe I learned perseverance from my dad, who was a Marine. Maybe I learned to keep on keeping on from my mother, who left him, taking a very big risk, financially and emotionally. Maybe that's why I refuse to back down. Despite everything in her life, my mother always landed on her feet. Today, she's in a leadership position in the community. At sixty-two, she runs a school for Indian youth in the inner city. This year, she'll graduate from Augsburg College as a licensed educator. She's a woman of courage.

I'm pushing thirty-eight and have done much. I try to surround myself with passionate people, people who are inspired to do this work, because that's what it takes to keep on with it. The job hazards and burn-out are big in this kind of work, when you're dealing with abused kids, youth who have had to use survival sex in order to have a place to stay, and women who are locked in domestic violence. It's easy to feel hopeless, to feel helpless. If you don't have a passion for the work, if you don't have inspiration and a sense of purpose, then what's the point? It's hard to ignite that in somebody if it's not already there, but I try to inspire and lead.

What drives me is looking beyond the hopelessness and the helplessness to the possibility. I don't get stuck in problems. I don't let obstacles get in my way; I can figure out a way around them. Whether in my own life or in the life of a youth or a woman, I ask: What's the possibility here? What's the possibility for you, for your family, despite what's going on? That's what keeps me going: possibility.

I still go to Sundance every year. In my Native tradition, all things begin with the spiritual. For four days, I'm with my people in that spirit realm. Sometimes it's hard coming home and getting back into the linear world. I've heard it called being a circle in a square world. I wrote a poem about it years ago:

They told me
the hardest thing you will ever do
is live a good life.
Because in the midst of all the
confusion,
noise,
insanity,
there seems to be no room
for goodness
for beauty.
I looked for goodness on street corners
and couldn't find it there.
I walked down alleys and passed through halls
and couldn't find it there.
I looked for it in the neon blackness
of night,
I searched for goodness inside a bottle
and found belligerence and ignorance.
I smoked the herb of apathy
and I didn't care anymore.
Then I went home and found beauty in
my son's laugh.
I went back to the womb of my mother

and found my spirit.
I looked to the sky
and found the prayers
and heard the songs.
Now I see, even in the cement of the city,
there walks a bear.
Among the lights and spiral
an eagle flies.
Our ways are so simple
yet so hard.
We are the circle in the square world.

In 1990, the Minnesota Citizens Council on Crime and Justice gave Gabrielle an award in recognition of her work at Ain Dah Yung. That same year, she married an Ojibway man whom she calls her "true companion, as dedicated to our community as I am." Last spring, she received a leadership grant to go to a Dakota language-immersion program for a year and stepped down from Ain Dah Yung. In May 2001, she received an Alumni of Color award from Macalester College.

Gabrielle's mentor, Lavon Lee, now directs the American Indian Family Center in St. Paul and is on the board of Ain Dah Yung.

SARK

"I was being plagued with flashbacks and nightmares to the point that I literally couldn't sleep. And late one night, I decided it would be better to be dead. I turned the oven on and stuck in my head."

Most of the world knows her simply as SARK. To a few, she's Susan Ariel Rainbow Kennedy. Author. Artist. Beloved idol of a million fans who are spiritually fueled by her colorful, handwritten, hand-drawn books packed with pure message and powerful insight. Her great love is bringing "magic into the most practical of lives."

Growing up in Minnesota, SARK's first (and favorite) job was as a wake-up fairy in kindergarten. She studied at the Minneapolis Art Institute and the University of Minnesota before focusing on radio and TV production at the School of Communication Arts. She likes to say that between the ages of fourteen and twenty-six she's had 250 jobs, some of them with exciting titles like "baby-sitter for millionaires," "artist available for dinner," "long-distance bicyclist," "incredible house sitter." From twenty-six on, she has been true to herself as an artist.

Arriving in San Francisco in 1982 with thirty dollars in her pocket, she bartered her art for rent and ate ketchup sandwiches. In 1983, the San Francisco Chronicle/Examiner *published her cartoon, "SARK's San Francisco" which ran for six years. It was just the beginning of a SARK empire of Spirit Cards, posters, and books, all available through Camp SARK, which you can reach through "snail mail" or online.*

Say the word, *courage,* and the first things that come to my mind are all the ways in which I am *not* courageous.

Suddenly, the room fills with all my inner critics. They crowd around me. "You were on the rowing machine at the gym, and you couldn't figure out how to use it," says one. "Your butt was going back and forth but your arms weren't going anywhere. You were convinced the woman behind you was making fun of you and laughing, and you didn't even have the guts to ask how to use the stupid piece of equipment. You pretended like you were done and got up and walked away." And then another elbows in to remind me that I'm an even bigger chicken a lot of the time: "You're so afraid of the dentist, he sent you an admonishing letter saying, 'If you don't get this treatment done, I can no longer work on you.' You burst into tears and vowed never to go to that dentist again." And then there's the perfectionist. And the inner angry mother and the kids, about eight of them. They get all excited. They want to be involved. "Let me play, let me play." So to even begin, I have to escort all these inner critics and "inside kids" out of the room.

The next thing that crosses my mind is that people often tell me that I'm courageous because I'm so honest. But I don't have a perception of being courageous when I tell the truth. I'm just being me. And there's freedom in that. I can't imagine not living authentically and speaking my mind.

It also fascinates me that people say, "You're so brave, how can you walk from your home near North Beach to downtown San Francisco and back, in the dark, like at midnight?" Well, I love walking in cities, because there's so much to feel and see, and the energy is so exciting. And yes, I use all the intuitive and psychic tools available to me, and I do all kinds of practical things like checking the doorways and staying in the middle of the road, and I pray that I won't ever meet up with someone who has bad intentions. But I am not going to trade walking for fear.

For the most part, what people perceive about me as courageous does not match up with my own perceptions. However, we unequivocally overlap on one thing — exposing the truth about being molested by my brother. Telling my parents, confronting my brother, was hands-down courageous.

Sometime in my thirties, I started having flashbacks and nightmares to the point that I literally couldn't sleep. It was terrifying.

Late one night, I decided it would be better to be dead. I turned on the oven and stuck in my head. In retrospect, it's funny because I didn't know that I needed to blow out the pilot light in order to have the gas suffocate me. I ended up with a terrible headache and smelling like pizza, and I didn't know why I wasn't dying. Thank God I didn't know better.

That episode scared me enough that I called a free suicide clinic in San Francisco. "Do you want to die or do you just want the pain to end?" asked the woman on the other end. "Oh, I definitely want the pain to end!" She encouraged me to come in. I took BART over to their office in the San Francisco Mission District and started going every week to talk with this wonderful young woman who had asked me that pivotal question. And that was the beginning of reclaiming myself. Coming head-on with incest as an adult is pretty common: You keep having this bad feeling and you try to explain it away, you use all these explanations, these rationalizations... you just don't want it to be true. For the next year or two, I continued to take BART to the Mission District to talk with the therapist. Eventually, I reached a point where I felt I had outgrown our work together. I was still keeping the secret. Why?

I started working with a psychotherapist. He asked me very personal questions about my sexuality, which was completely twisted by the experience of incest. I felt very ashamed and exposed. It was horrible to talk about, just torture. And I wanted desperately to get out of there, to stand up and walk out of the office and never go back. He often quoted to me from his own poetry, and I recalled one line about a tenacious extraction of weeds. I was definitely in the middle of a tenacious extraction of monstrous weeds.

I finally got up the nerve to tell my other brother. Being eleven years younger than me, he had no idea what had happened. He was just horrified. He cried. He hugged me. He asked what he could do. "Anything," he said. Even though he was still in school, he drove me to the therapist every week and sat in his car, doing his homework while he waited for me. In a way, he made sure I kept going and didn't bail. He was my champion, making up for some of what my brother had done.

At the time, I had already written my first book, *A Creative Companion.* In it, the only allusion to family problems was something like, "It was slightly less than happy." Some stupid line. The rest was what I call, "La la la." Don't get me wrong, I love that book. But I shared nothing, really, of my own story. I was working on my next book, *Inspiration Sandwich,* when my therapist challenged me, "Why aren't you saying more about your real experience? When are you going to start sharing your real self?" I was horrified. The last thing I would ever do was write about the incest.

It was time to tell my parents. But how? It was a terrible risk. I had no idea what would happen. They were still living in Minnesota, and I remember distinctly picking up the phone, starting to tremble, my folks answering, and my voice coming out high and shaky. I think I was probably very near hysteria. My brother was at their house; he may have been living with them at the time. The way I remember it, he said he was sorry, and that what he had done was wrong. However, he went on to say that I should just get over it. That wasn't a wise choice of things to say.

At first, my parents were upset and sympathetic. "We're so sorry." The initial response was one of love and concern. And then, as often happens in incest families, they began backpedaling. "Well, I don't know how this could go on with your mother not knowing," said my father. "She would never have let this happen."

The thing about incest is that everybody knows that something is wrong, very wrong. But nobody wants to talk about it. Especially people of my parents' generation. The thinking is, "If bad things happen, just put them behind you and go on." Well, you can put incest behind you, but it doesn't go away. It infects your entire life. Siblings can be in their seventies and still hate each other because they haven't talked about it or worked through the emotions or processed it. No healing. No forgiveness.

So when I dared to bring it back up, my parent's final words were, "Why are you dragging this back up? It can do nobody any good." We had just begun to peel away all the secrets.

Some time later, I sent my folks the book *The Courage to Heal* and asked them to read it. And I told them I was writing about the incest in my next book. Surprisingly, my mother said, "Oh, good. I think you should do that. You just write about what happened." She was very forthcoming with her support. My father was not: "Well, why can't you just wait until we're dead?"

What? "I'm not supposed to live a life until you're dead? Why don't you just die then?" I'm very grateful he didn't die then, but that was my initial response. I was so angry.

About a year later, my parents came to visit me and we had the most adult time we'd ever had. My father and I walked on the beach for hours. He apologized and told me some of his own family history, which had been very dysfunctional. He was at a loss as to how to be a good father, how he could have been blind to what happened. He was scared. It was the first time that I was able to see him as a parent who was flawed and as a person who was flawed, and to love him all together, all at once. There was nothing left but love.

We had five years of great communication after that, for which I'm very grateful. He loved that I was in business. He was so proud of me and went out of his way to tell anyone who would listen, "We didn't know that she could do it." Not like most parents who say, "We knew she could do it." He said the truth, in a self-deprecating way, "We didn't know. And we didn't help her, either!" It was very endearing.

My brother, on the other hand, never came around. After the awful and scary things he said to me when I confronted him, I realized that it was as if the incest were continuing and that I needed to stop communicating with him altogether. I haven't spoken to him in about six years, except for one time, at my father's funeral, four years ago.

Writing about the incest was huge. Revealing it to the world was very scary. I didn't know how people would respond. I thought they might turn against me, that they would judge me or blame me and write me mean letters. But I can't bear to be superficial, to look out at the world without people being able to look in at me. Where's the vision in that?

Once *Inspiration Sandwich* was published, my parents called to say how beautifully I'd written about the incest, how they were so surprised. I had agonized over what I'd written, taking great care to say what I truly wanted to say. And the message was that I had not simply suffered, but that I had also gained. Because of the incest, I disassociated as a child and lived so much in my imagination that I was spared many things, like conformity and being "normal." A lot of my creativity was also fostered during that time. I was constantly up in the apple tree in our backyard, reading book after book after book. I lived not only in books but also in the refuge of nature, which gave me an awareness of something much larger than me. The rhubarb came back every year; somehow, I would be okay as long as the rhubarb came back. I lived in that faith. And I'm sure that I am who I am today because of it.

Now, this is not a politically correct approach to the issue of incest. In fact, it's a very dangerous edge to walk. People wrote me saying things like, "Are you saying that this is good?" I've had people shred me during interviews when I bring up what I gained from the horrible experience. I'm not someone who takes confrontation well. I get really scared of conflict. I could just die. "Who would you have been if it hadn't happened?" asked a host testily. I don't know. I'll never know. It's irrelevant. What happened, happened. It shaped me. And here I am today, shaped and loving who I am. I'm like the kid in the story about the pony. A father gives his son a present, saying, "It's just behind the door." The kid opens the door, and the room is full of manure. "What's this?" says the kid. "It's just a bunch of shit!" And he leaves. The father goes to his other son and says, "There's a present behind the door." The other son opens the door, sees all the manure, and gets a shovel. His father asks, "What are you doing?" The kid starts digging and says, "There must be a pony in here somewhere."

I had to believe that something good came out of all the shit. My spirituality and faith don't support a random-victim mentality. I just know that nothing's lost, nothing's wasted. Would I like to redo that particular part of my history, just extract it? Of course. I'd also like to have been home schooled. I'd like to have had a father who wasn't a traveling salesman and was around more. I'd like to rewrite a number of things. And at the same time, those were the circumstances that set up the spiritual lessons I needed to learn. As my friend, a healer, says, "It was a curriculum for a course which you choose no longer to take." The legacy of abuse has stopped.

If people don't speak about these things, they keep growing and transferring from one generation to another. That's how it works. And I won't participate any more. No more secrets. It's a tremendous relief.

I believe fiercely in sharing our real lives. The response to my writing about the incest was that people wanted to know more. I went on to write *Living Juicy,* which also had many stories and references to the incest, and not just to the incest, but also to the self-destructive life that I had lived, which is common for people who have been molested. In many ways, I'm sure that I was trying to die through alcohol abuse and through dysfunctional sexual relationships. It's a miracle that I made it.

Eventually, I wrote an even riskier book, *Succulent Wild Woman.* I worked on it for ten years. It was a major break from my public image, which was "SARK in the magic cottage with fairy dust and snails and a little trail of cats following her." And it wasn't the kind of book a survivor of incest was supposed to write. One of the chapters was "Erotic Robot," about how I felt erotic but was like a robot. I wrote about my vibrator. I wrote about the real stuff of being a woman, like staining the sheets with menstrual blood. My God! How were people going to respond to that? How would they respond to SARK being sexual? I thought I was going to lose half my readers, maybe more. And what about the younger readers? What about their parents? Would they be furious with me? I had nightmares about it. I'd wake up in a sweat. Finally, I just closed my eyes and ... released it.

In some ways, I think my father's death set me free to write that book. I don't know whether I would have had the courage to publish it if my dad could have read it. My mom was extremely supportive. I told her I was scared, because I would be writing about her too. She said, "Well, you just write it. You write everything you need to write." After a pause, I said, "But, Mom, I have to tell you that sometimes when you've said 'write it all,' you've been supportive about it but sometimes not. I'm scared about how you might react to this."

"Well," she laughed, "I suppose I have done that. But you'll just have to learn to get over it."

What a gift. *Okay. I really have to let go. I can't keep measuring everything against what my mother thinks.*

When the book came out, she read it three times. When I asked her what she thought, the first thing she said was, "Your grandmother was not seventy-four, she was seventy-eight!" My mother is the meticulous date- and time-keeper of life. Her next comment was, "Why couldn't this have been fiction?" She went through a period of not being able to give it to certain people: "I'm not giving that book to anyone from church!" But in the end, I knew how much healing had gone on in our family the day that I called my mother, who had never been able to say the taboo word *incest,* and she answered the phone and said, "I can't talk to you right now. My neighbor is over, she has a masters degree and knows a lot about incest, and I am really learning so many things." My mother took on the issue and became very courageous. She even told her friends that my brother was a drug addict: "Well, he's a drug addict, and we don't know what to do." She was trying to get support and help in dealing with it. She needed people she could talk to. But nobody wanted to hear that. They wanted a more superficial relationship. I think she felt very alone.

People around me were resoundingly supportive of *Succulent Wild Women* — even those who said, "I love your books but I have to admit, I can't give this to my grandmother." I'd laugh to myself and think, "Your grandmother would love it!"

Succulent Wild Woman was a huge blessing for me. And a great healing. It gave me a lot of courage and confidence to go on and write more. I don't think anybody could have predicted it. I closed the circle in a way, having exposed the incest and with each new book coming closer to the healing. In my book, *Transformation Soup: Healing for the Splendidly Imperfect,* is a chapter titled, "My Mother Is No Longer the Problem: Now What?" And that's where I am now, with that splendidly existential challenge.

Bodaciously prolific, SARK has written ten books, with succulent titles like her most recent, Eat Mangoes Naked: Finding Pleasure Everywhere and Dancing with the Pits!

Cherie Carter-Scott

"It's one thing to live by my principles when everything is going well. It's quite another when everything falls apart. I had to find the courage to face life as it taunted, 'You really believe all this? Let's put you to the test!'"

Cherie Carter-Scott, Ph.D., is the founder of the MMS Institute, whose mission it is to support individuals and organizations in making their visions, dreams, and goals become a reality. She is the author of the best-selling books If Life Is a Game, These are the Rules: the Ten Rules for Being Human *and* If Love Is a Game, These are the Rules: Ten Rules for Finding Love and Creating Long-Lasting, Authentic Relationships.

For seven years, starting in 1979, everything in my life was tested. The challenges, tests, and obstacles made me look deeply at my core beliefs, to search for compassion, for perseverance. In my wildest imaginings, I could never have predicted what happened to me.

Before 1979, I experienced life as the Golden Girl; some jokingly called me the Queen of Consciousness. Everything I touched seemed to turn to gold. I started a business called Motivation Management Service in San

Francisco. We did individual coaching and corporate consulting. We conducted personal-development seminars to help people clarify what was meaningful to them, to change old behaviors, and to manifest their heart's desires, putting them in charge of their destinies. Every year, business doubled.

Then, suddenly, everything started to shift, as if someone had blown a whistle and said, "The game just changed." We leased a ten-thousand-square-foot building in San Francisco and discovered too late that the physical requirements for our business weren't possible. The building was instantly an albatross and our business projections completely invalid. I vividly remember a moment when I looked at my business partners and said, "We're either going to declare bankruptcy or we're going to dig ourselves out of this." We made the decision to hang in there, pay off our debts, and be diligent, even though we felt unable.

I had no idea that this was just the beginning.

A few years later, I found myself married and pregnant. My husband and I wanted to have a natural birth, so we went through both the Lamaze and Bradley methods, which were in fashion at that time. I did all the right things: ate well, exercised, took vitamins, kept away from coffee and alcohol. We were perfectly on track for a beautiful, mellow birth at home with soft lights and classical music. When the time came, I went into fifty-five hours of labor. I did the deep breathing, had tennis balls at my back, everything that I'd been taught to do, and nothing worked. Finally, I went to the hospital. They gave me a shot of morphine to organize my contractions. Another twelve hours of labor and Jennifer was, at last, born.

Does God still love me? Am I still blessed?

When I brought my baby girl home, I misguidedly thought I was safe in the glow of love from my husband and my father. I didn't know that my father, who called me "princess" even into adulthood, would soon die.

My father was a wealthy man, having inherited a hefty fortune. He had several homes, a substantial stock portfolio, plus my grandmother's townhouse on Fifty-seventh Street in New York, a significant property. Growing up, I heard over and over from my mother, who was very frugal, "I'm saving this for you girls. Someday, you'll get this china from *my* grandmother. You'll inherit these linens for your own table." I'm not talking about a single conversation, but a repeated litany of how we would receive family heirlooms. It became imprinted on my mind, *This is my future.*

Mommy died assuming her beloved daughters would inherit a beautiful estate made rich with the connection to her and to our ancestors, that she would live not only in our hearts but through her family treasures. This was not to be. In time, my father married a woman much younger than he and, to this day, I still don't know what happened between them. When he called to say he was scheduled for surgery, I was making plane reservations to go see him. Before I'd hung up, he said, "Wait until I'm home from the hospital." My intuition said, "Go, go now." But I agreed to wait. He died, and I never saw him again.

After the funeral, his wife met with my sisters and me and proclaimed that he had left everything to her. I went into shock.

Did my father really love me? What is the message?

I sank into a deep depression. Both my heritage and my future had just been claimed by a relative stranger. It shook the ground beneath my feet. Gone were my grandfather's hand-painted fish plates, my grandmother's monogrammed tea service, and other irreplaceable and priceless connections to my family heritage. They were the touchstones. Without them, I felt strangely orphaned. The fabric of our family tree was torn, and I felt a deep psychic wound as well.

I wrestled with what this meant about my father's true feelings for me. Looking for answers, the only place to go was within. I prayed. I meditated. I needed to know what he was saying with this act of disinheritance. I desperately wanted to understand. What was the message? What was he saying to his three daughters and to me, his favorite?

My sisters were as hurt as I was, and they wrestled with that same question: Why? We decided to go to a psychic who might be able to shed some light on the situation. Right or wrong, the psychic said, "Your father believed that you girls were so competent and capable that you didn't need his possessions or money." When she said this, something in me released. Yes, of course. It was the most empowering thing he could have done.

I didn't know it at the time, but I was learning rule number eight from the Rules for Being Human: What you make of your life is up to you. Years later, I would write about it in my book *If Life Is a Game, These are the Rules.*

The decision about how I was going to react to being deleted from my father's will was mine to make, and mine alone. I chose to have it empower me. I chose to take charge of my reality and manifest what I wanted, relying not on my father, not on his power, connections, or money, not on some future inheritance, but on me alone. Both my parents were gone now, and I had no cushion, no safety net. Now it was my game. I could mourn, I could feel victimized, hurt, and tormented over this incident or I could choose to say that it was my ultimate empowerment: My father believed in me; he believed that I could do anything.

It was a huge turning point in my life. A kind of rite of passage from child to adult. A passing of the torch in the truest sense: *Now it was up to me.*

I was only halfway through that seven-year cycle. Having stepped into a new level of responsibility for my life, I was about to learn my husband was a pathological liar. One lie after another began to surface, about his childhood, his family, where he'd gone to school, what he'd done in business. I felt like I was standing in the ocean and was being knocked down by one wave after another. When he left me, a friend said, "You're lucky he's gone." When I looked puzzled, she explained. "Because you never would have left."

I'm a very loyal person. Even though we'd experienced difficulties, I was determined to make our relationship work, believing that love conquers all. I wasn't ready to admit that he was a sociopath. No, these inconsistencies must be quirks. I tried harder, thinking that, if I could just love him enough, it would all work out and our marriage would be saved. Not in a million years.

I was now a single mother.

I scrambled to my feet, but another wave was about to knock me down, and I began to feel like I was caught, getting up as the waves receded but knocked down over and over again. Each time, I caught my breath. Each time, I wrestled with the questions, *Am I being tested to see whether I really believe what I'm teaching? Is this to see if I have the courage to hang in there with my beliefs when the going gets really tough? Is this about learning compassion for people who experience similar situations? Is this broadening me as a person, giving me dimension?*

It's one thing to live by my principles when everything is going well. It's quite another when everything falls apart. I had to find the courage to face life as it taunted, "You really believe all this? Let's see what you say when we put you to the test!"

I gained immeasurably from those seven years. The template throughout was, "There are no accidents." Each experience taught me something profound. Each made me ask, *What can I learn from this? What is the gift inside of this challenge?* Perhaps I was too attached to how I thought things should be, so that I wasn't seeing clearly. There were lessons in humility, especially when I was arrogant and thought I had life by the tail. There were lessons in gratitude, especially when I took my blessings for granted. I realized that the way I had things figured out wasn't always the "truth." Letting go of my images about the way life was supposed to be, letting go of my disappointment and anger when life didn't go that way, were important lessons for me.

We ended up subleasing the San Francisco building and changing our business direction, expanding nationally and then internationally and opening satellite offices across America and, eventually, in Europe and South Africa. If it hadn't happened that way, we would have become more and more embedded in San Francisco, in that building, in that reality, which was not to be the future for our organization. So I thank God for whispering, "No, no, no, this is not the direction to pursue."

In a similar way, Jennifer's birth was a great lesson in being unattached to how I thought life was supposed to be, learning to let go and allow life to be what it was, surrendering to *Not my will, but Thy will be done.* Her birth was peaceful and gentle, just not the way I had envisioned it. And, without my husband walking out, I would never have met Michael, who has shown me about authentic love in ways I never imagined. Without the divorce, I would have been slugging away, trying to make an impossible relationship work and I would never have experienced the kind of wonderful joy I share in my marriage now.

Today I feel incredibly blessed.

Life is never boring. I love being on the cutting edge. Where it seems impossible for people to find their dreams and live their passion, that's where I sizzle. I cherish making a difference in people's lives. Helping them birth their dreams and believe in themselves. Moving problems into solutions and making seemingly impossible things happen. That's what connects me with my soul, my reason for being, my purpose on earth. Being a part of people finding more peace and harmony, within themselves and with one another. Those seven years made me dig deeper into my essence to find peace, harmony, and the strength of my beliefs and teachings. By overcoming adversity and challenge, I connected with my true values. I connected with my spirit.

Cherie has also written Negaholics: How to Overcome Negativity and Turn Your Life Around *and* The Corporate Negaholic: How to Successfully Deal with Negative Colleagues, Managers, and Corporations. *In the* Game Rules *series, her latest books are* If Success is a Game, These Are the Rules *and* If High School Is a Game, Here's How to Break the Rules: A Cutting Edge Guide to Becoming Yourself. *Upcoming is* If Motherhood Is a Game.

Debbie Rosas

"I proposed . . . unorthodox ideas at a time when the business was doing better than it had ever done. I myself felt nuts at times. But then I'd be drawn back to that sensation, that little whisper, You're doing the right thing. I know it looks nuts, but you're doing the right thing."

One of the founders of the wildly successful Bod Squad in San Francisco in the eighties, Debbie Rosas was living a seemingly perfect life when a question hit her broadside.

Are you happy?

That was the question that changed my life. Utterly.

In 1982, I was living a perfectly wonderful, normal life. I was married and had two beautiful daughters. And I was a partner in a fitness business, the Bod Squad, in the San Francisco Bay Area. I had started it with two other women and it had become a great success, with fifty instructors teaching more than a hundred classes a week. Life was good.

One day, early in the fall, we hired a man named Carlos Rosas, a tennis pro who wanted to shift into aerobics — probably because of the music. I took him to lunch to get him on the same page with everyone, make him feel welcome, part of the family. Over salad and a Coke, he asked me about my life. I started telling him how perfect it was and launched into something of an oration. Done, I sat back. I lifted my fork and leaned forward to take a bite of salad when he looked up at me and asked, "Are you happy?" I bit down on the fork and almost lost a tooth. I can't explain it, but a shudder ran through my body. I'd never asked myself if I was happy. What a concept.

I was still shaking at the end of lunch when I went out to my car. My hand was trembling so much that I had a hard time getting my key in the door. Gripping the wheel, I tried to get hold of myself. *Okay, you're okay. Breathe, breathe.* As I reached to adjust the rearview mirror, the most startling thing happened. It jerked down, and I saw my reflection. But more than that, I saw myself, me. It was as if I were looking into my soul. Fixated, I felt cleaved open, exposed, emotionally dismembered. That same shuddering came over me. *This must be a nervous breakdown, you're having a nervous breakdown. You'll be okay, just drive home, you'll be okay.*

By now, it was mid-afternoon. As I pulled into my driveway, I heard a voice saying, clear as can be, "This is one of the last times you're going to drive into this driveway." Now I was scared. I hurried inside and thought, *Salad, make a salad. Get things ready for dinner.* In the kitchen, I focused on the refrigerator, got lettuce and started washing it. My girls, who were five and seven, came running in from school. *Normal, back to normal.* They hustled off to their rooms to play. I went back to making dinner and trying to breathe. Then I heard the door open. The center of the house was a garden with sliding glass doors. I looked up and saw my husband, George, walking in. Again, the voice came, "This is one of the last times you're going to see him coming home."

The panic I felt in that moment would only increase over the eight days that followed. I said nothing to George. I was too frightened. Then one night, for no good reason, I asked him, "Have you ever been attracted to anybody you work with?" As a sales rep in the women's clothing business, he worked with women all the time. Without answering, he got up, walked into the family room, and collapsed. *Oh my God.* I heard him fall and ran to him. He was passed out on the floor.

I rushed him to the emergency room. By then he was fine. Maybe it was stress, said the doctors. But we knew better. He had had that same kind of physical sensation that I had had over lunch with Carlos. He blacked out from fear. Because life as we knew it was over. Our perfect relationship, our perfect life had been dislodged by a question, making me realize that, after all this time, it was the first personal question I had asked my husband. Within three months, our eleven-year marriage had ended.

George and I had never an argument. He was the most loving husband, the most beautiful human being on the planet. I had never been unfaithful. I had never even looked at anybody else, and I wasn't attracted to Carlos. I had no reason to leave. How could I walk away? It made no sense. It was insane.

Listening to that voice meant I was following a feeling, a sensation, an intuition that this was what I was supposed to do. I had no idea where it would take me. I had no clarity other than the intangible. It was the first time I had paid attention to my voice rather than to my parents, my sister, my friends, society. The first time I had listened to the true me.

I remember vividly the first morning after I moved out. I was back at my folk's house, which is where I was when I married George. I'd gone from living with mom and dad to living with my husband. The house was in complete disarray because they were remodeling. Nevertheless, I woke up with a feeling of euphoria unlike anything I'd ever experienced. Even though I was afraid, even though the pain of the separation was heavy, I also had this other feeling. Exhilarated fear. The excitement of my soul moving me toward my greater good. To this day, this feeling continues to guide me whenever I confront challenges. It's a marker. If I have it, I know I'm going in the right direction.

What had happened with Carlos wasn't a physical attraction. It was something else. I found myself psychically drawn to him. I'd be picking up a stack of papers at work and walk into a room where he was, wondering, "What am I doing? How did I get in here?" It was odd, eerie. We began talking about life and going on walks and having very deep conversations. The connection between us grew stronger. And our conversations began to wind around the idea of a new way of working out, of moving. At the time, the media was breaking the news that people were injuring themselves with high-impact aerobics. The Bod Squad was built on high-impact, "no pain, no gain" aerobics. It had given me financial security and freedom. Yet I began to question it. Maybe there was something better that wouldn't injure people. Maybe there was something that would actually give people more than a physical workout.

My partners thought I was insane.

One day, a martial artist came to the Bod Squad to see what we were doing. He took me aside and said, "Come to my studio. I want to talk to you about the martial arts." When I told Carlos, he said, "Let's go."

The day we went to his martial arts studio was a turning point. At the beginning of our private class, he said, "Go ahead, move. Let me see how you move." We did some jumping jacks. And he said, "No, I mean move." We did kicks. He looked at us and said, "You don't know how to move." What? I'd been a fitness instructor for seven years. How could I not know how to move? I was the expert, the authority.

Wow, what a realization: I teach movement. I teach fitness. And I don't know how to move.

I was alarmed. I was overwhelmed. My God, I have to start all over. But I was also excited. Moving and jumping up and down are two very different things. Moving would open up a whole new world to me. It would answer that nagging feeling I had about people getting injured doing high-impact aerobics. It would begin a lifelong work that started out as NIA,

Non-Impact Aerobics and grow into NIA, Neuromuscular Integrative Action.

I knew that this wasn't going to be an easy road. Nobody was doing low-impact aerobics. My Bod Squad partners thought I was losing it. Our fifty instructors thought I was crazy. I wanted to stop jumping up and down. More, I wanted to take off my shoes, so that the movement could be better grounded and the feet could benefit. Heresy! Nobody, but nobody, took off their aerobic shoes. I proposed these unorthodox ideas at a time when the business was doing better then it had ever done. I myself felt nuts at times. But then I'd be drawn back to that sensation, that little whisper, *You're doing the right thing. I know it looks nuts, but you're doing the right thing.*

And then came the mutiny. One of my partners invited me to her house for dinner. I walked in on all our instructors gathered in the living room. They'd been having meetings behind my back and decided that I wasn't reliable, that I'd become emotionally unstable as a result of the divorce. And kaboom, kabang, kabong, I was out.

Staggered, I left. I felt utterly alone. I had just lost a business that I'd grown to a point that I'd always dreamt of, and I was adrift at the worst of times. I'd agreed to be equally responsible for the girls, and I'd just lost my financial security. George had kept the house. I'd accepted a small settlement. Now I was losing my only way to provide for the girls and me. It was huge.

I could have sued my partners. But the process would have been long, it would have been expensive, and it would have been vengeful. Instead, I chose to walk away and put my energy into starting something new. Starting fresh. That same sensation came over me, that exhilaration. *This is good. Painful, but good.*

The next day, I talked with Carlos about creating a new movement form that would not only exercise the body but the soul, the mind. Something that wouldn't hurt. That wouldn't injure people. Together, we made the commitment. That was the birth of NIA. It was born out of trust and faith in something I could feel powerfully inside me. The creative juice in me, the exhilaration of birthing NIA was stunning. I'd never experienced anything like it. I didn't have a clue what this movement was supposed to look like, but I could feel it, I could feel its power. And it carried me forward in the face of judgments from my family, from George, from my business partners, from the community. It carried me in the face of losing friends and feeling ashamed about not being financially successful.

That was eighteen years ago. Founded on the idea that fitness meant not only physical but also emotional and spiritual well-being and that pleasure and joy rather than pain and guilt produce lasting results, NIA carved new ground in the fitness field by combining aerobic movements with tai chi and other martial arts, ballet, modern and ethnic dance, and yoga. It wasn't easy. Sometimes I felt like an imposter. Who was I to talk about this new Eastern and Western movement form? But I knew I had to anyway. I had to be willing to trust it and let it be whole in each of its developmental stages. Not perfect but evolving. And, along the way, people gave us the courage and the strength to keep going, even though we couldn't give language to it from a scientific or a medical viewpoint.

Gradually, NIA found its legs in science as well as soul. One of the first doctors who endorsed it was the father of sports medicine, Dr. James Garrick, of the St. Francis Sports Medicine Clinic in San Francisco. Eventually, the American Council on Exercise accredited it. Over time, we developed an instructor training based on the belt system like the martial arts. Today, because it's adaptable to all models of health and fitness, NIA is used not only in traditional gyms and fitness settings, but also in college physical education, dance, and theater departments; in drug, alcohol, sex-abuse, and cardiac-rehabilitation clinics; and in spas, wellness centers, and martial-arts studios.

The mainstream media has begun to discover NIA. *Business Week* ran an article about it. *Self* magazine featured movements from NIA Dance, and the *Washington Post* proclaimed "Move over yoga, there's a new regime in town, NIA." A MS-NBC segment said, "Growing in popularity and increasingly offered at health clubs, NIA is also intended to be an outlet for creative expression, meditation, and emotional release... Incorporating tai chi, other martial arts, yoga, ballet, along with jazz, modern, and ethnic dance, what distinctively sets NIA apart from other New Age mind-body fitness pursuits is the emotional element." NIA is the antithesis of slaving at the gym. It is movement medicine.

People talk about NIA as though it were brand new. That's fine with me, because in a way it's always brand new, always getting better. The difference now is that there's a place for it. Personally, NIA has shown me about the courage to love, to love myself even as I was walking away from everything I knew, everything familiar, everything safe. It has been an affirmation that love is the only choice — it wasn't painless, but the direction it took me opened me to something profound: the courage to have faith and know that, by following my innermost guidance, I would travel the right path.

Debbie travels and teaches nationally and internationally with Carlos, doing seminars in Sweden, Switzerland, Germany, and England. According to American Fitness Magazine, *they are "the front-runners in mind-body integration. Their NIA Wave tapes sit head and shoulders above the crowded look-a-like market." Sharon Colgan, a southern California clinical sports psychologist who counsels elite athletes at the U.S. Olympic Trainer Center in Chula Vista, California, says part of the popularity of NIA comes from its ability to facilitate emotional release. "People I think are seeking answers for outside techniques*

and tools to better their lives and prevent illnesses and disease. NIA is a very playful kind of experience where you can still get your heart rate up, you can still get a good workout, but, as well, your mind and body and spirit is really integrated in every move that you're doing." Today, NIA is taught by four hundred black-belt trainers nationally.

Judith Light

"My mind can spin out in endless directions with excuses that keep me from moving ahead, from taking risks. It's exhausting. I analyze and analyze, getting stuck in my head rather than including my heart and listening to what my soul is trying to tell me."

In 1984 America came to love her as Angela Bower on the hit TV series Who's the Boss. *She has been an actress all her life. But it was her role as Vivian Bearing, professor of seventeenth-century poetry in the Pulitzer Prize–winning play* Wit *in 1999 that would challenge her as nothing else had. In a highly acclaimed performance that brought down houses with standing ovations, Judith earned stellar reviews, like the one from the* San Francisco Chronicle: *"Light seems transcendently moved... to find the flesh-and-blood reality of a character who's spent her life abstracting emotion." She began off-Broadway, in New York for five months, and then toured for four months. For those nine months, over and over, she dug deeper into her soul than she had ever gone.*

Playing the lead role in *Wit* was one of the most courageous things I have ever done. It made me look at myself more deeply than I ever had before.

For most of my life, my career has been everything to me, and my personal life just one of the things that fit into that career. Relationships have been the most difficult. Since *Wit,* I have moved toward having my life be the context of everything and my career one of things that fits into it. Believe me, this has been a very difficult process.

I was young when I decided to be an actress. I was good. And very successful. Acting was the vehicle through which I related to the world, the firm and solid ground beneath my feet. But over time, I would come to recognize that it perpetuated a kind of behavior that was unhealthy: wanting approval, wanting to be the center of attention. I would find myself being spoiled and petulant and angry. All ego.

From the summer of my sophomore year, while in the theater program at Carnegie-Mellon University, I toured Europe in *Guys and Dolls.* After Carnegie, I spent five years with repertory companies in Milwaukee and Seattle, doing lead roles from Shakespeare to Tennessee Williams. When I left repertory theater, I went to New York and landed on Broadway in 1975 in *A Doll's House.* Several jobs followed during the next couple of years. And then after a long period of being out of work, I was so frustrated that, one day, I said out loud to God, "What do you want? I'll do whatever you want." Now it took a leap of faith for me to even say the words, because I lived intellectually, from my head, not from my heart or from my spirit. But in that moment, I surrendered, really surrendered to whatever the universe had in mind for me. I put my ego aside, which made room for something else to come into my life.

Literally the next week, I got a call from *One Life to Live.* Oy. I didn't want to do a soap opera. I didn't want to do a sitcom. Ever. But as it turned out, it was right for me. Playing Karen Wolek on *One Life to Live* earned me a Soap Opera Hall of Fame Award and two Emmys. But more important, it put me in the company of Robert Desiderio, who was also on the show. We fell in love.

Life was good. Then one day, Robert went to California to be in a TV Movie of the Week. When he came home, he said, "You need to think about leaving New York and going to L.A. A lot of people don't know your work. Do you really want to stay on the soap for the rest of your life?" In a sense, he was speaking to my soul, to my higher self who wanted me to take a chance, to grow, to expand, who didn't want me to be on my deathbed saying, "Why didn't I try? Why didn't I take the chance? Why was I too afraid?"

Just before this, I had started working with Herb Hamsher, who would become my lifelong manager, personal advisor, and friend. Herb is a psychologist. At one time, he was professor of clinical psychology at Temple University. He's worked with multinational corporations and executives. He knows the human psyche, the human spirit, like no one I know. In the beginning, I'd call him up for advice in an informal sort of way. He said straight up that I probably wouldn't like what he said to me, that I might be taken aback by his suggestions.

Little did I know.

One of the first things he pointed out was that I was operating out of a child's view of what acting and "celebrity" was going to get me. It was all ego driven. I wanted approval. I wanted to be the center of attention, which I'd always been as the only child of very warm and attentive parents. Had I not woken up to this pattern of behavior, I might never have left New York or the soap opera.

I was terrified to leave the soap. But I did it anyway. I took the chance, with Robert's support. And it changed my life.

My last show was in December of 1982. And then Robert and I moved to California. I had no job, no prospects. I was on spec. Logic told me that was crazy: "You gotta be not thinking right to take that kind of a chance." In fact, I was going sane, not insane. It only felt crazy because it wasn't what I was used to, it wasn't comfortable. It wasn't rational. It was unreasonable.

But that's when life is most alive. Everything was new, everything was exciting, everything was scary.

I started talking with Herb about finding a way to use my career to be of service. Celebrity is hollow if you don't do something with it. "I can support you in that," said Herb. "It won't be comfortable, but I promise you it will be alive."

"Alive" I liked.

I did a television movie. I did an episode of *St. Elsewhere.* And then... nothing.

I called Herb. "What's the problem? What's going on? How come I can't get any work?"

He listened while I talked his ear off, and then he said something startling. "You're walking into auditions very angry. You're operating like a spoiled brat." There was the only child expecting to get what she wanted. Herb went on, "You're walking into the room furious. Like they owe you a living. That's the energy you're putting out, and I suspect that's why you're not getting jobs."

At first I was defensive. Which, to this day, continues to be a sure sign that what he's saying is absolutely on the money. But at the time, I didn't want to go there. Who wants to be told you can't cling to the very things that have kept you going for so long? Who wants to admit that you're behaving like a spoiled brat? Yet truth is the first step of change. By acknowledging my behavior, by being willing to move off it, to let go of it, I began to shift where I was coming from when I went into an audition.

Around that time, the networks were auditioning for their fall replacement series. I was up for three shows, *Command 5, Staff of Life,* and *You're the Boss.* Before they consider making a deal with you, the networks require that you put something in first position. I didn't know which show to pick. Herb finally said to me, "Just make a decision. Just land somewhere!" I chose *Staff of Life.* I would read for them on a Monday. The week before, I got a call from *You're the Boss.* They wanted me to come in that Friday and do a taped audition with Tony Danza, even though I had put them in second position. "I don't need to do that," I told Herb. "I put *Staff of Life* in first place."

"You're afraid."

Oh, come on.

"You're not going because you're afraid."

That made me mad. "Well, it's not what I want," said my ego, complaining that it was a royal pain in the ass to go in for that audition. My mind started to tick off reasons not to go...but they were all just excuses. Underneath, I was afraid. Afraid I wouldn't get the role. Afraid to go someplace where I didn't know people. Afraid they wouldn't like me. Afraid of a new situation. I was uncomfortable. Tony Danza was a big star...blah, blah, blah. My mind can spin out in endless directions with excuses that keep me from moving ahead, from taking risks. It's exhausting. I analyze and analyze, getting stuck in my head rather than including my heart and listening to what my soul is trying to tell me.

Fear does have its place. I'm not talking about jumping off a rooftop, yelling, "I can fly." We need to use fear in a healthy way. But auditioning with Tony Danza wasn't going to kill me.

I packed up my stuff and went to audition. It was sensational. I had the most incredible time. Tony was fabulous, and we connected in a way that left me feeling that this was the show I should do. Everybody in the room felt it.

When I left the audition, I called Herb and said, "I made a mistake by putting *Staff of Life* first."

"Pray that you don't get it."

Had I gotten *Staff of Life,* I would have had to take it. Both shows were at ABC. On Monday, when I went in to read for *Staff of Life,* apparently someone had seen the *You're the Boss* tape and knew that I was right for that show.

Sometimes, even when you stand in your own way, your higher self moves you toward the right thing. It's like driving down the road with the brake on, but you get where you're supposed to be nonetheless. And in this case, I was definitely being guided.

You're the Boss became *Who's the Boss* and ran for eight years, from September of 1984 to September of 1992. During most of that time, it was not only a top-ten hit, but was used as the launching pad for a large number of ABC shows that also went on to become hits.

Several years and many movies after *Who's the Boss,* my career was again shifting. I had the opportunity to audition for a play. "No," I said, "I don't think this is right for me." Which wasn't true. I loved the play. I loved the part, and it would have been great for me. But once again, I was afraid. And, once again, I dug in my heels. I didn't go up for the part.

When I realized what I'd done, I thought, "I don't like the way I'm operating. This has been going on for too long time. It has got to stop." By this time, I'd been doing, and continue to do, a lot of work in the AIDS arena and supporting the gay and lesbian community. It was ironic, because I spoke frequently about how the people in those communities inspired me because of the way they operated, the courage it took for them to come out in the face of possibly losing love and admiration, the approval of their parents, their clergy, their teachers, their world. They stood up anyway and said, "This is who I am." Publicly, I spoke about how they inspired me when I myself wasn't living with that level of courage and honesty. I didn't like it.

Fast-forward to *Wit.* This is a Pulitzer Prize–winning play in which the main character, Vivan Bearing, a brilliant and uncompromising scholar and professor of seventeenth-century poetry, is battling the final stages of ovarian cancer and finding her humanity. It is an emotionally daunting role. By this time, Herb and his partner, Jonathan Stoller, were managing me exclusively, as well as producing with me. With my husband, Robert, the four of us were like family.

Herb got the call from the producers of *Wit.* They were interested in having me read for the role of Vivian to take over from Kathleen Chalfant, who was in the original show that was playing in New York off-Broadway. "If you like the play," Herb said, "you have to go to New York to audition." I read the script and said, "First, I hate the way I've been operating. Second, this play is so overwhelmingly magnificent, I'm willing to throw my hat into the ring. I want to be the person I've talked about being and haven't been, the person I've wanted to be all my life."

I went to New York.

Herb suggested that I work with a coach before the audition. My knee-jerk reaction was, "What do I need to do that for?" Do it differently, said Herb. Operate differently. After arguing for a while, I decided to listen. As a result of working with a wonderful coach named John Kirby, for the first time in my life, I wasn't nervous for an audition. The casting director was there. One of the producers was there. Derek Anson Jones directed me . . . and I just did it. I was present in the moment with them; nothing else existed.

Interestingly, at that time, I was studying *A Course in Miracles,* and the lesson that day was, "There is nothing my holiness cannot do." Being in that state — not of the ego, but of the higher self, the soul — it didn't matter to me whether I got the part. What mattered was that I made the choice to go for it.

At the end of the reading, they said they had other people they wanted to audition, so they wouldn't be able to let me know right away.

Waiting gave me time to worry. What if I got the part? I would have to leave the comforts of my home, my husband, my life as I knew it in California, and move back to New York for some undetermined length of time, possibly even tour. If I toured, I might be away for close to a year. I'd done that before. I didn't want to do it again. Are you kidding? Also, I was completely obsessed with my hair. I had a lot of it. Long, thick, curly. Vivian had none as a result of chemotherapy. I would have to shave my head. I didn't know myself without this mane.

Finally, Herb got the call. The part was mine.

I was in my car in L.A. Herb was at his home in Aspen. He called me on the car phone. "Today's the day," he said, "you have to make the decision. You can use a lot of reasons not to do this, but they don't have anything to do with anything. There's an experience underneath, a "yes" or a "no," and you know what it is. Your soul knows." I pulled over and sat in the car at the side of the road. "I'm so scared," I said. He listened for an hour while I went through every consideration. What's it gonna mean? What's gonna happen to my relationship? What's it gonna mean to my life? How am I gonna be a different person?" I started to cry. I was so frightened. Because I knew that the answer was "yes," and it was like jumping off a cliff. I hadn't done a play in twenty-two years. Would my voice even hold up? How would I be received? What would the critics say? How could I ever follow Kathleen Chalfant, who had won every award, been lauded and lionized, and rightly so. I was absolutely terrified.

In the end, I told Herb, "I don't want to be on my deathbed saying, 'Why was I too scared? Why did I live like that, knowing the answer was 'yes' and saying 'no'?' So, the answer is yes."

The moment I made that decision, I started preparing. I wanted to learn the script before I got to New York for rehearsal. I wanted to impress people. I wanted them to think I was really good. When I realized what I was doing, I had to drop it. I needed to go about my business of being good and working hard, instead of trying to impress people. Having to prove I'm impressive comes from a place of deficiency. And I wasn't deficient.

This time, when Herb suggested that I work with someone — a voice teacher — rather than saying, "Oy-oy-oy! I don't want to go to a voice teacher, my voice is fine, I gonna get through this," I listened. I let myself be vulnerable and open. When we're in that state of availability, the universe comes to our aid. We allow ourselves things that we wouldn't allow otherwise. I found a wonderful opera teacher, Patricia McCaffrey, who worked with me on breathing and vocal production. It made the difference.

Partway through rehearsals, our director Derek Anson Jones was hospitalized with what was only later acknowledged as AIDS. His assistant director, Leah Gardiner, gave me his notes from the hospital as well as her own notes. I kept reminding myself to be flexible, to let the experience be exciting rather than nerve-racking. Excitement and nerves feel the same — your stomach has butterflies, your heart beats faster, your adrenaline rushes. It's all in what you call it, how you contextualize it.

Opening night. Derek was still in the hospital. I had a bite to eat with Herb and Leah. They talked with me about tightening the performance. There were places in me where I was still retreating from the piece, and I needed instead to come out with a kind of energy that would carry the whole play through to the end. Like in tennis, everything hinges on the serve. I needed to hit a heck of a first serve.

Back at the theater, in my dressing room, I prayed. I prayed before every show. I asked God, the universe, to help me deliver the play in the way it was meant to be delivered to the people who were there that night, that they would get whatever they were supposed to get from that particular performance.

It was time to go on. I felt a rush, an adrenaline kick that jettisoned me out, and I rode on it. Instead of letting it use me, I used it. I kept focusing on one center point to keep me in the moment, and I do mean every single moment, of the play. If my mind wandered in the least, I had to find my way back to that center, that moment, with nothing else going on.

The first night was astounding. And every night that followed. Every single performance. As I started getting great reviews and wonderful responses from the audience, it was difficult not to give it to my ego, not to get attached but rather to keep saying, "This isn't about me. I'm the vehicle. It comes through me, but it's not about me." I wasn't always successful at doing that. It's a paradox, how to be the star of something and yet not have that thing be about you but rather about how you can be of service.

Every time I did the show, I always had an adrenaline rush before going onstage, always. And in a way, I knew that rush was essential, because it gave me energy, kept me focused and present. See, I knew that I couldn't perform that piece if I had anything going on; I wouldn't get anything out of the performance that night and neither would the audience. Vivan Bearing demanded impeccable presence. At the beginning of the play, she learns she has cancer and is dying. She's acutely intellectual and, for the first time in her life, discovers that her intellect will not help her. She's forced into her emotions and her heart. Being her required that I be open and vulnerable, that I stay in the process with her and not get into my mind, that I be in the same process Vivian was in.

So that I could be emotionally clear for the role, I asked Herb to tour with me. During a period of nine months, I did 304 shows, and Herb was there, in the audience, for most of them. Before each show, if I had anything going on, I'd talk it out with him so that I was clean when I stepped into Vivian. To the degree that I got out of the way, I was in the moment and most powerfully Vivian. And I could feel the difference.

Doing *Wit* this way required a lot of me, but I felt a great responsibility to give the audience the best that I could give. And yet there were nights when I'd think, "Who's in the audience tonight?" Or if I knew that someone famous was there, I'd panic, "Oh my God, so-and-so is in the audience. . . !" And I'd have to really work with myself to drop it. "Am I being good? Am I being impressive? Do they think I'm great?" are all ego thoughts and the fastest way *not* to impress people. On the nights that I was either preoccupied or not as focused, noise in the audience or people talking would take me out of the moment.

After each show, Herb and I would talk about how it had gone that night, until I felt complete and done. I think it's the only way I could have lived with Vivian so intensely, for so long. I didn't carry her out of the theater with me. When I left at the end of the evening, I shifted entirely out of Vivian and back into me.

Being so clearly focused in the moment is a dynamic way to live, even outside the theater. For me, it's easier onstage than off. I don't live my everyday life with such emotional clarity and vulnerability; my ego is still too interested in being the center of attention and getting approval. But I'm learning. Living this way requires me to be centered and listen to what's essential on my path. It means being connected to God, the universe, and other people, being in the flow and letting that flow move in the way that it needs to move, not how I think it should move. That's how it was for me during *Wit,* and the experience was deeply profound and gratifying.

When *Wit* was over and I returned home after nine months of touring, I wanted to continue living with that same intimacy. I was wobbly. I needed to get my "life legs" back. Not the ones I had before, but the ones I have now, after *Wit.* It's scary for somebody who has been in her head so much to be completely open and vulnerable, especially in my relationship with Robert. I'm working on taking steps, having intimate conversations that make me uncomfortable. Sometimes I take the steps and sometimes, I don't. And you know what? I still find myself wanting to be perfect, to be impressive. I want to always do the great thing, the right thing, the bold thing...and I don't! Maybe I need to be patient with myself. Or maybe I need to "just do it." I was talking to Herb about something the other day, and he said, "You can think this to death. Just drop it. You know it doesn't work. So don't go there." It's like that old joke about the guy who goes to the doctor banging himself on the head and saying, "You know, doctor, it hurts me when I do this. What should I do?" And the doctor says, "Stop banging yourself on the head!"

So coming off the road after nine months with *Wit* was challenging. Just as making the decision to do *Wit* was challenging. It's all part of a long and ongoing process about making difficult choices that reflect my soul's path. *Wit* is about finding out what life is really about, and I had to immerse myself in it for almost a year to really get that lesson. It's a lesson I keep relearning.

It is ironic that *Wit* is the story of a woman who stays in her head all her life, protecting herself against her heart. When she's diagnosed with cancer, she's confronted with a medical community that operates in the same way. It isn't until moments before she dies that she realizes that life isn't about the intellect but about simplicity and kindness, connection and heart, intimacy and love. Our friend Paul Monette, who won the National Book Award for his memoir *Becoming a Man: Half a Life Story* and who died of AIDS, said to me, "All that will matter when you come to the end is how much you've managed to love and how much you've managed to give back. You will not have wanted to have read another script; you will not have wanted to spend another day at the office. You will have wanted to love and be intimate, and that's all that will matter."

In a way, that's what *Wit* has given me and that has been the great challenge. To live from my heart. To live in the moment. To be vulnerable with my living. To love. *Wit* was the culmination of my taking a stand as an adult. Now the context of my life is living fully, and my career is one of the things that fits into that context. I'm not where I want to be; there is a place where I still hold out and dig in my heels. But it's time now for me to take the brake off and let myself go.

In a San Francisco Chronicle *lead story about* Wit, *the writer says that, "Light . . . takes the audience on a devastating journey that goes to the heart of what theater can do. By penetrating to the core of this peculiar character's experience, she opens a window on the universal experience of death as a mysterious solo act — wider than Kathleen Chalfant's flintier creation of the role in New York did. Where the off-Broadway* Wit *was impressively fearsome and uncompromising, Light may even be more fearless in exposing the veins of tenderness and apprehension in Vivian along the way. Vivian's stony facade feels more real, with the cracks and flinches showing."*

Inspired to Take a STAND

Julia Butterfly Hill

"Of everything I've experienced here, the most demanding, the most courageous challenge has been to stay centered in love in the face of violence and anger, of frustration and fear and sadness."

In December 1997, twenty-three-year-old Julia Butterfly Hill climbed 180 feet up into a thousand-year-old redwood tree that was named Luna by Earth First! activists. She told this story a little over a year into her tree-sit. She was on a portable phone, and, during our interview, she would stop mid-sentence to say things like, "Oh wow, beautiful, hold on for a sec, I haven't seen a bird like that, ever." Little did Julia know when she climbed Luna that her feet would not touch the ground for more than two years and that her life would teeter precipitously close to the edge during that time.

Four years ago, in 1996, I was living in Fayetteville, Arkansas, a small college town of about 45,000 people. I was a Missouri-born kid of an itinerant preacher who had grown up in a camping trailer traveling from church to church, and it was my first sense of having my own home, of rooting. I was twenty-one. I had no idea that in one day my life would change dramatically and that I'd be set on a path that would lead me to a tree called Luna.

That day in August, I was driving a friend's hatchback when a Bronco rammed into me, slamming my head into the steering wheel and jamming my right eye into my skull. Treated at an emergency room, I was released, but I was far from whole. I began to experience short-term memory loss. Sometimes I would trip over nothing, fall for no reason, and have hot flashes so intense they'd make me throw up and pass out. I'd stutter, have crazy mood swings. My doctor, refusing to look into the real reasons behind my problems, decided that antidepressants would cure me. (I never took them.) My condition worsened.

I fully recovered only because a health practitioner who had traveled the world studying traditional medicines and ancient healing techniques recognized the implications of what had happened to me during the accident. It would take nearly a year to retrain my brain in motor skills and for my short-term memory to return. I grew acutely aware that every single moment, every single breath of every single day is an absolute gift.

So when I heard that some acquaintances were heading west on a month-long road trip, I jumped at the opportunity to go with them. It was a fortuitous decision, because it led me to the redwood forests of California. I'll never forget my first walk in a forest with trees so old it's hard to imagine their beginning. The people I was traveling with were eager to get out to the Pacific Coast, but I couldn't pull myself away and told them to go on without me. And then I walked deeper into the forest, alone.

Once I'd gotten far enough away from the highway to lose the sound and stench of the cars, I was overcome by the utter majesty that surrounded me. I dropped to my knees and began to cry. I sunk my fingers into the soil. I pressed my face against the earth. The experience was overpowering. This forest was a million years old. How does one grasp such a thing, such amazing power, such history and beauty, such knowledge and spirituality? It all came rushing over me like a tidal wave. And I felt suddenly awakened to the deep connection of all things, to a memory older than comprehension. In every microorganism in the soil, in the stars light years away, and within me, within all of us, resides that connection. We are all a part of creation, inherently linked. A spark lit, boooff, and I was on fire with the true essence of life.

I guess you could call it an epiphany.

Over the next few months, I camped and hiked up and down the Lost Coast of California. Periodically, I'd go into Garberville to restock on food and to do my laundry. A thread of events led me to EPIC, the Environmental Protection and Information Center, where I saw a photo collection documenting what was happening to the forests: the clear-cuts, the mud slides, and the activists fighting for the forests. I knew I had to get involved.

I called EPIC and asked them how to get plugged into the preservation scene. They told me about the Earth First! base camp, an activist camp where people train in backwoods actions, tree-sits, and other activities. After I had tried for two hours to get through to the base camp, a guy finally picked up the phone. I told him I wanted to get plugged in and he said, "Base camp is closing; we don't need you."

I felt like I'd been hit in the stomach. "I want to do something. Is there any way for me to get plugged in?"

He gave me another number and that person said the same thing: "Base camp is closing; we don't need you."

"I know base camp is closing, I don't care about base camp, I came here for the forest, not for base camp."

I ended up at a rally later that day, and one person after another kept turning me away. *Screw this,* I thought, *I'm going traveling. If it's this difficult to help, I don't want to help.* Still I felt so strongly that I was meant to be there. So I stayed. Eventually, a wonderful brother named Shakespeare overheard yet another person telling me that base camp was closing. Coming up to me, he said, "I'm at base camp, and it's not completely closed yet. Things are going on that we need help with, and it's the only way I know of to get you plugged in. You wanna go?"

So I ended up at base camp and spent the next several days wandering around still trying to get plugged in. I was lucky if someone would talk to me. Finally, a guy named Almond came around camp looking for someone to sit in an old-growth tree named Luna. I'd heard rumors about tree-sitting but didn't know much about it. I volunteered immediately. Almond looked me over; he didn't know me, and he wanted people he knew in Luna. But I was the only one raising my hand — except a guy known as Blue. (Front-line activists use names like Almond and Blue to slow down the police in the event of an arrest. Butterfly, by the way, isn't a woods name but one I've had since childhood.)

Earth First! base camps were held twice a year at the times when the logging company is allowed to go into the forest and cut or salvage; certain times are restricted because of the nesting of protected migratory birds. The front-line activists are in the trenches for a few months at a time. It was November when I arrived, and everybody was going home for a break, worn out from months of day-in, day-out actions, tree-sitting, and locking down, during which you chain or lock yourself to a tree or piece of machinery to stop the logging. No one else volunteered to stay and go up Luna. Just Blue (who later backed out) and me and, in the end, Shakespeare.

To avoid getting caught by the logging company, we hiked the two hours up the hill in the middle of the night and stayed at a satellite camp. The next morning, we climbed Luna. Yeah, I was scared. My legs were shaking as I went up with a harness and a rope, similar to the way rock climbers scale the face of a mountain. Only this harness was held together by duct tape! The wind had picked up, and I started to sway. About seventy-five feet up, I freaked out, hanging from this little rope. I placed my forehead and my hands and feet against Luna and closed my eyes and imagined the energy of my body going down Luna's trunk into the roots, into the earth. Doing that immediately grounded me.

My first sit in Luna lasted about a week. I did another one for a week, but I came down violently sick, apparently from water contamination at base camp. Almond befriended me then and took me to the doctor. After that I didn't want to do another week-long sit. Rotating in and out of the tree for such a short time wasn't enough for me. I wanted to have a bigger impact on those companies with seven-foot chain saws who can turn a forest into a clear-cut in a matter of days. I talked with Almond about this; he'd been involved with forest protection for years and was very savvy about politics and the environment. He agreed that I could stay in Luna for a month; he'd go in with me and would stay for most of it.

When we returned to Luna, we found not only the tree-sitter we were replacing but also another guy. Neither of them was leaving quite yet. They wanted another night in Luna. If we'd known, it would have given us precious extra time to make our preparations. As it was, we were now four people in a very small space with only three safety harnesses. That night in Luna, I couldn't sleep.

The next morning, the two guys were goofing around, dragging their heels about going back down. "You really need to go," I said, "because the loggers are going to be here any minute." Finally, they started down. Halfway down, they realized we were under attack. Pacific Lumber loggers were cutting Luna. I could feel the vibrations from the chain saw all 180 feet up. Down went the small trees growing from her base. A logger infamous for getting activists out of trees was climbing up the tree next to us. Seeing him sent terror through me. Word was he'd gotten fed up with tree-sitters and had become aggressive. Almond, who had never been out on a traverse line, went out to stop him. The traverse lines made it possible for us to climb over to other trees in the event that the logging company tried to take them down. If more than one tree was under attack, we could swing out into the middle of the traverse line to keep the loggers from cutting either tree.

Seeing that Almond had his harness on, the logger started cutting the traverse line. Almond pleaded with him to stop. He didn't have his safety lines attached. He backed toward Luna as the logger kept cutting. As the line gave, Almond dropped three feet before catching on a branch. It was the only thing that kept him from falling to his death.

That was the morning of December 10, 1997. For the next twelve days, the loggers cut trees around us, taunting that the "big trunk" was next.

They didn't get us out of Luna. But it was a portend of things to come.

In the beginning, I was tentative about living on a six-foot-by-eight-foot platform with a tarp roof 180 feet up; I was very apprehensive about going out on Luna's limbs. But little by little, I grew accustomed to climbing around and, when the others finally went down, to being alone. Being alone, I discovered, was the key. The space is simply too small. I could not have gone on as long as I have if I had had to share the space with other people. It would have driven me nuts.

During those first weeks of my sit, I kept trying to get the media to talk about what was happening out here on Pacific Lumber's land, a couple of miles above the little town of Stafford. If we were going to change things, people outside the local community needed to know. But mainstream media wasn't interested. That's the nature of the beast. At about day twenty, I concluded that I needed to give them a human-interest hook to get their attention. If I extended my sit beyond the national tree-sitting record, maybe the media would get curious. Then after a while, I recognized that being in Luna was more than just a way to get media attention for the forest. It was something far deeper for myself.

One thing after another happened to shake me loose from Luna. The logging, which had been further down the hill, relocated around Luna. It is horrifying to see a logging operation. The noise is deafening. The smell of fumes and exhaust and trees splitting and shattering is overwhelming. Seeing old-growth trees smash into the ground, knowing that we won't have any like them again, is devastating.

Redwoods are family trees; they often grow connected to one other. The loggers not only cut down the trees that grew at Luna's base, but in an attempt to scare me, they also made other cuts so that trees hit Luna on the way down. Then the helicopter came, a twin-propeller helicopter used to pull logs off the hills. It hovered right above my head as I dangled out on a branch filming it with a video camera. These things have three-hundred-mile-an-hour updrafts; they were trying to rip off my roof.

Men at the base of Luna yelled up at me that they were going to blow up the tree and when they got me down, they were going to do things to me and enjoy every second of it. Security guards were sent to cut off my supplies. They thought they could starve me down. I rationed and gathered water in my tarps and worried only that I had run out of battery power for my phones and so had no way to let people know what these men were doing to me. They used air horns all night to cause sleep deprivation. They brought in a dog that would bark every time they blew a shrill whistle. They tried everything they could to rip me apart on every level, emotional and physical, mental and spiritual.

And then the storms hit.

For weeks, the California coast was pounded with storms that grew worse and worse. It blew. It rained. It hailed. When my tarps ripped, everything became sopping wet, including me. I wrapped up in the torn tarp, trying to stay dry.

I had a little radio, left up here from a previous sit. It was on its last legs, but I fiddled with it during a lull, because I was worn out from the storms and in a mood to hear some music and just let go for a minute. Remarkably, I got the radio to work. I put on the headphones, and the first thing I heard was a warning that the worst storm in California history was on its way. I turned off the radio and sat numbly on my platform high above protection, fully exposed to what was coming. My phone was on extremely limited battery supply, but I called my direct ground-support person. "What should I do? Should I come down?"

"I don't know what to tell you."

I hung up and went through a very intense process of dealing with one of the most difficult decisions of my life. In a way, I'm glad I was alone. With another person around, I wouldn't have had the space I needed to flip out.

By this time, I had given my word that I wasn't going to allow my feet to touch the ground, no matter what, until I felt I had done everything within my power to make a difference in the preservation of old-growth forests. Coming down out of fear would be breaking my word. And I was raised with a very strong belief that I'm only worth my word, that I should never ever make a promise unless I can keep it. At the same time, would I be stupid to stay, hanging 180 feet off the ground, open to the full force of what was to be the worst storm in California history?

I remembered a story my father used to tell about a great flood that hit a small town. A man in the town prayed and knew that God was going to save him from the flood. When the water started rising up into his house, one of the townspeople came by in a rowboat, rescuing people who were stranded. "Get in," he yelled, but the man said, "No that's okay, God is going to protect me." The man in the boat couldn't believe his ears. "I'm trying to help you here, buddy." The man said, "No, no, God's gonna take care of me." The water kept rising, so he kept moving up the stairs in the house. Again, someone came by in a boat, a motor boat this time, the rescue squad. Again, he said, "No, it's okay, God's gonna take care of me." When the flood engulfed his house, he had to go up on the roof. But still, he believed that God would save him. A helicopter flew over and the pilot yelled, "Get in, we're here to save you." The man waved them away, "No, no God's gonna take care of me." Of course, he ended up drowning. As he stood before God, he asked, "God, you told me you would protect me; why did you let me die?" God said, "I sent three people to help you. What else did you want me to do?"

Had I been guided to turn on the radio? Was this God's way of helping me, letting me know that something terrible was about to happen and that I needed to get down out of the tree while I still could? I wrestled with the decision and, in the end, I felt that I couldn't come down out of fear, that I was not meant to touch the ground again, no matter what, until I had done everything in my power to change the logging of old-growth forests. There was still too much for me to do.

I picked up a microcassette recorder someone had given me, slipped in a tape, pressed "record," and started blabbering away. It took my mind off what was about to happen. It kept me sane. All through the storms, I came back to that recorder, as if it were a friend with a good ear.

When the big storm hit, the wind whipped up to ninety miles an hour. Branches were getting ripped off all over the place. Half my fort collapsed. I got thrown three feet and grabbed onto Luna. *Oh, my God, I'm going to die.* The wind was howling like a wild animal. I was trying so hard to stay alive that my fists were clenched, my muscles were clenched, my teeth were clenched, everything in me was clenched. And then Luna began to speak to me: *Julia, think of the trees in the storm.* An image came to me of the trees bending and blowing in the wind. *Trees that stand strong and straight in a storm break. The ones that survive bend and blow and flow with the wind. You need to learn the power of letting go. Become like a tree in a storm. If you try to hold on too tight and stand up straight and strong, you're going to break.*

I felt my muscles start to let go, shaking from the intensity of adrenaline. *Laugh, cry, scream, holler, hoop, do whatever it takes to become one with the wind, Julia. The wind is raging, so can you.* And so I did. I let go. I laughed. I screamed. I cried and cussed, whatever came flying out of me with the wind.

The storm lasted about sixteen hours. Later I wrote in my journal, "Approximately January 28: I'm not quite sure. I was scared. I take that back. I was terrified. When I was a child, I was in a tornado. That time I was scared. That was a walk in the park on a sunny Sunday afternoon compared to these last twenty-four hours. If I never, ever go through anything like that ever again, it will be way too soon." In the margin, I wrote: "Little did I know this was just the beginning of a horrendous onslaught of storms." Then I continued: "Helicopters no longer scare me. Pacific Lumber never did. The men at the base of the tree are a joke, but the awesome power of Mother Nature reduced me to a groveling half-wit fighting fear with a paper fork."

When the storms abated, I was changed. Every day in Luna now, I change. It's not simply that I free-climb barefoot, going all the way to the top, about two hundred feet, without a harness. It's that my commitment is more personal and deeper. I've been here for more than a year. In some ways, I can't imagine coming down. I don't know when I will. Day by day, prayer by prayer, I will come to that decision. Each day, I wake up and ask, "Am I still supposed to be here? Am I doing what I'm supposed to be doing? Please give me guidance." I can't think of a better way to live than to use the gift of being here as a way to give to others.

The work I've done here has gone way beyond my imagination. When I finally come down and look through the archives of the media coverage, it's going to hit me just how intense this whole experience has been. And yet of everything I've experienced here, the most demanding, the most courageous challenge has been to stay centered in love in the face of violence and anger, of frustration and fear and sadness. It's the hardest thing I've committed myself to, and I fall short. When the trees were smashing into the ground, I was consumed with sadness and fear and frustration and anger. I felt a piece of myself being ripped out, and I wanted to react like a wounded animal and strike out. I prayed to find a way to deal with these feelings, because I felt them enveloping me, so much so that I didn't think I could take any more. And then this amazing sense of love began to wash over me. Every time a tree smashed into the ground, with everything shaking and even the air shuddering, I also felt love filling up the great holes inside me. I realized that what I was feeling was unconditional love.

When I was growing up, my dad preached about agape, the highest order of pure, unconditional love. Agape, I suddenly recognized, was the love of the earth, the love of Creation. Every single day, we scorch and cut and burn and pollute and poison and yet Creation continues to give us life anyway. That's unconditional love. Wow. If Creation can have that kind of love for us, we should have it for the earth and for all life created here, including those who have lost touch with the earth.

That's when I started learning the power of love and the importance of my commitment to love. It's not easy, because to be open to love is to be open to all the pain and suffering of the world as well as to its joys and beauty. When I talk about it, I start to cry. I feel everything so intensely now. In my life down there, I had distractions to numb me and turn me away from what's happening to our world as a result of our disrespect for life, ripping out our roots to Creation. Up here, I can't hide behind the distraction. So I feel everything intensely: the anger, the sadness, the fear, everything. But love is what gives us the power to transform, and that's why love is the ultimate power.

When the Headwaters Forest Agreement — which in my opinion puts the environment in jeopardy in ways we will not be able to undo without a movement equivalent to the civil rights movement — came down the pike, when the California legislature passed its part of the funding even as people stood up and said, "No, no, no, no," the activists here, many of whom had been here for twelve years, felt like they'd been dealt a death blow. The local community was really low; you could feel a lot of despondency and despair. I prayed for guidance to find a way to transform the despair, to give us hope. The answer came: *Julia, sometimes you get so caught up in what you're struggling* against *that you forget what you stand* for, *and what you stand for is a love and respect for all life. That is something they cannot destroy. Love is the universal power. Man-made laws will never sign it away. It supersedes the power of technology and money. The only way for love to be destroyed is if you give it up. So as long as you have love in your heart, there is hope.*

I will never back down from taking a stand for life. And I will never let go of love. I've learned from my time with Luna that this is my biggest challenge. As long as you have love in your heart, there is hope.

In December 1999, satisfied with Pacific Lumber's covenant of protection for Luna and the area around her, Julia came down from her beloved tree and felt the earth again for the first time in two years. Her book The Legacy of Luna *was published shortly thereafter, and Julia began a media tour that put her squarely in the spotlight, bringing her message powerfully to people across America, England, and Europe.*

In the fall of 2000, Luna was attacked by someone with a chain saw who cut deep into her trunk. The assault brought a wave of outrage and an outpouring of support for both Luna and Julia, who fell to her knees sobbing when she first saw the wound on her beloved Luna. A team of arborists, foresters, mechanical engineers, and plant specialists responded quickly to secure Luna against the oncoming winter storms. The Circle of Life Foundation and Sanctuary Forest created a fund to help with the restoration, preservation, ongoing monitoring, and a criminal investigation. Julia founded the Circle of Life Foundation to inspire, support, and network with individuals and organizations working on environmental and social solutions that address threats to biological and cultural diversity. Sanctuary Forest is a land trust organization that holds the Deed of Covenant (similar to a conservation easement) that protects Luna and a three-acre grove around her. True to her mission, Julia responded to the attack, "Although symbols can be attacked, what they stand for can never be destroyed. Whenever Luna falls into the forest floor, she will feed and grow new life and what she stands for will live on forever. It's going to take people with diverse backgrounds coming together in unity and love to heal the wound in the tree and our world."

Julie Su

"I suppose it makes sense, then, that I would fight for people who cross continents and oceans for a chance at a better life, often with nothing more than hope and sheer determination to guide them in their journey. I am a product of that hope, and I carry that spirit in my heart, doing my best to fight poverty, exploitation, and suffering in a nation of plenty."

An attorney for the Asian Pacific American Legal Center in Los Angeles, California, Julie Su took on a behemoth: sweatshops in the garment industry.

One year out of law school, I walked into a case the likes of which I could never have imagined. It has defined me as an attorney, as a woman, and as an activist. In a way, it made complete sense.

My parents immigrated from China to Taiwan and then to the United States in the early sixties. Growing up, I felt the subtle, and often not-so-subtle, prejudice of people who looked on us with disdain because we were different. To this day, many people of color often view discrimination and racism as something they simply need to endure. Even though my parents knew in their hearts that the treatment they received was wrong, they couldn't take up the fight against it because, as poor Asian immigrants, they struggled just to get by.

For a while, my family had a Laundromat where my grandparents also worked. I remember going there on weekends, sitting on the dryers and watching my grandfather sort clothes. While my grandmother did alterations, she would talk about being poor in China, about fleeing the war, about the bombs falling. She told her stories without a trace of bitterness; she was simply talking about her life. Barely five feet tall and never weighing more than eighty pounds, she nevertheless possessed a tremendous strength that grew out of a lifetime of surviving hard times. Knowing that both she and my mother gave up everything they knew to build a new life in the States was profound for me.

My mother is a remarkable woman who not only made my clothes for years but also my first toys, a stuffed brown bear and gray mouse. Without complaint, she worked a number of jobs to support our family and to foster in my sister and me the conviction that our opportunities were limitless. Watching her work tirelessly, inside and outside the home, had a huge impact on me. She and my father made it their first priority to open the doors to our education and made us believe that, if we worked hard enough, we could do anything.

Ultimately, my parents saved enough to give us a comfortable life. I grew up in a middle-class suburb and went to a school where academics were strongly emphasized. Only as an adult did I realize how much my parents had to struggle. And only then, when asked, did they say, "Yes, it was very hard."

I suppose it makes sense, then, that I would fight for people who cross continents and oceans for a chance at a better life, often with nothing more than hope and sheer determination to guide them in their journey. I am a product of that hope, and I carry that spirit in my heart, doing my best to fight poverty, exploitation, and suffering in a nation of plenty. The struggle of garment workers against major, multimillion dollar corporations is a fundamental call for justice.

While an undergraduate at Stanford, I grew increasingly aware that law is not just a language, it is the language of power. Because I had grown up translating between Chinese and English, I knew that language often served to keep people at the margins of society. Going to law school would enable me to become a translator of the language of law for people who were disenfranchised or marginalized. A legal education would give me the tools to challenge laws written and enforced to preserve inequities.

When I graduated from Harvard Law School in 1994, I returned home to Los Angeles and received a fellowship to work at the Asian Pacific American Legal Center (APALC). My dream was to be a civil rights attorney working to end racism, sexism, poverty, and homophobia. To do that, it was important not only to translate the law for the disenfranchised but also to facilitate translations the other way around. Our legal system is ill-equipped to hear, and even hostile to, the stories of a large segment of society, stories that can't be fit into neat little legal boxes. I wanted to change that, to demand greater equality and inclusion, and to help people understand that they had power, that they could change their own lives.

During my first year at the APALC, I advocated for and represented low-wage workers in claims for unpaid wages and better working conditions. Periodically, state and federal labor agencies would call on us to go with them on garment sweatshop inspections, or "raids," to translate for the workers, who were almost all Asian and Latino. When I got a call a few days before a raid in El Monte, a suburb of Los Angeles, I had no reason to suspect that this raid would be any different from the others. The government was looking for Thai translators this time, and I referred them to people I knew.

Before dawn on August 2, 1995, a multiagency team stormed the sweatshop in El Monte. It was front-page news. Seventy-five women and five men had been locked in an apartment complex under armed guard for up to seven years, sewing garments that would be sold in national retail department stores. They'd been brought from rural areas of Thailand. Lured by the promise of good wages to send home to their families, they'd come to the States not knowing that they'd be forced to live, sleep, eat, and work as indentured servants. From dawn until deep into the night, they sewed garments until their fingers were raw and their vision blurred. Exhausted, they slept on the floor, eight or ten of them packed into a bedroom they shared with rats and roaches. The conditions in which they lived and toiled for years were unspeakable: no ventilation, boarded windows, razor wire atop the twelve-foot fence surrounding the complex.

The workers were paid less than a dollar an hour.

As the horrific story unraveled, we learned that the captors had used tourist visas to get the workers into the country. Once through customs at Los Angeles International Airport, they were put in the windowless back of a van and driven to the apartment complex southeast of downtown Los Angeles. They would not see the light of day again for years. Their passports and other identification were immediately confiscated by their captors, and they were told, "You've been brought here to work, and you're not going to be allowed to leave. If you try to escape, you'll be punished." A common threat used by employers of low-wage workers, it's regularly followed by, "Because you're an immigrant to this country, because you're poor, the government is not going to look favorably on you. Unless you obey me, I'll report you and the government will come after you." The Thai workers were also warned, "We will harm your families back home if you make trouble."

The next day, the Thais were put to work sewing garments for major manufacturers and retailers. If they got sick, they weren't allowed to see a doctor. Their phone calls were monitored, and all mail was censored. Over the years, nine of them escaped by jumping the fence or drugging a guard. One of the escapees sent an anonymous letter to the police about what was going on in El Monte. The police sent the letter to the Immigration and Naturalization Service (INS). Why the INS took three years to act remains a mystery. State authorities criticized the federal government, and the federal government pointed fingers at the State, each of them saying, "We got information, but we passed it on to someone else, and it was that agency's fault for not acting properly." So these workers' lives were caught up in the politics of blame.

When I read the *L.A. Times* story, my first thought was, "What happened to all the workers? Where were they sent?" I called my friend Chancee Martorell, founder and executive director of the Thai Community Development Center. She and I, with a small group of advocates, quickly mobilized. A year earlier, we had formed a coalition called Sweatshop Watch to bring together organizations across the state committed to eliminating sweatshops in the garment industry. Our coalition was young, made up mostly of Asian American activists and predominantly female.

We called around to find out where the workers had been taken and learned that the INS had incarcerated them in a downtown temporary holding area for immigrant detainees. When we went downtown and asked to see them, we were first told they weren't there. When we refused to leave, we were told, "Well, they're here, but you need their names and alien numbers to see them." It was a blatant attempt to keep the workers from any advocacy, legal or otherwise.

Why would the government want to hold these workers? First, because the U.S. Attorney's office wanted to make a case against the captors, and they needed the workers as witnesses in the criminal prosecution. Second, because the workers themselves were undocumented and so had broken the law. The latter was their primary justification. One INS agent said to me, "Two wrongs don't make a right. They're here without proper documents and, therefore, illegal and justifiably detained." I found it horrifying, that this blatant disregard for human rights was presented under the guise of the rule of law.

At the INS facility, I argued that detaining the workers sent the wrong message to other exploited workers by confirming what their employers were already telling them, "The INS is out to punish you, and if you report what is happening to you or try to raise your voice in protest, you're going to be deported." Because this was a high-profile case, the actions of the INS would create ripple effects across the entire garment industry and all low-wage industries, strengthening the hand of other exploitive employers.

My argument fell on deaf ears. After two days, the workers were transferred from downtown to the federal penitentiary on San Pedro Terminal Island in Long Beach. Once again, they were behind barbed wire, once again under armed guard.

At 6:00 the following morning, we went to Terminal Island and demanded to see them. We were told they were sleeping. Half an hour later, we approached a guard again. "They're eating breakfast," we were told. We waited a little longer and asked again. "They've been transferred." We would find out later that they'd been taken by bus, through a back gate, to the downtown holding center again.

After hours of phone calls and dogged persistence at the Terminal Island prison compound, the INS grudgingly agreed to bring the workers back so we could see them. I can still picture the prison buses as they came through the open gate. The workers, their faces pressed against the windows, looked lost and terrified. It is an image I will never forget. Later, they would tell me that, when the police knocked down the doors in El Monte and arrested their captors, they thought they had been saved and that they would be freed. Instead, they were put in prison jumpsuits and shackled. It was unconscionable.

When we finally gained entrance to the penitentiary at Terminal Island, we were told that we could see the workers only in groups of three and, by the way, that visiting hours were almost over. We were allowed just over an hour. In groups of three they came, dressed in prison jumpsuits, with a toothbrush and a document given to them by the INS rolled up in their chest pockets. They'd been tricked and brought to this country, forced to work eighteen hours a day in a place they couldn't see out of or leave. Food and basic necessities had been sold to them by their captors at four or five times the market price. Most of them were women between the ages of twenty and forty who had supported not only their own children but also their parents, siblings, and spouses back home in rural Thailand. They bore an incredible burden and, so, when the recruiter came with stories of America, they listened. They could make money by sewing garments in the States. "We will prepare the paperwork for you," said the recruiter. For these women, the opportunity to come to the States to work was tremendous. They were given no details of how they would get here; the recruiter said he would take care of that. And so they left behind their children and their families, not knowing that they wouldn't speak to them for years. Not knowing about the barbwire and armed guards and the dollar-an-hour wages.

We tried to make them feel more comfortable in the immediate sense, at the same time explaining that, if they didn't want to be deported, they had rights. They weren't criminals; they were being unjustly punished. We had to convey this very quickly while listening carefully to what each of them wanted. When advocating for people who are poor and who have very low levels of formal education, it's doubly important to really listen and to find out what they want instead of imposing our ideas of what we think they want. In the end, a number of them wanted legal representation.

We had begun what would be a period of intense advocacy, during which traps and barriers would be thrown in front of us constantly. Essentially, there was no established procedure for what we were doing. We were in uncharted waters, and, even though many people were on our side, even immigrant advocates would say to us, "This is just the way the INS works. You can't fight it." But we did, by refusing to accept no as an answer. When they slammed doors in our faces, we kept banging on them. In the waiting room, when INS agents seemed to be hiding in the back to avoid our demands, we used pay phones and called them. We were persistent. We approached windows outside of offices and shouted, "We're still here and demand to see the workers. You cannot hold people against their will and not let them know that they have rights." We called the media. At the end of the day, when the INS agents said, "We're closing up, you guys have to go home," we refused to leave, keeping the detention center open until midnight. Then we'd return to our offices and have strategy meetings lasting well into the night. After a few hours of sleep, we'd be up before dawn to start again.

At the same time that we fought for the workers' freedom, we mobilized to find temporary shelters for them in anticipation of their release. The outpouring of generosity was amazing. Churches came forward to offer space. Supermarkets called to offer food. Individuals donated clothing. Cedars-Sinai Medical Center, one of the premiere medical centers in the country, stepped forward to provide medical care. We found volunteers to teach the workers English so that they could become self-sufficient. AT&T donated phone cards so they could call their families. A dentist made a whole new set of teeth for one of the workers who, suffering from periodontal disease, had used pliers to extract eight of his abscessed teeth. We witnessed great humanity at the same time that we saw absolute indifference from the corporations in the garment industry that operated as though it was their unlimited right to use people for profit.

The second time I met with all the workers, they were being detained in a large INS holding tank in the federal building downtown. The room was hot as a sauna and stank. They had one toilet without a door; it wasn't even in a separate room. Some of the workers remember their imprisonment being as horrifying as El Monte, because it was at the hands of the federal government. They had no idea when it would end or what would happen. We brought in Buddhist monks to give spiritual comfort.

The workers were imprisoned by the INS for nine days. Finally, just after midnight on August 12, they were freed. A yellow school bus company donated their services to transport them. The initial group released was taken to a Thai temple in Hollywood. First were the calls home. The story had broken in Thailand, too, so families were extremely worried. Many of the workers had never used a phone, so we helped them make those calls. It was remarkable to witness them as they heard their children's voices for the first time in years.

As other workers were released, volunteers drove them to churches all across Los Angeles, where they'd be staying temporarily. When I dropped off the last worker at almost 3:00 in the morning, I sat in my car looking at her as she ran to rejoin her friends, and I could not imagine what they had been through or what was in store for all of us.

The workers' physical freedom was just the beginning. First and foremost, they wanted to find work, which runs counter to everything that the anti-immigrant school of thought says about poor immigrants in this country. We began the long process of helping them find jobs and apartments and teaching them how to use public transportation. At the same time, I had to convince the government to authorize them to work legally in the United States. I made the argument to federal prosecutors that, if the government was going to keep them as witnesses in the criminal case against the captors, then they had to be allowed to support themselves.

The overwhelming majority of the workers returned to the garment industry. Because some of the women had severe carpal tunnel syndrome, they couldn't sew garments anymore and found work as live-in housekeepers. Soon, under the leadership of the Thai Community Development Center, we found all of them apartments, near their work and accessible to public transportation. Then we taught them how to ride the bus, open bank accounts, and hook up their telephones and electricity. Every day for eight months, I and other advocates went to the shelters and then their apartments to make sure they had what they needed, to take them clothing, help them with health problems, get them to doctors or bring them medicine. It was important that we spend time with them to let them know we were there, to build solidarity and trust.

It was a tremendous undertaking. But there were many magical moments. Late one night, I drove to one of the apartments in a largely Latino neighborhood in East Los Angeles. When I got out of my car, I heard Spanish through open windows and in the common area. In the workers' apartment, we sat in the dark, because the electricity hadn't been turned on yet. I couldn't speak Thai, so we communicated with gestures. Together, we sat in the dark not speaking each other's language but communicating silently. This partnership, this sisterhood, would grow deeper. To this day, I use with them the Thai word for "big sister," a term of both respect and affection.

The U.S. Department of Justice and the U.S. Attorney's Office in Los Angeles prosecuted the workers' captors, a sixty-six-year-old Thai woman and three of her five sons. Before the case could be sent to a jury, they pled guilty to conspiracy, indentured servitude, and harboring immigrants. Some of the workers testified at the sentencing. I prepared them by explaining the criminal proceeding, making diagrams of the courtroom and explaining who does what and who sits where.

After the criminal case was resolved and the Thai family sent to jail — with prison terms of two to seven years — we encouraged the Department of Justice also to investigate the manufacturers and retailers to find out what they knew and whether they were complicit in the enslavement of the workers. They refused.

Frustrated that the real culprits were shielded from prosecution, the workers and I talked about fighting the garment industry. During many long hours over many days, I explained their rights, the legal system, its power and its limits, the potential benefits and the risks of such an undertaking. They could bring a civil suit against the manufacturers and retailers, whose demand for the cheapest labor at any cost had created the conditions for El Monte. But it would be anything but easy. Undeterred, they said they wanted to fight back.

In the months ahead, we would all need courage for what would become a tremendous battle against layers of oppressive institutions, from private corporations to state and federal authorities. It would take many people working together as a team to fight for the workers, most notably the Thai Community Development Center, the Korean Immigrant Workers' Advocates, and the Coalition for Humane Immigrant Rights of Los Angeles. It would take student activists, translators, sympathetic government officials, interested reporters, and innumerable volunteers.

The Asian Pacific American Legal Center threw its full support behind and resources into our legal challenge. We filed a lawsuit against manufacturers and retailers producing brand name labels, including B.U.M., High Sierra, Anchor Blue, Tomato, Clio, and many others. We named nearly a dozen corporate defendants, including Mervyn's, Montgomery Ward, and Miller's Outpost. It was the first federal lawsuit of its kind in which workers stood up to demand that manufacturers and retailers take full legal responsibility for the conditions in which their clothes are made.

At first, the manufacturers and retailers denied that their garments came from El Monte. But we had evidence: bundles of cut cloth and boxes and boxes of their labels found on unfinished garments in El Monte. With that tactic failing, they then claimed that they didn't know about the slave sweatshop and so couldn't be held liable. They moved to have the case dismissed.

The facts we presented to the court explained in detail how and why the manufacturers and retailers were responsible. A factory in downtown Los Angeles served as the front for the El Monte compound. Both locations were run by the Thai woman and her sons and operated under the name D & R Fashions and SK Fashions. The manufacturers and retailers employed garment workers through D & R Fashions and other entities that directly supervised the factories, so that they could claim they didn't hire or supervise the garment workers themselves and, therefore, were not responsible for paying them or treating them lawfully. But the manufacturers and retailers regularly sent representatives to the downtown "front" shop where only twenty to twenty-five workers were doing finishing work like buttons and buttonholes, putting garments onto hangers, and ironing. The actual labor of sewing garments wasn't done there, and the companies refused to ask where it was being done. They then used this self-imposed, willful ignorance to absolve themselves of any responsibility for the workers' suffering.

A federal judge denied the companies' motions to dismiss.

As a legal matter, this case was important because it helped establish a precedent for holding manufacturers and retailers responsible for the consequences of using sweatshop labor. When this case broke, other manufacturers and retailers tried to claim that it was simply a horrible aberration in an otherwise lawful industry. But sadly, El Monte was just one end of a continuum of abuse that is all too common in the industry. Because of the lack of regard for the human beings who make clothing — almost entirely women, women of color, immigrants — companies use cheap sweatshop labor and then claim that they have no control over the working conditions.

We fought an uphill battle to expose the lie behind the industry and to prove that manufacturers and retailers *do* exercise control. They reap the benefits of cheap labor and try to avoid any of the responsibility by using middlemen, so-called contractors, to watch over their workers. Lack of corporate accountability is what allows sweatshops to thrive.

When I talk about it now, I'm struck by how much we undertook. The case was highly controversial and unprecedented. I have no doubt that the legal opinions published in our case sent shockwaves through the garment industry. We would never have achieved such victories, and I myself would not have been able to stay the course, had it not been for the strength and courage of the workers. Periodically, they'd say to me, "You have so much energy, how do you do it?" I'd look at them in disbelief: "I'm just trying to keep up with you." They called me *ying lek,* which means "iron woman" in Thai. It's a term that applied far more to them.

Throughout the litigation, I did whatever I could to ensure that the workers wouldn't feel like they were just names on a piece of paper. The way in which we conducted the case was very important to me. I didn't want it to be a typical lawsuit in which the attorneys make fancy arguments and the clients sit back and wait for the outcome. That would have reinforced the marginalization the workers already felt. Instead, engaging them fully in all aspects of the legal decision-making and planning process served to empower them and reinforced their commitment to the broader implications of the case. So in addition to meeting with them and constantly explaining what I was doing, I took them to the retail stores where the clothes they had made were still hanging on racks. There they saw the connection firsthand, from El Monte to the retail stores. They would look at a garment, see the price tag, and a cloud would come over their faces. "So expensive," they whispered. One dollar an hour they had made sewing that garment.

Communicating with all the workers was daunting, but I needed to keep them abreast of the case and so met with them all as a group monthly. The workers themselves came up with the idea of also electing representatives. This was remarkable, because none of them had thought of themselves as leaders or representatives, nor had they ever cast a vote. After lengthy explanations and careful consideration, they held elections to choose representatives who would help me to ensure that everybody understood what was going on with the lawsuit. This was participatory democracy in action.

The litigation was fought long and hard. The manufacturers and retailers hired what seemed like every major law firm in Los Angeles to fight us. We were inundated with discovery, which are legal requests for information, and countless questions that were entirely irrelevant to the case, a legal strategy to bury our side, especially effective when the plaintiffs are poor and their attorneys are a nonprofit organization. I countered by bringing the workers in to answer specific questions, which also gave them an opportunity to tell their stories personally. "On exactly what day did you sew B.U.M. shorts?" asked the defendant's lawyer. "How many did you sew? What did the shorts look like? How many stitches did you do?" At first, the workers were concerned that if they didn't remember precisely, they would undermine the case. Absolutely not, I said. Just explain what you do remember. What's important is that you're heard — by the judge and by the corporations. They gave poignant answers: "I don't remember the exact date I sewed those shorts, but that's because, for years, day in and day out, this is all I did. While I may not remember the exact day, I may not remember the exact stitch, I do remember that I saw your label, and I still see it in my sleep at night."

Throughout the case, attorneys on the other side would offer small amounts of money and say, "Come on, your clients are poor, they have to take it." As the case dragged on, I knew they thought the workers would burn out, that I wouldn't even be able to find them when needed for the lawsuit. To the contrary, with just a few hours' notice, I could call a meeting and all of them would show up. Their presence and tenacity were powerful. They stood up against huge odds.

Just as the workers faced prejudice, so did I. Lawyers on the other side were dismissive of me, an Asian American woman, only twenty-seven years old. Once, when we were appearing at a big law firm for settlement discussions among all the companies, I took some of the women workers with me. I was in a suit, carrying my briefcase. As we approached, one of the attorneys said to me, very slowly and with exaggerated pull on the vowels, "Where's your lawyer?" The first time we appeared before the judge, I was in the courtroom with two of my cocounsel, both of whom are white men. The defendants' attorneys came over and introduced themselves to the men, completely ignoring me.

I had never presented an argument before a federal judge, and I struggled with whether to do it myself or give it to one of my cocounsel who were long-time, experienced civil rights attorneys brought in precisely for their expertise. With so much at stake, I nevertheless made the decision to argue it myself. From the beginning, I had told the workers that it was their voices that needed to be heard, their stories that needed to be told. Since I was the one they knew and trusted, it was important for them to see me standing up to represent them. It was also significant that they see me, an Asian American woman like them, presenting legal arguments before the court. Too often in our society, we equate passion or emotion with a lack of clear reasoning or strong analytical skills. However, my passion for our cause and my personal commitment to the workers made me a better, not worse, advocate. It was important to keep that heart in the case, including in the courtroom and in front of the judge.

Although we never went to trial, we made several appearances before the judge. I knew that the outcome of the lawsuit could depend on who was assigned to hear the case. We were fortunate that our judge was a brilliant African American woman who was willing to give the workers a chance to be heard. Her respect for them, and her respect for the law, was invaluable to our success in later reaching a landmark settlement with the defendants.

The lawsuit dragged on for four years, and I can't remember a time when I wasn't scared. Some of my fear came from the sheer sense of responsibility

I felt to do things right, because what we were doing was so very, very important. The stakes were high, and the pressure intense. My fear was alleviated, in part, by the fact that the workers were, in all ways, my partners. At the same time, I remember being scared when they'd ask me what to do, because I needed to advise them while also giving them a sense of their own power.

Our whole approach to social justice work — emphasizing client participation and power — would either break new ground or fail. We were setting precedent, not just in terms of the lawsuit but also by trying a different way of lawyering, by challenging a system that privileges the attorney over anybody else, including the client. Because we couldn't rely on a positive outcome at the end — indeed, the challenges were too great and the legal system too biased against us for us to focus on the distant possibility of victory — the process itself had to be valuable. The naysayers were everywhere, insisting that it wouldn't work.

One by one, the companies settled.

To help us prepare for trial against the last defendant, I brought in an old friend from law school whose firm had agreed to work pro bono. I was at his firm when the last company agreed to pay 1.2 million dollars. I called my office to get all the workers together for a meeting. My heart was racing as I drove to the meeting, thinking, "Wow, this could be it. It could be over." We had come so far; it had been a long time since all the early meetings by candlelight. And here we were, with a final 1.2 million dollars on the table.

By the time I got to my office, all the workers were there. I had just been in an eight-hour negotiation with the company's lawyers and chief executive officer, dealing with men, all men. When I walked into the room and saw the workers, I put my hands over my face and started to cry. It was very emotional. When I looked up, many of the workers were crying too. We had grown very close and been through a great deal together. Later, some of them said they thought I was crying because we had lost the case. Some of them thought I was simply too exhausted to speak. Others said, "No, she's crying because something great has happened." When I saw them, all together after four years, defying everyone who had predicted that they'd run away in fear or never understand such a complex case, I was overwhelmed by the power of them all.

We had truly done this together. They could have given up at any time. Instead, they became powerful decision makers. Early on, they'd say, "Julie, what do you want? What do you want us to do?" By the end, they wouldn't even ask. The dynamic had changed entirely. I'd give them an update and they'd talk among themselves to decide what to do next, generating their own ideas and proposals. They had learned to speak for themselves. And, in a very profound way, they understood the significance of what they were attempting to change in the garment industry.

With this final settlement offer, we had three options: we could settle; we could ask the judge to decide the case as a matter of law, which meant it would be decided without a jury; or we could go to trial. The workers broke up into groups and discussed, argued, debated, and advocated for different positions, trying to balance the myriad factors involved. Articulating what they wanted, coming to a consensus, would take four or five hours. But at the end, they decided clearly for themselves.

They accepted the final settlement. It was the spring of 1999. The overall settlements from all the companies totaled a little more than four million dollars. They had taken on the challenge of fighting the corporations so the garment industry would realize that the workers who sew their clothes are people, individuals with humanity and dreams.

Most of the women still work in the garment industry, earning minimum wage. Some saved their settlement money. Others sent it to their parents and children in Thailand. Some even bought homes for their families or paid for a sibling's education or started a small business in Los Angeles. Yet the most radical transformation would not be measured in dollars. The most profound changes were personal: standing up, speaking out, daring to take on the seemingly impossible. They gained tremendous confidence.

In the beginning, the women would tell me that I needed to find a boyfriend. "If you talk so much," they warned me, "you're never going to find a boyfriend." Or "If your opinions are so strong, no one's ever going to want to be with you." They also worried about their own futures without a man. By the end of the case, they said instead, "I can take care of myself. Why would I want to be with someone unless he's good to me, unless he respects my opinions and my strength?" Those were dramatic changes.

Another landmark victory was getting visas for the workers to stay in this country. At every turn, I was told, "It doesn't happen that way. It can't be done. They don't deserve it. What kind of precedent will this set? People will be knocking down the borders to come to this country if your clients are allowed to stay." When I couldn't get the results I wanted in Los Angeles, I went to Washington D.C., where I met with congressional representatives, senators, the staff of the Department of Justice and the Department of Labor. When I learned that Attorney General Janet Reno would be in Los Angeles, I stayed up all night preparing for a meeting with her. After that meeting, some of the barriers started to fall. When we finally won the visas, we celebrated with Thai food, music, and a big cake I had bought that said, "To justice, freedom, and to all of you."

Our legal battle became the catalyst for enormous changes in the garment industry. A couple of published opinions by the court gave the green light to garment workers to sue manufacturers and retailers. It's a green light that we've used again and again in subsequent cases.

Fighting this battle, we all learned much about the legal system, and we also helped to change it. As an attorney, that change was pivotal to me: the legal system has to be able to respond to genuine demands for justice and not just be there to arbitrate different claims of self-interest. We have a long way to go before all have true equal access to justice, but our case was one small step toward that ideal.

I have been accused of being too emotional in my work. During this lawsuit, it happened often. I'd be sitting across the table from one of the workers or about to make an argument to the opposing side when incredible emotion would sweep over me. It was so powerful that often I'd get tears in my eyes. This was viewed as a sign of weakness. But looking back, I see that it was the source of my strength. I believed deeply, passionately, in what we were doing. The depth of that feeling would give me the courage to fight for the workers, to accept nothing less than what I knew they deserved.

For her work on the El Monte case, Julie was awarded the Reebok Human Rights Award, given to individuals under thirty who have made significant contributions to human rights. The executive director of the Reebok Human Rights Foundation, Sharon Cohen, said, "My esteem for Julie Su is so high. Every law firm wanted her when she got out of Harvard, so she could have been on a partner track by now, looking at millions of dollars. But she chose a course as a human rights activist. She's just amazing." Julie shared her twenty-five-thousand-dollar award check with the Thai Community Development Center and the Korean Immigrant Workers' Advocates.

During the El Monte lawsuit, Julie met Hernán Vera, also an attorney. On the third anniversary of the El Monte raid, they had a traditional Thai wedding, planned and attended by most of the workers. On October 3, 2000, they had a baby daughter, LiMei.

The women who courageously stood up for their right to be treated humanely are:

Sukunya Sutthiprapha
Chamnien Toratsami
Klaikaeo Naokhamphaeng
Bunta Phondet
Nuntha Praean-Patthamakun
SutchaiChisuneee
Suchada Iamphon
Mali Burilong
Samruam Wankham
Umaphon Phowon
Khanit Phu-phanchit
Phaonapha Phensuk
La-ong Kitcharoen
Siwan Techadi
Chamnien Thaweewat Thomas
Ruchirat Sibunkham
Phatchari Thamasali
Rungthiwa McAllister
Suphaphon Kingchan
Bunlum Chanbowon
Wina Namtham
Wari Kaeopraditphon
Saman Wiphanna
Supawadee Phromwiint
Sombun Phaengkaeo
Nitaya Soikhoksung
Sawiang Singsathit
Duangsaeng Krajangsri Suvanich
Prasop Thuaiychun
Wannipha Sichaichanc
Phanthong Khamphira
Sombat Puritsaphan
Bunlai Misi Vancura
Runglawan Rutthidet
Sompong Samudpeud
Lamphu Songkhram
Sirilak Rongsak
Buppha Chaemchoi
Lampang Sisa
Phattharaphon Nuni
Chammari Onchairat
Suni Chaemchukun
Manun Phalat
Sa-ngob Chanwichian
Siriphan Rakkhong
Bumsom Phalat
Somphit Sinsurin
Sutta Kiangsung Phillips
Kanchana Suriyatraku
Waeo Saengtarat
Sangwan Watthanaphong
Phitsamai Baothong
Phaisan Kaeobunpan
Wasana Buasing
Bunchan Butdi
Somyong Malison
Somchit Nonsila
Rotchana Chuchuchit Sassman
Lamphoon Angkhom
Suphaphon Khamsutthi
Sunan Chao-op-tom
Maliwan Radomphon Clinton
Suphawan Simarak
Rosalba Cadena
Elvira Damian
Pilar Iglesias Gracia
Maira Delfin Montalvo
Concepcion Rivas
Adriana Zaragoza Navaro
Gladys Bardales
Araceli Castro
Aquelina Gaspar
Gladis Lopez
Anabel Rivas
Rosina Villanueva

Joanne Spencer

"If anyone had told me what I was about to become involved in, I would have said they were just plain crazy... I'm a mother of three and a grandmother of three. I'm too old to be marching around the jail with a group of people and standing on the jailhouse steps talking over a loudspeaker about how Tyrone Briggs was innocent and that he should be free."

Joanne Spencer is a homemaker, wife of a physician, mother, and grandmother who was living a comfortable life on the upscale shores of Lake Washington in Seattle until her call to jury duty.

There it was, lying among my mail that day in April of 1987.

I picked up the plain manila card addressed to me and turned it over. I was being called to jury duty and could expect to spend about eight days, more or less, at the courthouse. I had never sat on a jury. Those eight days turned into eight years of seeking justice.

The first case on which I was seated was a criminal case that lasted fewer than three days. We came in with a conviction, and I experienced for the first time how hard it is to call another human guilty even when the evidence proves him to be. He would do time and, hopefully, be rehabilitated, but that last part was up to him and a justice system which, at the time, I thought was working just fine.

Three of us from that case were called to serve on yet another jury, again a criminal trial. It turned out to be a case in which a young black man was accused of attacking, robbing, and raping women. There were five victims — three Caucasians and two Asians.

As soon as I got into the courtroom, I knew this case was going to be different. Armed guards sat on each side of Tyrone Briggs, the accused. *This guy must really be dangerous,* I thought, as a strange queasiness churned in my stomach. The trial began with the prosecutor describing the attacks. Chills went up my spine. I was nervous and repulsed just sitting in the same courtroom with Briggs. But I took my duty as a juror very seriously and kept reminding myself of the judge's instructions to keep an open mind and not make any decision until we had heard all the facts of the case. The judge also instructed us to take notes, which would be destroyed after the trial. I filled an entire spiral notebook.

I knew nothing about the case going into it, because I had been in Japan vacationing with my husband when the attacks occurred. I was a completely untainted juror. I gathered from what was said that there had been a great deal of publicity about the case in Seattle, and many women were scared to death. All kinds of safety precautions had been taken to protect women working at Harborview Medical Center, since three of the victims had worked there and all five incidents took place within a short distance of the hospital.

As the women testified about the attacks, I empathized so strongly that I wanted to reach out and wrap my arms around them. Yet as the case progressed, I began to see that something was wrong. Descriptions of the assailant given to police right after the attacks were dramatically different from those given in the courtroom. An artist's sketch done by one of the victims and a composite drawing done by a man who came to the aid of one of the victims were shown as evidence. Neither of them resembled Tyrone Briggs. They showed a man with a short Afro, matching the description given by other victims. Our jury was shown a photo of Briggs, who had long jeri curls down past his collar when he was arrested. Numerous people testified that he had worn his hair like that for two years. The sketch and composite showed a man with average-sized nose and lips. The defendant sitting in front of me had a very prominent nose and lips.

One woman said, right after her attack, that her assailant was balding. The man who made up the composite drawing said the assailant had a receding hairline, which his drawing showed. Briggs didn't have a receding hairline, nor was he balding.

The height of the attacker, given by the five victims, ranged from five foot eight inches to six foot two. Briggs was six foot one. The age of the attacker varied from fourteen years to twenty-five. *Why such a wide age range?*

One witness said her attacker had a space between his front teeth and that they were "yellowed, spacey teeth that looked like they needed a lot of dental work." When she saw Briggs in the lineup, she noticed that he didn't have a space between his teeth and changed her description to say the space was in his back teeth. Briggs was instructed to open his mouth wide and show his teeth to each individual juror. He had nice white teeth, no spaces, not yellowed, not looking like they needed dental work.

Another one of the victims described her attacker immediately after the attack as having freckles across the middle part of his face. Briggs had no freckles. However, he did have a very large, black, distinctive mole over his upper lip. It was an easy facial feature to spot, even from the jury box, yet no victim or witness saw or described a mole on the face of their attacker. In the courtroom, all of them admitted they could see Briggs's mole clearly and from a great distance.

As a juror, I found it curious that Briggs had prominent features that were clearly visible in the courtroom but never described by the witnesses. I was frustrated that none of my questions were being answered. I was only finding more questions. None of this was fitting together. The only thing that was fairly consistent was that the attacker and the defendant were both light-skinned black men.

Perhaps the greatest discrepancy was the stutter. Briggs had a bad one. We hardly needed the testimony of his high school basketball coach and two teachers who worked closely with him that he stuttered, always, no matter what. When Briggs took the witness stand, occasionally the cords on his neck stood out with the great effort it took for him to get out what he wanted to say. As he testified, I noticed the shock on the faces of three of the victims who were sitting together, listening. Their mouths literally dropped open. I wondered how they could have been attacked by this man and yet be so surprised that he stuttered dramatically. During all five crimes, the attacker had spoken and the dialogue had usually been extensive. And yet Briggs couldn't get a sentence started without saying, "Ahahahaha," stopping mid-sentence and repeating it before he could continue. His family said Tyrone had always been like this.

After the detective had arrested Briggs, she put together a six-person photomontage. One of the victims, herself a deputy prosecutor, picked two men who resembled her attacker: Briggs, who was number four, and a man in the number-one position. But throughout the trial, she said she wasn't really sure Briggs was the one who attacked her. Another victim's statement read, "I'm not positive it's number four; he could be the person. It's definitely not numbers one, two, three, five, or six." The statements made by all the victims were tentative.

Finally, the trial got around to how Briggs was arrested. Since the attacks had all happened in the same area, during the same early morning hours, they were considered the work of a serial attacker. Because of the close proximity of the attacks to the hospital, they became known jointly as the "Harborview Rape Case." Harborview Medical Center was next to a public housing project called Yesler Terrace, which is a high-density, low-income housing project run by the city.

Tyrone Briggs had lived in Yesler Terrace with his parents, brothers, and sister for about a dozen years and was living there at the time of the attacks. Hundreds of young black men lived there, and the police were picking up those between the ages of fourteen and thirty for questioning.

A police stakeout was conducted in the neighborhood to try to catch the assailant. During this time, even though Briggs didn't fit the description of the person they were looking for, a policeman, stopped him for routine questioning to see what he was doing in that area. Briggs told him he lived there. The officer talked to him for a few minutes and noticed that he stuttered, writing this in his police notes. After a minute or two, he motioned to the detective in charge of the case to come over and talk with Briggs. She was sitting in her police car with her coffee and didn't bother to get out. It was raining. She motioned Briggs over and talked to him for a short time, then left.

Briggs didn't fit the descriptions given by the witnesses, and the two police had no reason to detain him. However, when they returned to the station, they put the information Briggs had given them into their computer as a routine check. He had lied about his name. As a juror, I thought, *Lying to the police officer about his name, that sounds pretty bad.* I thought maybe this was going to turn out to be the "smoking gun." But it turned out to be something a kid, who had just turned nineteen, might do if he was afraid of getting busted for a fifty-six-dollar traffic ticket he hadn't paid. Late one afternoon, after his dad had gotten off work, Briggs had jumped into his car to go over to a friend's house and had left his driver's license in another pair of jeans. He was stopped by a policeman for a routine check in the neighborhood and given a ticket for driving without his license. When the officer questioned Briggs in the stakeout, he was nervous because he hadn't paid the ticket, and so he lied about his name, but he was naive enough to give his correct address, phone number, and birth date.

The detective got a warrant for Tyrone's arrest and went to his house. Briggs's mother, Dorothy, told the police that her son was at the gym two blocks away. The detective arrested him right off the basketball court for the unpaid traffic ticket, took him to the police station, booked him, and took a mug shot of him.

The next morning, Tyrone's father paid the traffic ticket and took his son home. But the detective wasn't done with him. She got another arrest warrant and knocked on Briggs's door again. She wanted to talk to Tyrone. Dorothy told her that Tyrone was at the basketball gym shooting hoops, as usual, but she would send his father to get him. The detective gave Dorothy her card and asked her to call as soon as Tyrone got home.

When the detective went back, this time she took five other officers with her. They walked in and, after a brief conversation, she said, "Tyrone, I'm placing you under arrest for assault, robbery, and rape."

It occurred to me, that if I'd committed those crimes, if I was that kind of person and I heard the police were looking for me, I'd split. I wouldn't wait around for them to handcuff me and take me off to jail, like they did Briggs. It didn't make sense to me.

After the detective got Briggs booked, she went back to his house with a search warrant and, with the other officers, went through the house. They took a lot of clothing, photographed different rooms, searched drawers, but didn't turn up anything to tie Briggs to the crimes.

The next day, the detective called all the witnesses down, telling them she was going to conduct a lineup. When they arrived, they were kept waiting while she decided to make up a six-person photomontage instead.

The photomontage was something of a problem. Briggs had a conspicuous, dark mole over his upper lip, and the attacker didn't have one. The detective took care of this problem with her pen. She drew over Briggs's natural mole and then placed a corresponding ink dot over the upper lip of the other five in the montage. As a juror, I was shocked that a police officer would tamper with evidence. It was obvious that her actions would plant the thought of a mole in the witnesses' minds.

Weeks later, the detective conducted a lineup. Tyrone Briggs was the only one repeated from the photomontage and the only one with a mole. When this came out during the trial, I came unglued. Police tampering with evidence. Suggestive remarks made by the officers in charge of the line-up. All this would have greatly influenced the witnesses to pick Tyrone Briggs as the perpetrator of the crimes, whether he was guilty or innocent. It was outrageous.

Throughout the trial, the prosecutor seemed adamant that Tyrone Briggs was the attacker of these women. *If that was true, then why didn't any evidence point to Briggs?* One poor victim had been bludgeoned with a stick that had visible bloody fingerprints on it. The fingerprints weren't Briggs's. There was no saliva, semen, or any other forensic evidence to point to Briggs. Nothing the police found while searching Briggs's house tied him to these crimes. Briggs had alibis — twice from his family, once from his teachers.

A few other things seemed strange to me. I wondered why a kid who lived in the neighborhood all those years and was kind of a neighborhood hero because of his basketball fame — a kid who was known as one of the good guys in the neighborhood — why would *he* commit these kinds of crimes and commit them *right in his own backyard?* Why wouldn't he go at least a short distance away? Why during the day, when people who knew him would see him? It didn't make sense. And it didn't add up that after one bloody attack, Briggs walked right by the scene of the crime, with the police K-9 unit looking for the attacker, and the dogs didn't even give him a whiff.

The only possible explanation that made any sense to me was that the public outcry put pressure on the police to find the criminal. They must not have done a thorough investigation and hastily arrested the wrong person. In light of nothing but doubts and discrepancies, I didn't see how I could call this guy anything but innocent. Nine other jurors felt the same way, including the two who had brought a guilty verdict in the previous case. We ended as a hung jury. Two men voted guilty and were solid as stone no matter how much the rest of us argued with them. They said they had the right to vote as they wished, and they wouldn't let the rest of us confuse them, period. It was one of the most frustrating things I've ever experienced. It made me fear some jurors and shook my faith in our justice system.

Following the verdict, both the prosecution and defense attorneys spoke with the jury. I told Tyrone's lawyer, Richard Hansen, that I was heartsick. "If there's anything I can do, please let me know," I said. He gave me his card. I felt terribly depressed about the fact that our jury came so near to, and yet so far from, acquitting Briggs. That night, after we were declared a hung jury, I sat down and wrote Briggs a letter, which I sent to Hansen to deliver to him in jail. I wanted the poor kid to know that ten of us on that jury had voted innocent. I wanted him to know that ten of us out of the twelve didn't think he was the horrible, sick criminal the police and prosecutor had made him out to be.

Four jurors and I stayed in contact after the trial. It was good therapy. No one else could understand what we had been through and our shared frustration over not having reached an out-and-out innocent verdict. The prosecution decided to retry Briggs, and we were all glued to the TV during Briggs's second trial. We thought surely this jury would acquit him. We were stunned when, instead, they convicted him. What was it about the word *"doubt"* that this jury didn't understand, when there was nothing in this case *but* doubt? A guilty verdict was incomprehensible.

The frustrating injustice of the whole case made my blood boil. I couldn't imagine how it felt to be Tyrone Briggs, star high school basketball player now locked up in prison for something he didn't do. He wasn't just a good basketball player but an "outstanding basketball talent." Several college coaches had asked about him. His coach was sure that Briggs had a brilliant future awaiting him. Basketball was something he could do without his stutter holding him back.

It was heartbreaking to see the outpouring of hate directed at Tyrone from people who didn't know the true facts in the case. Simply by virtue of being arrested and tried for this crime, he was the target of all the venom and cries for revenge as if he were truly guilty. People took what the police and the prosecutors said as gospel. I understood. Before this case, when I heard about a crime and that someone had been arrested, my first thought was always, *"Thank God, they got the guy."* But no more. My first thought now was, *"Dear God, I hope they got the* right *guy."*

Many things were hidden in Tyrone's case, things that our jury wasn't allowed to know. I learned about them later. I found out that there were seven other people who had been victims around the same time, in the same general location. Those seven were called in to identify Briggs, and they said he wasn't their attacker. But they had seen the sketch done by one of the victims and thought it looked just like the man who had attacked them. I also learned something about the state's star witness. He had often been in trouble with the police and one of the charges against him, just prior to the Briggs trial, was committing perjury in a murder trial.

Richard Hansen hired a detective to depose the second jury and found that there was jury misconduct. Based on the evidence, the judge overturned the guilty verdict. But then pressure from the prosecutor's office and the public made her change her mind. Hansen filed an appeal. The appellate courts were full, so a long wait was in order. In the meantime, Tyrone Briggs remained in jail.

Tyrone was becoming very depressed and Hansen thought it might cheer him up if some of his former jurors who believed in his innocence went to visit him. I had never been in a jail before, so my husband went with me the first time. Tyrone was so happy to see us. He was claustrophobic and would hyperventilate at times. My husband, a physician, told him some things he could do to help himself. I, and all the others who would work with him, came to know Tyrone as a sensitive, polite person and a gentle soul. The first time I went to the jail alone at night, he was concerned and told me it was dangerous, that I should be very careful.

Owing to his pronounced stutter, Tyrone was a good listener and not much of a talker. Before I'd leave, he would put his hand up to the glass that separated visitor and prisoner, and I would put mine in front of his. Most times, he would wave all the way until I disappeared into the elevator.

If anyone had told me what I was about to become involved in, I would have said they were just plain crazy. First of all, I'm a mother of three and a grandmother of three. I'm too old to be marching around the jail with a group of people and standing on the jailhouse steps talking over a loudspeaker about how Tyrone Briggs was innocent and that he should be free. My husband was at the hospital when that happened. Some of his colleagues told him they'd seen his wife on TV. He knew how strongly I believed in Briggs's innocence, how the injustice of the whole thing was driving me crazy. He knew that I had to stand up for my beliefs. His support never wavered, but he wasn't without concern that I was becoming so visibly involved in such a high-profile case.

The appeals court date was a long way down the road, and the judge had set bail at a hundred thousand dollars. Someone who didn't know Tyrone but believed him to be innocent put his house up for the bail. Tyrone was released, but had to have around-the-clock monitoring. Electronic monitors weren't available in our state at that time, so human monitors were needed. I volunteered, even though I didn't know where I'd find the time.

The day after we were sworn in by the judge as monitors, our pictures appeared on the front page of the newspaper. Soon after, I started noticing police cars everywhere I went. One would be in front of me at the same time that one was behind me and one beside me in the next lane. I found out the same thing was happening to Tyrone's dad and one other monitor.

This is when I began to understand the esprit de corps among police. Since I was standing up for Briggs, I was going against the prosecutors and the police. And boy, do they stick together. I think they were trying to scare me off. This went on for two-and-a-half weeks. I guess they gave up when they found out I wasn't going to knuckle under.

Right after Tyrone was released on bail, the prosecutor sent notices to all his neighbors that a dangerous, sexual predator was going to be living in their midst. His address was listed in the news media. He and his family were frightened by this. They no longer lived in Yesler Terrace but another neighborhood where they weren't known. To counter the scare tactics of the prosecutor, some of us went door to door, talking to the neighbors to reassure them that they had nothing to fear. People looked puzzled and some a little frightened when they saw me, this short, white woman at the door with this tall, young, black man who was Tyrone's brother.

Mr. Briggs's boss gave Tyrone a job as a stevedore on the docks. He was allowed to go to and from work with his dad, but the rest of the time it was up to the monitors to constantly check on him to make sure he was home. On special occasions, he was allowed a brief outing with a monitor accompanying him. Sometimes I took him to his old high school to shoot baskets with his buddies on the school's free-shoot night. For the briefest of time, he was back in his element, on the basketball court.

Other times, I took him to his church for Sunday service. His minister would greet me as Sister Spencer. I found a wonderful spirit there, and even though I was the only white face, people were friendly to me.

Each monitor had a special logbook to keep records of every contact or outing with Tyrone. We had to send in a weekly report to his parole officers. During the twenty-four-hour period I was responsible for him, I was required to go to his house both announced and unannounced. I set my alarm at different times throughout the night to call him on the telephone.

I became chair of a support group called "Justice for Tyrone Briggs." We spoke before churches and other organizations about the case and raised a little money to help with his defense. One of our objectives was to let the general public know that Briggs was innocent, to inform them of the facts not told in the media. My grown son and one daughter became involved. My son wrote newsletters that a coworker printed on her computer. A few of us sat around stamping and addressing thousands of envelopes to judges, attorneys, news media, and anyone in the general public we knew. Our efforts almost amounted to a full-time job. We held some of our meetings at Briggs's house so that Tyrone and his parents could be a part of it.

The appeal was finally heard and the decision made to try Tyrone again. The prosecution had nothing new to present. But the new defense team had hired a private detective who discovered new evidence for the defense.

I was approved as Tyrone's adult supervisor to take him to the breaks and lunches during the month-long trial. Reactions in the courthouse and on the street during lunch breaks were diverse and sometimes amusing. Publicity was incredible. Some people would look terrified. Many would grin as we walked by, and whisper, "Good luck, we think you're innocent." Almost everyone had a strong opinion one way or the other about his guilt or innocence.

It had been three and a half years.

The third jury voted ten for innocent and two for guilty. The state dropped all charges with prejudice, which means Tyrone can never be tried on these charges again. He's free now, but deeply scarred.

And I, mother of three and grandmother of three, have learned to be a mouthy woman in the best sense, to take a stand for what I believe, to not be intimidated, and to demand justice.

Joanne has written about her experiences with Tyrone Briggs in her book, The Seventh Victim, *and is looking for the right publisher.*

Carrie Barefoot Dickerson

"Our attorneys had withdrawn because of our huge debt to them, and they advised me to withdraw... 'You can't win.... ' I told them we *had* to win and I would never withdraw. That's when I offered to mortgage my property."

A teacher for many years before becoming a nurse, Carrie Barefoot Dickerson was a fifty-six-year-old farm wife when she went to battle with the federal government in the town of Claremore, Oklahoma, a place made famous as the setting for the musical Oklahoma! *She would persevere for nine years and do the impossible.*

"Carrie, this is the last of our money."

My husband Robert handed me a three-thousand-dollar check to pay our attorney. "You'll have to find another way to finance your fight."

For more than four years, we had spent thousands of dollars of our own money — from calf sales and the profits of our hundred-bed Aunt Carrie's Nursing Home — in an effort to prevent the Black Fox Nuclear Power Plant from being built near Inola, twelve miles south of our Claremore, Oklahoma, farm.

On May 8, 1973, I had read a newspaper article about Public Service Company of Oklahoma's plans to install two General Electric boiling water nuclear reactors. I had little knowledge of the implications of nuclear power, but the article made me think of something I'd seen in a magazine twenty years earlier. It was a picture of a muskrat, and the caption beneath it said that the muskrat developed cancer from the radioactive effluents released into tributaries from the Oak Ridge Nuclear Facility in Tennessee where the muskrat had been found. I remember thinking at that time, "Our government will take care of this problem. It will protect us. It won't allow more cancer cases to occur from radiation." I was very naive.

Twenty years later, after reading in the newspaper about Public Service Company of Oklahoma's plans, I wondered if it were true that the government would protect us. For my own peace of mind, I decided to call the Atomic Energy Commission (AEC) — now the Nuclear Regulatory Commission (NRC) — and ask them to send me information about nuclear power plants. One of the packets I received contained a 1965 study that had been commissioned by the AEC and kept secret for eight years. The five scientists who conducted the study concluded that if the water were cut off to a nuclear power plant, a meltdown would occur and radiation would be released that would render an area the size of Pennsylvania uninhabitable for countless centuries; hundreds of thousands of people would die of acute radiation poisoning; others would develop cancer and leukemia, and infants would be born with severe birth defects. (The study, eerily, predicted what would happen at the nuclear power plant at Chernobyl, in the Ukraine, on April 26, 1986.)

I was enraged by what I read. Oklahoma is about the size of Pennsylvania. The entire state and all its people could be eradicated by a nuclear power plant accident. How on earth could the government and the utility company approve and promote the use of an energy source with such devastating risks? I could not allow this threat to hang over our state and our people, our families, our children. At that moment, I knew in my heart that beyond any doubt I had to use every power within me to prevent the construction of the proposed Black Fox Nuclear Power Plant. I could not — I would not — allow the plant to be built.

As we watched our two-year-old grandson play in the yard, Robert protested that one cannot fight big business and the government and win. And he was concerned that my life could be endangered in the process. I told him that another thing I had learned was that even if a devastating accident never occurred, the nuclear power plant would produce long-lived, high-level radioactive waste that wouldn't decay for many thousands of years. During all that time, future generations would be burdened with the task of using their tax dollars and their time and efforts to keep the waste under surveillance and out of the biosphere to prevent it from destroying them. I told him that the radioactive effluents from a nuclear power plant can cause infants to be born with birth defects and children and adults to develop leukemia and cancer. I asked Robert, "Can we live with ourselves if we sit and hold our hands and allow J. J. (our little grandson) or other children to develop leukemia? Or allow future grandchildren (ours or others) to be born with birth defects?" That convinced Robert, and he became my most ardent supporter.

In 1976, the hearing process for the plant began. The law requires that a hearing be held, and, if there are no protesters or interveners, it usually lasts only two days. The Nuclear Regulatory Commission did not wish the hearing to last beyond those two days, so they tried to persuade us not to intervene. "You'll be wasting your time, your energy, and your money," someone from the commission said to me, "because the law doesn't allow an intervener to stop a nuclear power plant. All you can expect to accomplish is to change the site of the plant if it's not suitable or to change the design if you can prove there are flaws." I told them that, regardless of such an unconstitutional law, we *would* intervene and we *would* stop Black Fox, because we had to.

It was difficult to raise money to pay the fees for our attorneys and expert witnesses who represented us in our intervention in the hearings. Even people who believed in the cause would say, "I'm not going to put my money down a bottomless hole. You're not going to win, so why try?" To which I would reply, "If we don't try, we won't have a *chance* to win!" Our family had to bear much of the burden of funding the fight against the construction of the plant. But now, with that last check, our bank account had dried up.

That night, knowing I couldn't sustain the fight without more money, I prayed, "God, I can't sing and I can't pick a guitar, so I can't have a concert to raise money. I'm just a registered nurse and a former schoolteacher. What can I do to raise money? We can't quit, we must stop that plant!"

At 5:00 the next morning, I awoke from a Technicolor dream about a beautiful sunburst quilt. Usually my dreams vanish when I go back to sleep, but this time I said to myself, "God has given you the answer to your prayer. You get up and sketch that dream quilt." So I did. It had been forty-two years since I had quilted, and I told God, "You'll have to help me remember how Grandmother Perry taught me to cut out the pieces and sew them together and to use the thimble and needle to make tiny, tiny stitches."

Somehow I made that quilt and I thank God for his divine inspiration. Working with those beautiful, bright colors and becoming absorbed in the repetitious process of stitching — working the needle in and out of the fabric — helped to give me the sense of tranquility and peace that I needed. In the end, the quilt was so radiant that my daughter, Patricia, named it *Sun in Splendor.* We raffled it at the fall 1977 alternative energy fair — the Energy Exposition at the Tulsa State Fairgrounds — and raised three thousand dollars. Soon other women began to pitch in and help to make quilts and, working together, we eventually raised sixty thousand dollars.

For five more years, I continued to lead what would be, in the end, a nine-year battle to stop the Black Fox Nuclear Power Plant. Earlier, when I had first read about the secret study that predicted the possibility of a nuclear power plant meltdown, I had become so angry with the government and the utility company for failing to uphold their responsibility to protect our health and safety and the viability of our land that I had made myself physically sick. Large sores had appeared on my scalp and I had had trouble with my gall bladder and liver. It became difficult for me to carry out my duties at the nursing home and to be kind to the residents and employees. My anger totally consumed my life.

Very soon, I had to face the fact that my anger was not having any effect on the government or the utility company — only me. It dawned on me that I couldn't have anger in my heart and be healthy, and that to be successful in my efforts to stop Black Fox Nuclear Power Plant, I had to be healthy and vibrant.

To help dispel my anger, I took time out to quietly contemplate scenes from my youth: our family heritage of love, loyalty, and honesty, and of accepting the challenges of life and overcoming hardships; mother teaching us to love our neighbors as ourselves; our little country school where we were taught to be responsible citizens; our small Methodist church where our minister had taught us to never relinquish our faith and where we learned social responsibility.

Taking contemplative time helped me change my attitude, keep an objective eye on what I was trying to accomplish, and remember to love my neighbors as myself. I started treating people from the utility company and the government with respect and kindness. And they began treating me the same way. And, honestly, if I didn't become well.

My first public appearance was at a hearing in front of the Claremore city council only four months after I learned about plans for Black Fox.

The utility company had requested the city councils or commissions of each town and city within a twenty-five mile radius of the plant site to give their approval of the nuclear power plant. I reminded the council members that, as businessmen, they wouldn't make business decisions without first studying the facts on both sides of an issue, and that, in this case, they needed to study all the facts before making a decision about whether or not to approve a nuclear facility. I laid out detailed information about the dangers of nuclear power and gave each of them a packet with more data, which I asked them to study. Since I had never before attended a council meeting and didn't know how well I would be received, I was surprised and pleased that the councilmen agreed to postpone the decision about giving their approval of Black Fox. The next evening's newspaper ran a front-page article headlined, "Council Reviews Inola Plant Opposition," citing the reasons I had given for opposing the plant. Like it or not, I had been launched as a public figure.

The first person to interview me was popular radio talk show host Hugh Garnett at KWHW in Altus, Oklahoma. He asked me the name of my organization. My organization? I thought, if I admit I'm alone, I'm a dead duck. "Citizens' Action Group," I said. A few days earlier, I'd been visiting with one of the residents of our nursing home when I saw Ralph Nader on the TV talking about his Citizens' Action Groups and their moral outrage about creating a radioactive legacy that would mortgage the future for the next fifty generations in exchange for a little electricity today. I told myself Ralph wouldn't mind if I borrowed his groups' name for a while. After all, our goals and philosophies were the same. (I often regret that I didn't take the time, after the fact, to ask for his permission.)

My mother had taught me never to lie and that if I did, I'd have to defend it with a second lie. Sure enough, Garnett's second question was, "And how many members are in your organization?" I breathed a quick prayer: Oh, God, don't let this be a lie. Please bring forth one hundred people who believe as I do! "Oh, about a hundred," I answered.

The news went out, and more reporters from newspapers and from radio and TV stations started calling and reporting. People called wanting to be the one-hundred-and-first member of my Citizens' Action Group. In barely any time, we had more than a hundred members. I bought a film projector and a film, "What's Wrong with America's Reactors?" and started traveling across Oklahoma, Arkansas, and Missouri to educate people about the need to prevent the construction of Black Fox. I organized and attended conferences, seminars, and rallies.

Public reaction wasn't all positive. One day, three acquaintances of mine came by to tell me that what I was doing wasn't Christian, that God had given us uranium to use and by opposing it, I was going against God. Well, the only thing I could say in response was, "God made rattlesnakes, too, but he also gave me the sense not to step on one!" My husband's Aunt Ruth cornered me one day and said, "Do you know what people are saying about you? They're saying you're a radical." That took me by surprise. I couldn't do anything but laugh. She scolded me but good. "It's nothing to laugh about, you're destroying our family name!" (She soon came to realize that I was right and even invited me to speak at her women's club meetings.) Prominent businessmen I had known during my teaching career phoned my home and called me terrible names — one of them even said, "Why don't you put your apron on and get back in the kitchen where you belong?" (It dawned on me that some of these hysterical people probably owned stock in Public Service Company of Oklahoma or its parent company, Central and Southwest of Dallas, Texas, or General Electric Company, or maybe in uranium.)

Friends and teaching colleagues began to turn and walk away as fast as they could when they'd see me coming down the street. I started to feel ostracized, and then I started to feel afraid. When I rented space at the county fair to gather signatures on an antinuclear petition, a group of young men surrounded the booth and started calling me names. I was too frightened to speak. When the threatening phone calls started, I realized how close I was to danger. I remembered something Norine Hughes, Okmulgee County Home Demonstration Agent, had said to me: "You'll step on toes and make enemies when you stand for something, and you won't be as popular as the fence sitter. But the friends you make will be worth having. Stay off the fence and make your life count!" During my teenage years, Mrs. Hughes had come to our school every month to supervise our 4-H Club activities and had been very influential in helping me to overcome my shyness and self-consciousness. She worked with us on our demonstrations and taught us to prepare our clothing exhibits and our canning and food preparation exhibits for the county fairs. She also taught us to give our five-minute speeches on timely topics, helping prepare me to win the state contest when I was a senior in high school. She had believed in me then, and now, without her inspiration, I would have had a much harder time dealing with the calls and the rejection.

The severity of the treatment I received from some of the community made me examine my motives more deeply. What I was doing wasn't about me. It was about something bigger. I was merely the catalyst to a larger purpose, helping to bring together people — expert witnesses, attorneys, common folk — to accomplish a very worthy goal. My feelings had nothing to do with that goal, so what did it matter if my feelings were hurt? I was intent on preventing the construction of Black Fox Nuclear Power Plant and, in so doing, protecting the health and safety of the people of Oklahoma and preventing the decimation of our soil. I was not doing this to inflate my ego or to achieve fame. What did it matter if people thought I was a radical or an alarmist or off my rocker? I knew I wasn't.

By now I had incorporated my organization and changed the name to

Citizens' Action for Safe Energy (CASE). At the same time that we were fighting nuclear power, we were promoting clean, safe energy. Because the activities and hearings were taking so much of my time, we sold our nursing home so I could be relieved of my nursing duties and could devote full time to stopping Black Fox. And it was a good thing we did, because the attorney and witness fees were so high that, eventually, the total amount of the sale was used to pay expenses for the fight.

From the beginning, our strategy was to try to stall the progress of the hearings, to throw whatever stumbling blocks we could in the path of the licensing process. The longer we could postpone the issuance of the construction permit, the more likely it was that Public Service Company would ask for a rate increase called Construction-Work-in-Progress (CWIP). In my early research, I had learned that, invariably, when a nuclear power plant was planned, the utility company eventually asked the state's utility commission to grant a rate increase, to allow the ratepayers to pick up the tab for building the plant. I knew that when that happened, we would go to the Oklahoma Corporation Commission hearing and prove that the electricity from Black Fox would be too expensive for people to pay for it. I knew that was how we would stop Black Fox.

When the first hearing — the Environmental and Site Suitability hearing — was over, a Limited Work Authorization (LWA) was granted in the summer of 1978, which allowed for the clearing of trees and the building of roads on the site. Because of our delay strategy, the hearing — which was to have lasted less than a week — had been drawn out to eighteen months. When the LWA was finally granted, our attorney immediately appealed the ruling, which took all his time — so it was necessary to hire a new set of attorneys to prepare for the next hearing, the Health and Safety hearing.

During the last half of 1978 and the early part of 1979, we were occupied with the Nuclear Regulatory Commission Health and Safety hearing.

Again, we used every delay tactic we could conjure. General Electric Company had the first of their two planned reactors built in the Netherlands. It was shipped across the Atlantic and up the Mississippi River to Tennessee, where more tons of steel were added. We were terribly concerned about the safety of G.E. reactors and eventually were able to have a hearing on the "G.E. Reed Report," an in-house study done by G.E. and kept secret, which found numerous problems with G.E. reactors. We had to go through a hearing just to get the right to have a hearing on the G.E. Reed Report. In the end we prevailed. The newspaper headlines read: "Black Fox: David vs. Goliath." We had won our first victory.

In early 1979, our funds were again depleted, and it was necessary for me to mortgage forty acres to keep the hearing going. Our attorneys had withdrawn because of our huge debt to them, and they advised me to withdraw, saying, "You can't win. You cannot stop Black Fox." I told them we *had* to win and I would never withdraw. That's when I offered to mortgage my property if they would continue with the hearing. The hearing ended on February 28, 1979, and a construction permit was expected by the utility company in early June. We were apprehensive. Would the company ask for CWIP in time for us to prevent the issuance of a construction permit?

One month to the day later, on March 28, 1979, a partial meltdown occurred at Three Mile Island nuclear power plant in Pennsylvania. It was horrible. Had we not intervened in Oklahoma, Black Fox would have been under construction by then. After the accident, a temporary moratorium was issued on nuclear power plant licensing.

Knowing the moratorium would be lifted, in late 1980, the utility company asked the Oklahoma Corporation Commission (OCC) for a rate increase to pay for the building of the Black Fox plant. It was what we had been waiting for. We hired yet another attorney to represent us in that hearing, and it took the attorney and expert witness almost a year to prepare.

Two other organizations intervened with CASE in the hearing. It began on September 15, 1981.

In the end, as I had anticipated, the OCC found that electricity from Black Fox would be too expensive for the consumers to pay for, and they informed the utility company that they would not be allowed to charge the ratepayers for building the plant. They were given the choice of canceling their plans or finding funds elsewhere for the construction of the plant.

On February 16, 1982, I was sitting in my living room, waiting impatiently for the news. Would they or wouldn't they cancel their plans to build Black Fox? Finally, the phone rang and OCC member Norma Eagleton told me the news. The Public Service Company of Oklahoma had canceled their plans to build Black Fox Nuclear Power Plant. Immediately, another phone rang and *Tulsa World* reporter Bob Mycue was on the line, bursting with excitement. And there I sat with a phone to each ear, TV and radio reporters recording the momentous event. Victory at long last.

We were told it was impossible to stop a nuclear power plant and, yet, through unrelenting effort, perseverance, and faith we fought city hall — the U.S. Nuclear Regulatory Commission, our local utility company, multinational giant General Electric Company, and the lobbyist-controlled congressmen — *and won!*

Carrie Barefoot Dickerson, now eighty-four, wrote about her struggle in Aunt Carrie's War Against Black Fox Nuclear Power Plant, *which she dedicated to her husband, Robert, who died nine months before the Black Fox victory. She continues her vigilance against nuclear pollution and unsafe transportation of high-level nuclear waste, believing passionately that we must look to sun and wind power and other safe technologies for sources of alternative energy.*

Susan Sweetser

"In the years since the rape, I had become the first woman attorney in a prominent law firm, specializing in corporate and commercial law. How would they treat me if they knew my secret?"

In 1980 Susan Sweetser was kidnapped and brutally raped. After spending the next ten years trying to close that chapter of her life, she stepped out from behind her veil of privacy in order to focus attention on the treatment of crime victims and to force a change in Vermont's laws. Her advocacy and undaunted determination to challenge the criminal justice system led her to a successful run for the Vermont Senate. As state senator, she launched, and fervently pushed through, a body of legislation to protect victims.

In 1980, having served eight years for sexual assault, Robert Percy filed a successful postconviction release motion with the court, got his sentence reduced, and was released.

Three weeks later, Robert Percy raped me, and my life was changed forever. I was married, pregnant, an honors student in college in a small town and working part-time in a country store. Only weeks after he attacked me, I identified Percy in a photo lineup, and he was arrested. However, Vermont law at that time required that he be released on bail. I was terrified — I had talked to the police and identified him. What if he found out where I lived and came after me again?

Within weeks of Percy's release, he kidnapped another woman, robbed her, raped her repeatedly over an eight-hour period and forced her to drive to Connecticut, where she finally escaped. He was again apprehended and thrown back in jail.

In my case, Percy had a jury trial and was convicted. He appealed his conviction to the Vermont Supreme Court, which reversed his conviction based on what it perceived as prejudicial remarks made by the prosecutor in her closing arguments. The court ordered a new trial. In Vermont, when a case is retried, it goes back to the day of arrest, unlike any other state, where it goes back to the day of trial. In other words, the prosecution and the defense have to do everything over again, pretrial motions, the entire discovery process. It means new defense material, new paperwork, new deadlines, new lawyers, new jury, new judge.

Percy was convicted for the kidnapping, robbery, and rape of the other woman as well, and appealed his conviction to the Vermont Supreme Court, which, based on a technicality, reversed the conviction and sent it back for a new trial. This guy was one dangerous S.O.B. and, as long as there was a chance that he could get out, I was scared to death, for myself and for my family.

During this same time, he was retried in my case and was again found guilty and again appealed to the Vermont Supreme Court. Now, in addition to being afraid, I was outraged and disgusted. Everyone has a right to a fair trial, but they don't have a right to make up things, which is what he was doing to try to get out of prison. He used a threefold defense: first, that I had picked out the wrong guy in the line-up; second, that if I had picked the right guy, then it wasn't rape but consensual; and third, if it wasn't consensual, then he was crazy. The entire defense was ludicrous, one lie after the other. This time, the Vermont Supreme Court affirmed the conviction. Percy appealed to the U.S. Supreme Court. It took the U.S. Supreme Court about six months, but they eventually denied the petition for writ of certiorari (a request to the Supreme Court to hear the appeal), so the appeal was never heard.

Ten years later, I was still reliving my attack and still waiting for justice to claim its due from Robert Percy. Robert Percy raped me, he was convicted, and yet he still played games with the legal system, with other women's lives and, ultimately, with me. I wanted it to be over with. I wanted to heal and it was impossible, because I had to keep all the details of the attack in the forefront of my mind. I had to remember, I couldn't forget anything. I would need those details in the event of yet another trial, where I could count on the defense lawyers to attempt to discredit my memory to a jury in order to bolster their case. I could not forget; I could not put it behind me and move on. That is what made these years so painful.

It was shocking to see how the criminal justice system got away with mishandling, not just me, but victims in general. I was disrespected both by the defense attorneys and the media, who referred to me as the "alleged" victim — as if I was the person who had committed the wrong and it was my burden to prove otherwise. When trials and decisions on pretrial motions were delayed six months, nine months, twelve months, I wouldn't be told. When the judge granted continuances asked for by the defense, I wouldn't be given any reason for the postponement. The Supreme Court routinely waived appellate deadlines for the defense without my being notified. The continuances and extensions were for indefinite periods. The prosecutors did all they could to expedite this, and the defense counsel did all it could to drag it out, often arguing that they needed the extra time to prepare an adequate defense. I would find myself calling the court clerks and prosecutor's office and saying, "What the hell is going on?" Through it all, I felt like I was being victimized again, this time by the very system that I was turning to for justice.

One cold day in February 1990, the *Free Press,* our local paper, ran a synopsis of the story of Nancy Ziegenmeyer, an Iowa rape victim who had gone public after waiting over a year for her case to go to trial. Buttressed by Nancy's story, I knew I needed to tell my own.

In the years since the rape, I had become the first woman attorney in a prominent law firm, specializing in corporate and commercial law. How would they treat me if they knew my secret? People often treat a rape victim like someone suffering from mental illness — fragile, damaged. Others feel that the victim is somehow to blame for the attack. Or simply not to be believed. It's not just men, but women, who respond this way. A great distance lay between that young college coed and the successful attorney I had become, and, although my name had appeared in the newspaper when the rape first occurred, I had done everything I could to keep my secret. I had talked to hardly anyone about it other than my husband and my family, about how I felt and about how poorly the criminal justice system had treated me. For me to finally open up about my horrifying experience meant putting a great deal at risk. How would my colleagues at work react? How would clients react? More important, how would my ten-year-old daughter react? I was pregnant with her when Percy raped me.

I picked up the phone and called the *Free Press* editor, who was a client of our firm. It was difficult to broach the topic with him, because I didn't know him that well and the rape was still very painful for me to talk about. I finally plunged in and said, "Look Ron, you ran this story about a rape case in Iowa and I think that's great, but you guys are missing an even bigger story, which is the huge problem in the criminal justice system here in Vermont."

His interest piqued, he asked, "What are you talking about?"

I told him about cases — I knew of at least five others at the time — left to wither on the vine, cases that were three and four, nine and ten, years old that just went on and on and on.

"Where did you get this information?" he asked.

I was vague at first, but then I just finally said, "One of those cases is mine. And one of them involves another woman who was attacked by the same guy."

He immediately said he wanted to do the story and make it big, but he said to me, "In order for this story to have the impact that you really want it to have, we have to use your name."

I told him to forget it. I had been identified by name only twice when the case first went to trial ten years earlier and seemingly lifetimes ago in that small country town of seven hundred where I was then living. I'd done everything I could to protect my privacy since then. I was the "pregnant twenty-two-year-old Worcester woman" attacked by Percy.

"Okay, I respect that," he said, "I understand. If you change your mind, let me know."

Around this same time, Jeffrey Amestoy, our attorney general, was lobbying for the legislature to pass a law to increase the maximum penalties for rape and kidnapping; a law that would have changed Vermont's legal definition of kidnapping. If it had been the law at the time I was attacked it would have made Robert Percy subject to a maximum penalty of life imprisonment, while giving a judge the ability to withhold bail. The Senate had already passed the bill by a very narrow margin and only after a bloodbath on the Senate floor, with ugly debates and highly contentious arguments. It went over to the House Judiciary Committee for a vote, and, because it was late in the session and there was precious little time left to schedule testimony, it looked like the bill was going to die.

Jeff had worked on my case initially and was also a friend. I called him after I read about the bill and said, "Look, I can't let this bill die. What can I do to help?"

He said to me, "The best thing you can do is to testify about how you feel about the bill and why. But I'm not going to ask you to do that. That's something you've got to decide, if and when you're ready."

I thought about it overnight. I knew I had to testify, to do what I could to save the bill, and to make sure that other women were protected. I needed to do something to bring a greater sense of reason to what had happened to me. One of the hardest things for me had been the question, "Why?" When you have faith, when you believe in God, you can't help but question, "Why did this happen to me? Why did You allow this? I'm not a bad person." I had struggled with that for a very long time. That night, it started to sink in that maybe God needed to use me as a tool to make it better for other people. Making that decision was hard enough, but following through was even harder, although ultimately one of the most healing and rewarding things I have ever done. For all my anxiety about breaking my silence, it was the beginning of a catharsis that was long overdue.

By the next morning, I had decided. And I was ready.

I called Representative Amy Davenport, at the time chairwoman of the House Judiciary Committee and who later became a Vermont judge, and asked her if I could come in and testify on behalf of the bill. She didn't understand my motivation, but she scheduled me to testify a week later. It was late March 1990.

I was truly scared and extremely nervous. I put together some of the news clippings about my case to show the whole sequence of events: my reporting the case, Robert Percy being charged and then released on bail, him committing another offense while out on bail; my trial; the other woman's trial. I wanted to show that, if this bill had been law back in 1980, this entire chain of events would have been very different. The other woman wouldn't have been kidnapped and raped — maybe even I wouldn't have been raped.

The afternoon I was scheduled to testify, I used some vacation time to leave my office. I didn't want anybody to know where I was going or what I was doing. Testifying ahead of me was one of Vermont's more liberal judges. I sat there in a small, stuffy committee room with a dozen legislators and listened for half an hour while he talked about how we didn't need this bill, we shouldn't be withholding bail from people, and so forth. Throughout his testimony, I struggled with anger and the pain of knowing that so many people looked to him for justice when he didn't have a clue; he just didn't get it. As he finished, the bell rang, signaling a House roll call vote on the floor. This was fairly routine when the legislative session was in its last weeks. The House would be in session debating a bill while House Committees were meeting. When the debate ended, a roll call would be held and the bell would alert members who weren't on the House floor that they had ten minutes to get to the floor to vote. Which meant the committee hearing was over. I was told in essence, "Sorry, Susan, we couldn't get to you today, we'll call you, don't call us." I drove back to my office.

It had been hard enough to psyche myself up to go to the hearing and then to sit through the judge's testimony knowing that his power would influence the committee members. Being denied time to testify pushed me to the brink. When I got back to my office, I called the *Free Press* editor and said "I'm ready to talk, but you'd better send someone right now, because tomorrow I could very well change my mind." He sent over a young reporter, and she and I spent the next seven hours together, until 2:00 in the morning, talking about what had happened and why. Why it was wrong and what needed to be changed.

We spent the next few months putting the story together, gathering the material they needed to write the series, which they called "Searching for

Justice." During that time, I was called back to testify on the bill. I passed out my newspaper clippings and told them why I was there. "This is my story, it happened to me in Vermont, it can happen to anybody, and this is your chance to make sure it doesn't." I tried to stay calm and told myself I was not going to cry. But in the end, I cried anyway. I brought up other cases in which women had been victims as a result of someone being let out on bail. My testimony had a huge impact on the committee and made it very difficult for them to offer excuses, about how late it was in the session, how they just didn't have time to get to this particular bill, or how it would just have to wait until the next session. They passed the bill.

The *Free Press* writer came to the hearing, and I knew my testimony would be in the paper the next day. I still hadn't told my colleagues anything.

When the "Searching for Justice" series was published, it was difficult to see my name in print. And it was painful and difficult trying to explain rape to my daughter. I cried and so did she. She understood that someone had done something bad to me, and it made her angry. During the three days that the series ran, she had a hard time coping with her feelings. She wanted me to read her the stories, but I told her I would put them away and she could read them for herself when she was older. It was heartbreaking. I wanted her to be able to just be a kid, to have a normal life, to not always be looking over her shoulder. I wanted her to be careful, but to have trust. When the first story ran, one of the boys in her day camp asked her if that was her mother in the newspaper, and when she told him it was, he hugged her.

The "Searching for Justice" series rocked the consciousness of Vermonters: The editorial pages were filled with letters of outrage. *CBS This Morning* broadcast interviews with me and Percy's other victim. Other rape victims at last started coming forward. I think my story and all the publicity surrounding it, and the passing of the bill helped the movement toward victims going public and persuading legislators to change laws.

After this ordeal was over, I started Survivors of Crime, a grassroots organization and resource for victims, their families, and concerned citizens. It's a place where people can research their rights, get advice, and help make changes in the criminal justice system. At that time, Vermont had one of the most liberal criminal justice systems in the country, pro defendant and almost hostile to crime victims.

I also set out to change the Vermont Constitution, so that judges would be able to withhold bail on someone charged with a violent felony that didn't carry a maximum sentence of life imprisonment — crimes like aggravated assault, reckless endangerment, domestic abuse, and child molesting. The way the state constitution read when we started, a judge couldn't withhold bail on these crimes even if convinced that the person would commit the same crime while out on bail.

I started using all my vacation time going to the legislature to try to get the constitution amended, an arduous five-year process. In Vermont, you have to get the amendment passed through two separate sessions of the legislature and then have it put to the voters. I spent months in our Senate Judiciary Committee simply trying to get the amendment out of committee and onto the floor, but it finally passed both the Senate and the House. That tremendous amount of work to get the state's Constitution amended made me think that I could have more impact if I were on the inside with the power of a vote rather than on the outside asking for change.

That's when I decided to run for the Senate.

I was elected in 1992 and re-elected in 1994. In 1994, we passed the most comprehensive antistalking legislation in the country. We also passed the constitutional bail amendment, paving the way for the people of Vermont to vote on this issue. In the 1995 to 1996 session, I was given the chairmanship of the Judiciary Committee, a turning point for me: I had gone from being a citizen advocate to being one voice of a six-member committee, chairing the committee and setting the agenda. During that session, we passed a crime victim's bill of rights, a sex offender registry bill, and a bill making resisting arrest a crime in Vermont. We closed loopholes in our negligent driving statute, in our attempted murder statute, and our leaving the scene of an accident statute. We increased parental responsibility for certain juvenile crimes. All these not only passed our committee and the Senate, but they also passed the House and were signed into law by the governor. Each was a victory won and my ultimate justice in a long struggle.

Still — fifteen years later — I got a notice in the mail that Percy had filed another postconviction release petition trying to have his sentence in my case reduced. The local district court denied his motion, and I expect that in the next thirty days I'll get a copy of his appeal of that denial. People think these cases end — but this stuff goes on and on and on. As long as Percy is incarcerated, as long as he wants to be a jailhouse lawyer, and as long as he has full access to the public defense system, this case will never end for me. Even though he was convicted not just once but twice for rape and sentenced to eighteen to twenty years, and even though he was convicted in the other case of rape, kidnapping, armed robbery, and possession of a firearm and sentenced to forty to sixty years, to be served consecutively with the sentence in my case, it isn't over.

Those ten years I had a lot of dark nights, during which I didn't think I'd ever see the light of day. There were times when I felt like I was teetering on an abyss, that I was going to go over the edge and that there was no coming out of it. But through all those years, the most profound thing I learned was that when hard things happen and difficult situations arise, and they do still arise, I know I can handle them. It doesn't mean that something isn't going to be difficult, that it isn't tough or unpleasant, but I have found the inner strength to get through. I know that I may teeter, but I won't go over the edge. And that strength certainly isn't something that only I possess

— we all have it. If we persevere, if we don't give up, that inner strength comes unlocked when we need it most.

In 1991, Susan was selected by the American Bar Association as one of twenty young lawyers in the United States whose work has made a difference. Five years later, she ran for U.S. Congress and lost. "I was the Republican candidate running against a three-term, incumbent (the only Independent in Congress) whose supporters wrote vicious letters to the editor repeatedly accusing me of 'cashing in' on being a rape victim," she says. "It was awful. There was also a Democrat in the race. The incumbent got 53 percent of the vote, I got 37 percent, and the Democrat got 9." In 1998, as a result of a letter her oldest daughter sent to Working Mother *magazine, the magazine named Susan the National Working Mother of the Year. She spent a year lecturing around the country on balancing family and career and on the great need to substantially increase the woefully low numbers of women on corporate boards of directors.*

Presently, Susan is enrolled in the Wharton Executive M.B.A. program (graduating in May 2002) and continues to fight injustices when she sees them. She hopes to become a corporate CEO and philanthropist.

Inspired to Be
YOU

Judy Collins

"The words fell out . . . 'I can't do it, I'm not going to do this.' I don't know how those words came out of my mouth, because I was in a state of total fear and anxiety. Once again, I wasn't living up to her expectations. It was a crushing moment."

Folk icon Judy Collins first came to prominence as one of the defining musicians of the sixties, giving voice to and galvanizing a generation. Throughout her forty-year career, she's recorded many top-ten hits, earned numerous Grammy nominations, and released more than thirty albums, many of them going gold or platinum. Last year, she formed her own record label, Wildflower Records, and made a PBS TV special, "Judy Collins Live at Wolf Trap." In the summer of 2001, she produced the Judy Collins Wildflower Festival with Janis Ian, Ritchie Havens, Roger McGuinn, Tom Paxton, and John Sebastian. She's given eighty concerts in the last year and recently rereleased on CD Golden Apples of the Sun *and* Maid of Constant Sorrow.

From the time I could reach the keys of my father's piano by standing on tiptoe, I remember tapping on the ivories. I began classical training early and was destined to be a concert pianist. Daring to step off that path at age sixteen was one of the hardest things I've ever done.

I grew up with music. My father was one of the pioneers of the golden age of radio and had his own show. My first memory of him was his singing. That he was blind made no difference to him. He was a man with great vision and even greater belief in his ability to do whatever he desired. I was heir to that confidence; my parents taught me that I could do anything I put my mind to.

I started taking piano lessons at age four, first with Mrs. Munson in California and later with Walter Raft when we moved to Denver. I loved the piano with a passion. My mother once said, "We never had to force you to practice. But I always had to remind you to wash your hands first."

Daddy was forever looking for the best teachers for me and, one day, he found the brilliant Brico. Dr. Antonia Brico had conducted orchestras all around the world. I first met her at her magnificent studio made of marble from the quarry at Marble, Colorado, its massive walls covered with climbing ivy. With my music crumpled under my arm and my pigtails in disarray from a day at school, I entered through the carved wooden door. Inside stood a matched pair of Steinway grand pianos flanked by statues, photographs, and death masks of Beethoven, Bach, Sibelius.

Unimpressed with my technique, Brico nevertheless saw promise in me and set out to groom me for greatness. I became her protégée and worked hard, very hard. The intensity of study, however, was not without consequence. Often Brico and I had tumultuous, emotional sessions. "Why can't you practice more, little Judy?" she would chide. I'd cry and try to do my best, but her expectations of me were very high.

At the same time that I was studying to become a grand classical pianist, I was learning Dr. Brico's personal story. After my Saturday lesson, I'd stay for a lunch of chicken and yogurt and cucumber salad with apple tarts and listen to the opera, paging through her endless press clipping books and discovering her extraordinary life. In 1923, at a time when women were rarely allowed into the hallowed halls of orchestral conducting, she was one of two musicians from America chosen to study conducting in Germany at the Academy of Music. After graduating, Brico made her debut with the Berlin Philharmonic. *The Paris Match* and the German newspapers raved, and she returned home a star. The Los Angeles and San Francisco symphonies fought to be the first to showcase her, and New York, Chicago, and Boston followed. She was flooded with invitations from all over Europe. She conducted Sibelius's orchestra in Helsinki, and they became close friends.

Brico was dazzling to me. Once, when Arturo Toscanini came to conduct in Denver, I trailed around behind her and the great conductor, carrying his music and listening to the two friends laugh and carry on in German. At the time, I was practicing a Mozart piano concerto that I would later play with Brico's orchestra, and Toscanini told me I'd do well. To an aspiring pianist, this was heady stuff.

Because she put so much into my grooming, Brico was constantly afraid that I'd be lured away by popular music. She knew my home was filled with music, all kinds of it. At times, Daddy would invite me to go to the studio with him and be on his radio show. We'd sing pop ballads like "Grab Your Coat and Get Your Hat" or "The Sunny Side of the Street." This, I'm sure, was terrifying to Brico. When I learned the fingering to the jazz version of "Laura" from George Shearing, who came to dinner after being a guest on Daddy's show, Brico had a fit. "I don't want you to play that jazz!"

Still, the centerpiece of my life was practicing to be a classical pianist, and I was devoted to Brico. I thought she was the cat's pajamas. At thirteen, I had my debut with her symphony, playing Mozart. It was the beginning of grand things I would do as a pianist for the next three years.

But then came folk music. I first heard it on the radio. "The Gypsy Rover" and "Barbara Allan." The Kingston Trio. Harry Belafonte singing "Scarlett Ribbons." I fell head over heels in love with this music. It stirred something in me. It spoke to my soul. It wasn't Daddy's popular music, and it wasn't Brico's classical. It was my own. Daddy rented me a banged-up guitar, and I started to find my way around on it.

Afraid to tell Brico, I simply mentioned, in an offhanded way, that I'd learned a song on the guitar. She winced. And turned my attention back to the Rachmaninoff Piano Concerto no. 2, an extremely demanding piece I was memorizing to play with her orchestra.

The day came when I knew that I had to tell her the truth. As much as I loved the Rachmaninoff concerto, I didn't want to play it with her orchestra. I didn't want to be a classical pianist. I wanted to be a folk singer. The choice I was about to make would forever alter my life. I was sixteen.

How would I tell her? When would I tell her? I had lessons on Tuesdays and Thursdays, and then I'd usually go back for another on Saturday. I decided Saturday would be the best time to tell her, because things were a little calmer then.

As always, the studio that day smelled of grapefruit and tea and honey. I sat down on the piano bench. "Let's see those nails," said Brico. It was our ritual. She clipped my nails, and then I started to play the concerto. She was very pleased with my progress and, at the end of the lesson, wanted to set my practice schedule for playing with the symphony. I couldn't face having lunch with her, I couldn't sit there knowing that I wasn't going to continue to play.

The words fell out...

"I can't do it, I'm not going to do this."

I don't know how those words came out of my mouth, because I was in a state of total fear and anxiety. Once again, I wasn't living up to her expectations. It was a crushing moment. If I hadn't had a long relationship with her and felt very close to her, maybe I could have just blown everything off and gone away and never come back. But I had to say to her, face-to-face, that this wasn't going to work out the way she wanted. Because she believed so fervently in me, it was terribly difficult.

We both cried. It was my first major experience of having to explain that I couldn't do what somebody wanted me to do.

She told me I was ruined.

I was so heartbroken that I didn't play the piano again seriously until I moved to New York years later and first rented, and then bought, the Steinway piano I own to this day and on which I do most of my composing.

Even after I became quite successful, Brico remained unconvinced that I'd made the right decision. After one of my concerts, she came backstage and took my hands in hers and said remorsefully, "Little Judy, you really could have gone places." She was still dazzling to me nevertheless, and I was indebted to her for all that she'd taught me. Regardless of our tumultuous times together, my studying with her all those years is fundamental to the fact that I'm still in the music business and that I don't see the end anywhere in sight. I started my own record company and continue to create wonderful things, and it's all because I had that firm foundation in music. And because Brico believed in me.

In 1972, I made a documentary about her called *Antonia: Portrait of the Woman.* It was nominated for an Academy Award and gave her a new burst of exposure that brought her opportunities to conduct all over the world again. Once more, she was in demand and celebrated for what she had accomplished not only as a conductor but also as a woman. For me, it was wonderful to give back to a woman who had given me so much.

Brico was in New York a few years before she died. We had lunch, as usual, at the Russian Tea Room. Afterward, I took her to a rehearsal at the National Dance Institute, which Jacques D'Amboise founded to teach children of all social and ethnic backgrounds. Jacques's work inspires in children a confidence not just on the dance floor but in life. Every year, for twenty-five years, I'd written songs for their performances. And now Brico watched as a thousand kids on the floor danced and sang with me "On the Other Side of My World." At the end, she came up to me and said, "You're wonderful. You're remarkable." It was the first and only time that she said anything like that to me, except when I was playing Mozart at thirteen. I think she finally understood.

Judy wrote two autobiographical books, Trust Your Heart *and* Singing Lessons, *as well as a novel,* Shameless. *She also produced and codirected the Academy Award–nominated documentary,* Antonia: A Portrait of the Woman, *about her first music teacher, who was a pioneer in her time as a female orchestral conductor.*

A UNICEF Special Representative for the Arts, Judy has traveled to the former Yugoslavia and Vietnam and taken up the crusade against land mines, creating a foundation for land mine education, awareness, and removal and providing prosthetic limbs to victims. "I hope to shine a light on something that I think is terrible," she says.

Kathy Buckley

"Overcompensating to be liked and wanting to "save" people who were hurting, I had learned how to give but not how to receive. The most courageous thing I have ever had to do, hands down, is learning to receive. I'm doing that gracefully and letting other people feel good."

As a child, Kathy Buckley was sent to a school for the mentally retarded. It took school administrators, psychologists, and audiologists almost a year to discover that her slow speech and language development was not the result of retardation but of hearing loss. Today Kathy shakes her head: "And they called me *slow?" Her hearing loss was only one of many challenges she's faced.*

Being born with a hearing loss and not having language as a way to bond with people, I didn't start speaking until I was eight years old. That's a long time to be trying to bond with my family. I couldn't connect. And that was the hardest thing, wanting desperately to make a connection and, instead, having people poking and probing and making fun of me and making me feel like I was retarded and dumb. I didn't know until I was almost thirty-four years old that I wasn't really retarded. I still play with it, to be honest.

So, receiving? I certainly didn't feel worthy of it. Not only that, but my mother was one of those people who, if she were to give to you, you'd have to give something back. She evaluated and judged me on what I gave her in return. As a result, I always associated receiving with an expectation that I had to give something in return. Ergo, I didn't want to receive, because I didn't want to be obligated.

I'm a very giving person. I'm always giving. Unconditionally. But, for someone to give to me? No, no. Nobody can give to me. "Can I do this for you?" someone might ask. My response? "Oh no, that's okay. I'll take care of it." I don't want people going out of their way for me.

My best friend, Jane, is the one who put this issue in front of me in such a way that I couldn't avoid it.

As a comedienne and public speaker, I had been traveling a lot that year. I was on the road so much that it took three months to move into my new house in Burbank. I'd be gone for three weeks, come back for four days, and run out again. I didn't have time to unpack the boxes stacked in my living room. I didn't have time to hang curtains and kept complaining that, without curtains in the bedroom, how could a person sleep? I needed to sleep, I was tired, blah, blah, blah.

One night, I came home from a whirlwind trip. I'd been in ten states in nine days. I had one outfit that I'd change in and out of while in flight; I burned it on day ten. As I drove home from the airport, I was really grouchy, because I knew what a mess I'd be walking into, that I didn't even have my bed set up right. It was late. I was exhausted. I opened the front door and got a whiff of Pinesol.

It was dark inside, and I kind of stumbled around the boxes to turn on the lights.

And.
Everything.
Was.
In.
Its.
Place.
Everything.

I started to cry. Jane had cleaned my house, unpacked all my boxes, hung beautiful curtains in the bedroom, and put my bed together. On the bed stand was a bouquet of roses. And a note from my godchild, who was only a year old, so I was kind of surprised that she wrote so well. "I love you, Aunt Kathy," it read.

From room to room I went, sobbing. I had never felt so loved. There, alone, at night, I had no escape from that love. Nobody there for me to joke with, nothing to do but absorb it, take it in. It was the most incredible moment in my life. Even though Jane wasn't there, she was very present — not physically, but in my heart. No one had ever done anything like that for me.

Nothing is as great as a woman friend whom you can talk with and yell at and love. Jane and I have that kind of friendship. She'll say to me, "Please don't put yourself down in front of me." It's all about respect with Jane. She makes me aware. She helped me break my patterns by bringing them to my attention. Being able to take criticism and not go on the defensive is my number-two challenge. I've had to learn that criticism is a way to grow, a chance to take a look at myself from a different perspective, inside out, upside down, and see what I want to change.

Since that night alone in my newly unpacked house, I've been learning to receive. And to receive gracefully. Some time ago, my brother called in tears. "I'm inviting your friends to a surprise birthday party for you," he said, making me wonder about the "surprise" element. He was undone by the fact that everybody was so excited to have an opportunity to do something for me. "What can we do to make this a great party for Kathy?" they were asking. It was the first time I realized that because I got such joy from giving, I was taking that very joy away from my friends.

It was my way of overcompensating. I wanted to make sure that I was accepted, that people liked me. I didn't want anybody to feel my pain of rejection. I didn't want anybody to feel the negativity of what that was like. "You're too stupid, you're too tall, you're dumb, you can't, you won't..." That's the vocabulary I learned when I finally learned to understand language. People were actually saying these things to me, and I was believing them.

Most people who have a disability find that one of their other senses becomes stronger. In my case, it was intuition. I *feel* when somebody is suffering. And I don't want them to suffer because I know what it's like. So overcompensating to be liked and wanting to "save" people who were hurting, I had learned how to give but not how to receive. The most courageous thing I have ever had to do, hands down, is learning to receive. I'm doing that gracefully and letting other people feel good.

Learning to receive is learning to love myself. To respect myself. To feel that I'm worthy. All those things come when I receive unconditionally. It's been a challenge for me. It continues to be a challenge. But I'm getting better at it.

I had to get out of my own way to let the love in. I will never forget that feeling as long as I live. It was like Jane went in with a nutcracker and opened my heart for the first time. I was so vulnerable. I was exhausted. There was nothing I could do but absorb the love like a sponge. Just take it all in. It was one of the biggest turning points in my life.

Doing comedy was the last thing on Kathy's mind thirteen years ago. She did her first stand-up on a dare from a friend. At the comedy contest, she was nervous not because it was her first time or because she couldn't hear the audience clapping. What made her nervous was that she was competing against comedians who had been in the business for years. She took fourth place.

Today, Kathy is billed as "America's First Hearing-Impaired Comedienne." She's a four-time American Comedy Award nominee as Best Stand-Up Female Comedienne. In June, 1998, her one-woman show, Don't Buck with Me, *had a three-month run at the prestigious Tiffany Theater in West Hollywood, California, and won the entertainment industry's coveted Media Access Award as Best Play of the Year. It went on to play in New York.*

A guest on the TV series Touched by an Angel, *Kathy has also appeared on* The Tonight Show *and been featured on* The Today Show, Good Morning America, Entertainment Tonight, Extra, Inside Edition, CNN'S Show Biz Today, *and others. In 1997,* People *magazine tagged her's as one of their most touching stories of the year. She was also featured in the HBO TV special "Women of the Night," filmed at the U.S. Comedy Festival in Aspen, Colorado, and she was included in the E! Entertainment TV special "The World's Most Intriguing Women."*

"Anything can be achieved when the heart and the mind work together," she says.

Paula Brisker

"The reality of what I was about to do hit me.
I was going out there to sing, and I felt scared and excited,
and my whole body was buzzing."

Paula Brisker is a singer/songwriter who lives on the California coast with her husband, Jeff Worley, her dogs, George and Haley, her five cats, and three horses, the newest a filly named Rennie.

Several years ago, I was at a crossroads in my singing career. My spirit was calling me to take the road that would challenge and change me. I hadn't sung for an audience in a long time, and I had a burning desire to perform again. No, not just perform. I wanted to write my own songs, listening to the voice of my soul. I wanted to produce my own show.

You're not qualified. You're not ready. Your songs aren't that good. This is the voice of the struggling artist in me who is always ready with criticism, blame, excuses. Where does this voice come from? I can't tell you. I grew up in a loving home with parents who encouraged me in whatever I wanted to try. Yet here I was, afraid to express myself and full of self-doubt. Maybe it was only stage fright. Maybe it was deeper. I believe that we all come into our lives with lessons to learn. Maybe one of my lessons was learning to express my deepest emotions and insights, to be all that I can be, to be startlingly true. It took nerve for me not to listen to my critical voice. It took guts to make the commitment: I *will* perform my own music, from the depth of my soul. I set a date... and my own private transformation began.

I had always thought it was the visibility of performing that scared me, but I discovered that it is the vulnerability: to stand in front of people with my heart wide open. It terrified me. No performance is ever good enough for a perfectionist, and I am a perfectionist par excellence. The voice in my head always lectures, "If you make mistakes, people will say you're not good enough to call yourself a singer or a songwriter." With this performance, I hoped to quiet that voice and allow my true essence to come through. I gave myself permission to make mistakes. In fact, I told myself up front that I could *count* on making mistakes, and what mattered was not that I made them but how I handled them. I would be kind to myself. I even allowed myself the option of pulling out — I didn't have to do this performance, I could stop at any point.

Knowing that I could trip on any number of emotional roadblocks, I decided to go looking for them ahead of time. I asked myself what could go wrong. I was keenly aware of how terrified I became when I walked onto a stage, afraid to look at the faces in the audience, afraid that I would turn to stone. I craved that connection, and yet I was afraid. What if I said something stupid? I had never felt comfortable speaking at a performance. What if I stumbled over the equipment? I was usually so tense that this was a real possibility. What if my throat closed up? It had happened before, and the audience had strained to hear me, so much so that I had had to signal the other singer to take over. Even though that happened years ago, the memory of that helpless feeling when my voice wasn't cooperating with my mind and my heart stayed with me — and it was a fresh fear now.

I mentally and emotionally dove into those terrors, imagining everything that could go wrong, feeling the fear deep in my belly and not knowing at times if I'd get through it. Some nights, I'd wake up in a cold sweat. I'd lie there feeling paralyzed. Some days, I had no clue what I was doing. I just kept moving forward, not hiding the dread but trusting that my passion and spirit would lead me.

Facing my fears rather than denying them was key. I shared them with my partner, Jeff, who had seen me grow and change over the years and had always supported my independence and power. He brought out the best and I could count on him to make sure I plumbed the depth of my emotions. Rather than try to assuage my fears, he assured me that he was there to lean on, which gave me tremendous room to look deeper, knowing he was right there. And I leaned on my rituals and spirituality. I took long walks in nature and talked to the Goddess and to the earth. I asked them to help me lift the anxiety and turn it into excitement.

The pressures gradually started to lift, and my fears began to subside. Perceptibly, all the *What if this's* and *What if that's* dissipated. I had never created a space in which my voice and my music would be able to come alive freely. It was exhilarating. Now rather than feeling paralyzed, I was ablaze.

I think it was no coincidence that the practical pieces of organizing the performance now came together effortlessly. I booked the ideal performance space. The date that I wanted was available. My mentor, Raz Kennedy, who is also a dear friend, agreed to be musical director of the show, and I secured an opening act that fit right in with what I was doing. I had ample rehearsals with my backup group and felt confident with the musical arrangements. I was ready.

The morning of my performance, I woke up feeling very quiet, very solemn. I grounded myself with a short meditation about how I wanted the day to feel to me. Then I went out into the field below my house to a large patch of "pink ladies." There were hundreds of them all around me, dancing with the breeze and shimmering in the morning light. As I walked through them, absorbing their beauty, I noticed one flower quite a distance away from all the others. It drew me, a sturdy little thing, standing all alone in its own pick of soil. It made me think how, sometimes, I must step away from the crowd and into my own desires and convictions to see clearly where I am and what's ahead. And it reminded me of how much I had changed in the process of getting ready for my performance, of who I had become, of the adventure ahead. I felt liberated, no longer at the mercy of my fear, and I knew now that I could turn it into a powerful energy. I had leaned on Jeff in a way I'd never done before, letting myself be more supported by him. And I felt less afraid to reveal who I was and what I wanted to say through my songwriting, more focused on writing music from my heart than music to please.

The night of the show, people packed the room. The opening act began. In the past, I would have hidden from the audience, paralyzed with fear. The fear of facing the faces. The fear of their rejecting me and my music. It's not that I wasn't afraid or nervous, but I stayed in the moment and the fear began to turn into excitement. I stood in the back of the room and watched my opening act as the audience responded. The energy in the room was building, and I knew I would be just fine.

The opening act finished. It was time. My time.

Before going on, I asked the musicians and background singers to join hands with me and my musical director in a circle behind the stage. This ritual allowed us to warm up our vocal chords and to create a musical resonance and harmony before going on stage. It also created unity and cohesion and was a way to align our souls and spirits with the muse. My musical director reminded us to breathe into the music and above all to have fun with it. He said a prayer to connect us all in spirit, and I felt an enormous rush of emotion. The reality of what I was about to do hit me. I was going out there to sing, and I felt scared and excited, and my whole body was buzzing.

As I walked toward the stage, I imagined a door in front of me, a door made of fear, and I walked through it with purpose and I was swept away by love as I came center stage. In the front row sat Jeff, the one who had seen me through to this moment. My mother sat with him. I had written a song for her that she would be hearing for the first time that night. I had also written a song about my father, who was my biggest fan and had recently died. I opened the show with it as a way of bringing him into the room so that all who knew him could feel his spirit. I closed my eyes and visualized him and how much he had loved my music... and I began "Into the Light" for my father, who surely was watching and was everywhere in my heart:

> You gave me the freedom to follow my dreams,
> I'll never forget you, you're still with me now,
> It feels like a miracle to see you go into the Light....

Before I knew it, I had finished my last song, and I was floating on a feeling of triumph and celebration. The audience came to their feet, applauding for more. We sang an encore.

When the performance was over, many people told me how moved they were by my voice and my songs. Someone I respected said, "You're on your way." Another told me that they were inspired to continue with their own music. As we packed up the equipment and drove home, I was elated. I had not simply done what I had set out to do, but I had flourished with the experience. I will never be the same.

Paula continues to perform her original music in the San Francisco Bay Area. Her new CD, Narrow Road, *is a powerful collection of her original work and was released in the spring of 2001. "My hope is that it inspires people to ponder the notion that we can fulfill our dreams and craft the lives we want at any age," she says.*

Susan Point

"Still working as a secretary to provide for my kids, I'd sit up late at night rocking my son in his cradle with my foot while I designed and engraved."

Like her ancestors before her, Susan Point (Ē'ixwe'tiye) lives at the mouth of the Fraser River on the Musqueam Indian Reserve in Canada. The Musqueam Band are "people of the grass," taking their name from the grassy banks of that river, an image seen often in her work. A painter, printmaker, and sculptor, she revived the two-thousand-year-old art of her Coast Salish tribe, now thought to be the prototype for the northern Northwest Coast art seen frequently in galleries. For Susan, making the leap to artist was one thing, but breaking from traditional art was yet another.

As a child, I knew very little of traditional Coast Salish art. Few did. Much had been lost. Making the commitment to be an artist and to the unearthing of our tribal art, much of which is still lost to this day, I would know both joy and frustration. It would require great discipline and patience.

I was raised on the Musqueam Indian Reserve, one of several Coast

Salish nations whose people originally lived in the southern British Columbia region. When I was a child, the houses numbered no more than three dozen. Water was carried in buckets from a communal tap. Electricity and indoor plumbing didn't exist on the reserve.

My mum and dad were fisher people and seasonally traveled 250 miles north to River's Inlet for the salmon run, taking their whole brood of kids with them. My dad would fish, and my mum would work in the canneries. I was born there, in Alert Bay, the fifth of what would be seven children and half sister to eight older children from mum's and dad's previous marriages. When the fishing season ended, we'd return home to the reserve, sandwiched within a city of two million people. To our north is Vancouver. To our south is the international airport. We're urbanized, but we're on land set aside for Native people. Many people on the outside don't even know we're here.

Growing up, I never saw my mum idle. She was a very hard worker and always doing something. In addition to working in Vancouver canneries or the reserve's market gardens rented out to Chinese tenant farmers, she was busy gathering shoots of salmonberry bushes; harvesting and preserving cherries, blackberries, and salal berries; smoking sockeye salmon; plucking the ducks that would give her the feathers to make our pillows and mattresses; cutting cordwood; or cleaning, teasing, carding, and spinning fleece from domestic sheep from which to knit sweaters, vests, socks, and mittens. She was one of the last Musqueam women who knew how to make the cedar-root coiled baskets and one of the last to make the sewn cattail mats used at one time to line the inside walls of Musqueam longhouses. One of my most cherished possessions to this day is a basket made by my mum. Others in my collection go back three generations of women in my family.

Although I've always loved to draw, I didn't know I'd become an artist. "Artist" wasn't a recognized profession in traditional Coast Salish life. Rather, the perfection of one's craft was respected, as was one's skill in performing it and the pleasure it elicited. In our community, music, dance, storytelling, and oratory were also respected forms of art and essential to religious and ceremonial activities. These art forms were private and not to be seen or heard outside our community. The scarcity of Coast Salish art today is, in part, a result of European contact and settlement of Salish lands.

When I was sixteen, I left school and went to work alongside my mum at the cannery. At seventeen, I married. At eighteen, I had my first child. During the next ten years, I worked as a secretary, first for the Musqueam Band, then with the Union of British Columbian Indian Chiefs and, eventually, as executive secretary with the Alliance Tribal Council. I might still be there today were it not for a course in jewelry making offered to First Nations peoples by Vancouver Community College. Having just had my third child and on maternity leave, I thought, Why not?

With the jewelry making class, I put my feet on the path to becoming an artist. At that time, I didn't know anything about our Coast Salish art form, so I practiced the northern-style art. One day, my husband, Jeff Cannell, asked the pivotal question, "Susan, don't you have your own art form?"

Fortunately for me, my aunt Della was married to Michael Kew, an anthropologist and professor at the University of British Columbia who specialized in Coast Salish art and culture. Over the years, unbeknownst to me, he had collected much documentation about Coast Salish art and culture — a collection of slides, photographs, and published images. "Yes, of course," he said when I asked him to tell me about our art. He took me through the Museum of Anthropology at the university, where he introduced me to Coast Salish artifacts.

Wow.

I was captivated. Salish art is beautiful in a way I'd never experienced. *I want to bring this back*, I thought. *I want to revive my people's art, continue their story, so others know that it existed, that the northern style was not the only art form.* The art of the Coast Salish was sacred and private, whereas the art of the northern Northwest Coast people was secular and public. In the Salish tradition, one didn't talk about the meaning of a piece of art for fear of tempting danger, because to speak was to reveal sources of power, the visions and dreams of the creator of the piece.

Seeing my excitement and realizing that I might be able to help revive Salish art, my uncle passed on to me everything he knew and helped me discover what he didn't know. I felt a calling to make people aware of our art, to let them know that it had almost been lost altogether. I would spend years researching, going to museums and libraries. Much remains a mystery. Even the elders within our community don't know why certain images were used, what some of the designs mean. All that was lost long ago.

I began experimenting with Coast Salish art by sketching, simply pencil on paper. Over time on quiet evenings, I designed what would become my first black-on-white painting of four salmon balanced in a circle. I titled it *Salmon.* It would be reproduced as a serigraph and was the first of a hundred different prints I would produce in the ten years that followed. In the beginning, galleries didn't know what to think of my work, because it was a departure from the northern style, distinguishable by the use of two colors, black and red. They'd never seen anything like what I was doing. What was Coast Salish art? And who was Susan Point?

Still working as a secretary to provide for my kids, I'd sit up late at night rocking my son in his cradle with my foot while I designed and engraved. When it came time to print, my older kids would hover over the kitchen table while Jeff and I pulled the prints, and then they'd run them over to whatever flat surface they could find that would make a good drying place. I didn't preconceive an edition size; it was whatever we could successfully pull at that moment.

All my work has been self-taught. I've learnt as I go. After ten years, I started to agonize over whether I should do my art full-time. Having grown up poor, I had promised myself that, when my time came, I'd make sure my children had what I didn't have, that they would have the best. My job as a secretary gave me a secure paycheck every two weeks. My art, on the other hand, would be pure speculation, and I didn't know whether I could survive on it. It would be a big step for me.

Galleries and their clientele began to respond to my work. It was finally becoming evident that there was interest in the Salish art form. But still the question remained, *Would I make it as an artist?* I'd have to apply myself diligently and motivate myself to make sure that I regularly had pieces to bring out to the public. But even then, would anyone buy? Even with all these questions knocking around my head, I decided to take the plunge.

Leaving the security of my job was scary. I now had no reliable income to support my family, my work was on spec, and my buyers were galleries that have their own highs and lows. Christmas was good for a month. Spring wasn't. Nobody bought in the spring. I had to learn to balance the best time to create with the best time to sell.

Throughout it all, Jeff was always supportive. A non-Native from back east, he became my agent when I began doing limited-edition silk screens. I'm not good at banging on gallery doors, it's nerve-wracking to me. So I was grateful when he started pounding the pavement for me, going door-to-door with my prints.

In 1986, a piece of mail came addressed to me. It was an announcement of a commission from the city of Seattle to do cast-iron tree grates. Why they sent it to me, I don't know, because it was for U.S. artists. Never mind. I applied, drawing on the fact that I'm Coast Salish and that Coast Salish people also resided in the southern area of Washington state. Five small commissions were awarded to five artists. I was one of them. They assigned me the red oaks, and my first public commission became part of the Municipality of Metropolitan Seattle Art Collection.

That was my first step toward working in mediums other than paint and prints and precious metals. Once I'd done that job, others followed. Eventually, I was working full-time on large-scale public art commissions, which forced me to expand artistically because I had to create with new and unexpected mediums — concrete or wood or glass — to fit the site criteria. Knowing artists who worked in those mediums made it possible. When I started a big glass carving commission for the Vancouver airport, I worked alongside two friends who work in glass as I created the *Land, Sea, and Sky* installation. I've learnt from my artist friends, as they've learnt from me. It's all been hands-on.

At times, I thought this great undertaking wouldn't work. At times, I was afraid to branch out and work in new areas, new mediums, because of the flak I might get from my peers, who are more inclined to stay within their traditional mediums.

I'll never forget how scary it was for me to simply introduce nontraditional color into my prints. *Kwantlen* was the first serigraph to incorporate the blending of colors. It got a quick response from the Native arts community, who said it wasn't authentic Coast Salish art. It took a long time to be accepted. When I began to work in glass in 1986, I was nervous, anticipating the critics who, as expected, lambasted me, saying, "That's not Native art. They never used glass." In the beginning, the criticism was hard. Then suddenly in 2000, glass became a medium practiced by many Native artists, and it's now an accepted Native art form. I consider any medium acceptable that allows the opportunity to place the Salish footprint upon our lands, making our art known.

Sometimes I go back to the traditional. But I like to experiment; it's just in me, wanting to try something totally new, going beyond, working in new mediums. I don't want to confine myself to doing only traditional work. In a sense, I've gone quite contemporary. A number of young, up-and-coming Salish artists are following in my direction now, and that feels good.

Certain artists reach a stalemate, doing the same thing for years and years. I started out doing traditional art and over time got more into the contemporary art form, always using elements of the Salish in my work. Times change. So do I. And so does my art. Who knows what I'll be doing fifteen, twenty years from now. Hopefully something exciting on the road of my ongoing evolution as an artist. Along that road, in that evolution, I will always feel the honor of my role as an artist in continuing my ancestor's visual art form.

Acclaimed worldwide for her large-scale work in wood and glass, Susan has won some of the most prestigious commissions awarded to any Canadian artist in recent years, thirty-five of them for public art pieces. Self-taught and uniquely original — she has been called one of the most innovative Northwest Coast artists at work today — she combines a deep respect for the ancestral with a passion for contemporary exploration. An artist with a diverse and devoted audience, she has participated in more than sixty group exhibitions and has had a dozen solo shows. In the spring of 2000, Susan received an honorary Doctorate of Arts from the University of Victoria for her contributions to the art world. In the recent book Susan Point: Coast Salish Artist, *Michael Kew talks about her "vision and stature as an artist." Her work, he says, "proclaims the enduring presence of her people in their land."*

Rayla Allison

"It had been a long, sometimes tenuous journey to this spot, this time when two countries, at odds with one another, would play a friendship game on a makeshift softball field."

An attorney in sports law, including Title IX work, Rayla Allison was, at one time, league director of Women's Professional Fastpitch. As a young woman, she was the catcher of the Connecticut Falcons, four-time world champions. "Without the old days, both the good and the bad," she says, "I don't think the new league would be having such success. A lot of what we have today — softball in the Olympics, women's World Cup soccer — has been built on the successes along the way and the lessons learned from the failures." Twenty years ago, the world of women's softball was a much different place. "You'd get the questions: 'When are you going to get a real job? What does your boyfriend think? When are you going to settle down?' That was quite a hurdle."

Waves of sea-green, deep dark blue, and khaki, classless uniforms filled the stadium from ground to horizon, in every direction I turned.

Tens upon ten thousands of pairs of dark eyes peered out from under their color-coordinated Mao caps at our light-skinned formation as we entered the Beijing Municipal Soccer Stadium. In a world of unfamiliar faces, customs, people, and politics, we marched in a column one behind the other across the skinned expanse of field to the cadence of the wedding march. It was the beginning of the end of decades of China's isolation from the West and, apparently, the furling banner of stars and stripes at the head of our column had made the transition, but not our national anthem that accompanied Old Glory.

I, along with the other two dozen players, coaches, and leaders, reached across one by one to our Chinese counterparts and clasped hands above our heads, parading across the field the one hundred yards to our designated mark, united in friendship. Parting hands, bowing, and exchanging gifts, we honored one another by our presentation, then turned and bowed to the dignitaries of the state seated in the front rows.

It had been a long, sometimes tenuous journey to this spot, this time when two countries at odds with each other would play a friendship game on a makeshift softball field. Had it been my dream? No, it was a planned mission, an aspiration that I tasted, touched, and molded in my mind at a very early age. My mother had said I could make anything happen, and I had believed her. Of course, back then, I didn't know the goal would take me halfway around the world to play my sport in front of more than sixty thousand blue, green, and khaki clad Chinese fans. I had not known that the sport I lived and breathed, that brought me a beautiful feeling of accomplishment, capability, strength, and success, would lead me to represent my country in an overflowing stadium in Beijing.

The ability to let fly a ball, hurtling it at great speeds to its destination with pinpoint accuracy, thrilled me and had thrilled me since that first day of catch with my mother in the backyard. The smell of the leather, the smooth finished grain of the bat, these were my fun, my inspiration, my opportunity. Opponents became friends, coaches my role models, my family the supporting unit. To be sure, there had been failure, obstacles, lessons learned. Skinned knees, broken fingers, a crushed ego. Yet the sound of *"Play ball!"* beckoned to me every springtime and held me through late September each year.

And now, walking the length of the tunnel, the sun hitting my face as I stepped out onto the field with the finest of the game, this was my arrival. I would share the sport with those I admired and respected. It had been a worthwhile journey.

Our interpreter explained the Chinese public address announcements and introductions. The crowd was being informed that a complete circle in this American game was a score of one point and that the most points by either team would determine the championship. Only the equipment and the sounds were the same. Fifteen wash basins perched upon fifteen pedestals stood behind our bench. Delicate lace towels for wiping our sweat were assembled on a stool. A large urn of hot tea, to quench our thirst, was stationed at the end of the dugout. A blue-Mao-suited umpire swept home plate with a long-handled house broom, while the other umpire watered the batter's box from a flower watering pitcher.

Nine dark-eyed athletes in red uniforms took the field and loosened up with ground balls, fly balls, and throws to the bases. Their compatriots clapped softly as they took the field. We laced up our cleats, stretched our muscles, and listened to the pregame speech by the coach. It was springtime in China, the year 1979, and it was time to play ball....

In August, 1999, the Connecticut Falcons gathered for their twenty-year reunion and played a scrimmage game at Falcon Field in Meriden, Connecticut. It was a Friday night,

and the stadium was sold out. "People who had followed the team in the seventies came," recalls Rayla. "Some brought their old programs and pennants. They sat where they had held season ticket seats twenty years before. Children and grandchildren were introduced to us." It was a far cry from the days when women and girls weren't accepted as athletes.

Elaine Suranie

"I was acutely aware that I had an inner strength far greater than was socially acceptable for a girl to reveal. Having finally been given permission to be strong, I wasn't about to waste it."

Elaine Suranie is a respiratory therapist who works with end-stage respiratory patients, teaches seminars on coping with stress, and occasionally dabbles in Hollywood. She has participated in writing, directing, and producing several stage, film, and TV projects, including assistant directing the Emmy-Award–winning ABC special Peter and the Wolf, *starring Kirstie Alley and Lloyd Bridges, and coproducing the 1999 Hollywood Bowl tribute to NASA and JPL, "From the Bowl to the Moon." She is currently writing a script for the new PBS animated children's series,* The Chinese Siamese Cat.

Kathy was a few years older than I and about thirty pounds heavier. Not what you would call a trim girl.

She had been held back in school (they did that back then) and to me, a sweet, skinny, Catholic girl, she looked more like a high schooler than a grade schooler. Her long, bright red hair, wall-to-wall freckles, and longshoreman personality made her a real standout in any crowd.

Until I moved into the neighborhood, she and her sidekick, Pam, were the star kickball players and generally feared by all — girls and boys alike. For whatever reason, Kathy decided that it was time for a sacrificial lamb to remind the masses who was in control. I was the chosen, her new handpicked object of ridicule and terror. Why she chose me I will never know; maybe it was because I was a teacher's pet, well liked by everyone and just as good as she in sports.

One Monday during recess, Kathy casually walked up to me and my friends to announce that, come Friday, she would be waiting for me in the field that stood between the school and the housing tract where I lived. With a menacing look and a sneer that made my stomach churn, she pushed me up hard against the wall to underscore her intention. I was horrified. Who was this girl and why me? I had never even been in a fight before. Oh, sure, little stuff with my sister and some of the neighbor kids, but never a real fight! I was not *allowed* to fight, which, of course, meant that I was not even allowed to defend myself. Even if I had been, it was obvious that Kathy, by sheer mass, was going to pulverize me.

After spending the rest of the day listening to my sympathetic friends tell me graphic details of what Kathy had done to other poor defenseless souls, I resolved that what I needed were reinforcements. So I told my mom.

My mom, who is French Canadian, was in her youth a tough farm girl who went through her own trials, including the early death of her mother from tuberculosis and seven years in a Catholic orphanage. She eloped at age nineteen with a Polish farm boy whose mother kept chickens in the house and, sixteen years later, divorced him. She suffered poverty and humiliation and, over the course of her life, tempered herself into a "good woman" who didn't complain and cried in private. When I told her about Kathy, she pragmatically stated that "good girls don't fight" and that the best thing to do was to "avoid the troublemaker." It was painfully disappointing that she, who had survived so much childhood abuse herself, would automatically defend the rules of proper behavior. Having children who were clean and well mannered had become more important than defending me. To act unladylike, whatever the reason, was not acceptable.

Today I understand this dichotomy. To be a good wife had become everything to her; she had subjugated herself to it, and a good wife made sure that her children were socially in step and properly behaved. To fight was ill mannered. But as a child, I responded less sympathetically. My conclusion was that mothers who stay at home to cook, clean house, do laundry, play solitaire, and watch TV soap operas often do not have well-developed coping skills to deal with the real world. I was going to be ripped to shreds in a large empty field while the whole world watched, and the only thing my mother cared about was that I acted like a "good girl." Image is everything, especially in a small neighborhood where people feel free to walk into your house if you don't answer by the third knock.

That week was one of the longest weeks of my life. I remember lying in bed at night, crying silently out of fear and humiliation. All I wanted to do was mind my own business and be a happy kid, but by sheer default my mother had offered me up as a sacrifice to the social gods of Image and Virtue by which she herself had been crushed.

Come Thursday, I tried to fake a fever by putting my face up to the bathroom heater, but my mother didn't buy it. Kathy threw rocks at me during recess that day, and I went home crying. This disturbed my mother more than anything I could have ever told her. It must have touched some familiar place deep inside her. She knew that I was not a crybaby. I could rough and tumble with the best of the boys, would hurl myself off the block fence to tackle my stepdad, and had been tossed and trampled by my horse with never a whimper. I collected snakes, spiders, and an odd assortment of insects, much to her chagrin. I was afraid of little and had more than once overheard my mother describe me to relatives as a "tough little shit."

My mother called the school to complain that I was being harassed and was told casually that there was nothing they could do about it, especially if the fight was to take place off school property. This made my mom angry. (Whoever taught us that anger is not a good thing lied.) She didn't like to make complicated spiritual, social, or moral decisions, but after looking at my pleading face, she said, "If that girl lays a hand on you, let her have it, and let her have it good. Nobody touches my kid and gets away with it." With that, she promptly went back into the living room to watch her soaps.

Why this proclamation was a comfort to me, I will never know. Certainly, my common sense told me that I was still going to be mutilated. But my spirit soared. To have been given *permission* to stand up for myself, even if that meant coming to blows, was thrilling. Thrilling in a way that was so liberating and so self-affirming that I was completely washed over with love for my mother. I knew without question now that she loved me more than Image and Virtue. I was a valued person who had a right to defend herself, no matter how much good-girl status I lost in the process. In retrospect, this moment, this feeling, was very life changing for me and represented a part of my character that would be challenged again and again in the years to come. Even as a silly ten-year-old, I was acutely aware that I had an inner strength far greater than was socially acceptable for a girl to reveal. Having finally been given permission to be strong, I wasn't about to waste it.

Come Friday, I had knots in my stomach and was thinking of ways to run for my life rather than to fight. Most little girls are not accustomed to violence, other than from adults, and have trouble with the physical threats from their peers. Boys take it for granted.

That day I did a lot of praying. During recess, Kathy came up to me and echoed her same old warnings. Surrounded by my friends, I remember looking her straight in the eye and saying very forcefully, "I'm looking forward to it!" I'll never forget the shock on her face, the confusion. In that one spontaneous moment, I knew that I was going to be a hero. I was going to give Kathy what she had never gotten from anyone before. A fight. A real honest-to-goodness, punching, kicking, rolling-in-the-dirt fight. My fear was suddenly replaced by excitement and purpose. A just cause had been placed before me, and no matter how much I got hurt, I was committed to win or die because it was the right thing to do. When Kathy regrouped, she actually looked angrier than she had before and sneered, "Good!" and stormed off. My newfound courage wavered.

After school, I started walking home through the field with my two friends, Connie and Patty. (Patty, who was an ultrawimp back then, went on to become a police officer, and Connie died of asthma the following year.) They were true-blue scaredy-cats who were also forbidden to fight but were willing to come along so that they could drag my body home.

Kathy and her sidekick Pam were waiting for me. Without a pause, I handed my books to Patty, picked up the largest, strongest branch I could find, walked right up to Kathy, and swung with all my might. She put her arm up to block the blow, but the branch ripped through her skin, knocking her down. Pam was thunderstruck. I lifted the branch again, swung, and hit her hard in the arm a second time, yelling, "Come on, you big bully! Come beat up on the little kid!" Kathy started wailing about her arm as blood ran to her elbow. "That's not fair!" she screamed, pointing to the branch. (Fighting in those days meant fists.) My whole body was shaking. I yelled something back about it not being fair for her to pick a fight with me.

We yelled a few more words at each other, and she ended up calling off the fight and going home. (You could call off fights in those days. It was a sign of bad sportsmanship if you didn't allow the other side to save face.) I had won. Suddenly, an inexhaustible sense of power came over me. It was clear that there was a force inside me to be reckoned with. The wonder was that I still felt like a good girl. Amazing!

My memory is that, shortly after that day, we all became friends and made a pretty unbeatable kickball team. The tough girl softened, and the soft girl got tougher. All the way through junior high school, Kathy used to tell other kids about the day this skinny little girl clobbered her with a tree branch and made her cry.

Having wrestled with Hollywood, Elaine is currently having a life. "Being politically correct has never been my strong suit," she says. "I have spent half my life wrestling the world for approval and only ended up trampling the gentleness in my own soul. The second half of my life is dedicated to learning to enjoy the things that inspire me without feeling like I need to be doing more. Long walks with my dog, good music, breaking bread with friends, laughter with my sister, working on my golf swing, writing what I want. God is in the simplicity of life."

Sonya Bell

"By being a blind runner and doing what a sighted person can do, I'm living a big part of my dream. I'll always have this voice inside me saying, *Don't give up.*"

Among her many awards, at age fourteen, Sonya Bell won the 1994 Arete Award, junior category. Given annually by Intersport Television for courage in sports, the award takes into consideration not only what athletes have accomplished but also what they were up against and how they refused to be held back by limitations. To present the award to Sonya, tennis great Monica Seles made her first public appearance in more than a year. "I wanted to meet her and do something for an athlete who was so brave," Monica writes in her autobiography. "This girl did somersaults on the balance beam, technical floor routines, swung from the uneven bars!" Sonya Bell is blind.

I was born a seven-month, premature twin.

I weighed a pound, and my sister weighed a pound and a half. The doctor told my mother that we only had a 50 percent chance of living. Because I couldn't breathe on my own at first, I was given oxygen, which caused some damage to my eyes. Eventually, I went blind.

When I was eight years old, I left home to attend the South Carolina School for the Deaf and the Blind as a residential student. Because the schools where I lived weren't equipped to teach the blind, I didn't have any other choice. I guess I knew at some point that I would have to go to a special school, but I didn't think it would happen so soon. It was the scariest thing I've ever done, and the hardest, too.

On Sundays, I'd get on the bus at 6:00 in the evening and ride the hour to the school. I'd stay for the week and come back on Fridays. I wasn't used to riding the bus, and I didn't like it. I wasn't used to going away from home, period.

When I first got to the school, I had nightmares every night. A youth counselor would come in and sit with me for a few hours to help me calm down. I missed my family and my friends, and especially my twin sister, Tonya. And I was scared, because the people in my family were the only ones I knew I could depend on to help me. Later on, my mom told me it took a lot for her to let me go, that she had to put aside her own feelings and think about me and my future, because we weren't always going to be together and she wanted to give me the best chance in life.

In the beginning, I didn't know how to get around the school. I had to ask for help and hold onto somebody's arm wherever I went. Then one day I met a lady who pointed out to me that I didn't have to ask for help all the time — I could find my own way. She taught me how to be independent by using a cane. It made me really nervous in the beginning, but I built up self-esteem by doing things on my own and trusting people to steer me right.

Everything changed for me when I met Mrs. Bowen. I went to physical education one day and there she was, asking me if I knew any athletics. I told her no. She asked if I'd like to learn how to roller-skate, and I said sure. She started by teaching me certain skills, how to move my body in different ways. Then one day, she handed me some skates and told me to put them on. The first thing that came into my head was, *Please do not let me bump into anything.* Mrs. Bowen promised she wouldn't. She told me to skate forward. I skated forward. She told me to stop. I stopped. I was scared, because I didn't really trust her to keep me from bumping into the wall. She took my hand and said, "Sonya, if you will trust me, and I trust you, everything will be all right."

I've been trusting her for many years now. She taught me other sports: ice skating, gymnastics. I was so excited to learn. And then, one day, I started to run track.

When I run, I have a guide, Jack Todd, who goes with me. The first time we met, we spent some time just getting to know each other: I told him a little about myself and he told me a little bit about himself. When we got out on the track, I had that same fear that I had had the first time I roller-skated: *This guy's gonna run me into a pole or make me trip and fall and hurt myself.* I asked him right off, "Please don't let me run into anything," and I kept asking him that every time we'd run. Finally, when I started to race, Mrs. Bowen had to say to me, "Sonya, just trust your guide — he won't let you run into anything." It took me a while, but as I got older, I began to trust Jack more and more. Now it just comes naturally.

When I was nine, I started competing in the Special Olympics. I ran track and also competed in gymnastics, speed skating, and figure skating. Mrs. Bowen saw that I had a talent for sports, and I went on to race for a local track club, the Spartanburg Striders, which was integrated with kids from public schools. By thirteen, I was running interscholastic track and, eventually, I entered meets of the U.S. Association of Blind athletes, an arm of the Olympics for athletes who are blind or visually impaired.

When I run in a meet, the first thing I do is to walk the track with Mrs. Bowen so I get to know it. All tracks are pretty much alike, but it's a way to give me "visual" cues, setting a picture in my mind about where I am, helping orient me to that particular track. As we walk around it, we talk about my goals, my expectations for the meet. Mrs. Bowen does this to get me focused on what I'm there for and to get an idea of how I'm feeling, how I think I'm going to do. It relaxes me too, which is really important because if athletes are tense and tight when they compete, they usually don't do well. So this is part of my way to relax and focus.

We usually walk a few laps, and then Mrs. Bowen gets me a schedule of the track events so I know when mine start: the two-hundred meter, the four-hundred meter, and the relays.

Just before a race begins, Mrs. Bowen says to me, "You know what you're here for and what you have to do to get it." I nod at her and ask my guide if I'm set up straight. And then, the gun goes off and he yells "Go!" When we get to a curve or into the straight-away, he says, "Curve" or "Straight-away," and he cues me to kick it or to come in or go faster. Whenever I race, I think of the track as a racetrack with all the cars going around and around just like I'm going around and around, and it helps me keep going faster and faster. And I get this feeling building — *Come on, just keep going, push, push, push* — until I get to the finish line. And if I win, that's good. If I don't, then I just keep on trying until I do. That's what counts, having faith in God and knowing that I can do it, believing in myself more and more, having determination and concentration, and knowing that I can do what I put my mind to if I go 100 percent.

By being a blind runner and doing what a sighted person can do, I'm living a big part of my dream. I'll always have this voice inside me saying, *Don't give up.* It's just this thing with running, this sensation that you can't ever give up. You've got to have that feeling not to back down from the challenge.

My coach and my parents and I work as a team. I couldn't do it without them, period. I've got the will to race, but they give me the love and support — which is why I'm a little nervous now, because I know the next step for me is college and going out into a bigger world, kind of like when I first went to the South Carolina School for the Deaf and Blind. That scares me, but, like my mom said before, we're not going to be together forever and I have to look to my future.

I get my strength by having faith and believing in myself. I want to do well, not just in athletics, but also in life. And the thing that keeps me going is people. I love hearing people cheer for me. I love having people congratulate me when I do well. I love that feeling of euphoria when I've done my best and given my best. That's when you'll see me smiling and laughing. That's when I'm really living my dream.

In the fall of 2001, Sonya graduated from the South Carolina School for the Deaf and the Blind and made the rather giant leap to a technical college, where she is majoring in music and computer sciences. She's also become an accomplished soprano, singing gospel and often performing the national anthem "anywhere, anytime," which includes school, local events, the regional convention for the Alpha Kappa Alpha Sorority, and the U.S. Association for Blind Athlete's national competition at Colorado Springs.

Inspired to CHALLENGE

Penny Harrington

"Stay true to what you know is right, even when it's damn painful."

Penny Harrington had been a cop in Portland, Oregon, for nineteen years when she was named chief of police. She was the first woman in the country to rise so high in the police ranks of a major city. It was a tumultuous time in Portland, and her appointment would be short-lived and her life threatened.

In 1985, I was appointed chief of police of Portland, Oregon. It was a dream come true. Eighteen months later, it would become my worst nightmare. To this day, it's difficult for me to talk about it.

I had been on the force since I was twenty-two. I loved my career, despite all the inherent traumas of being a woman in a man's world. I felt I was doing something important, that I was helping people. It was very fulfilling. Sure, I dreamed of making chief, the zenith, the highlight of any police officer's career. But for all my dreaming, I was still a woman. And I knew that regardless of talent, regardless of ability, regardless of how hard I worked, I would never be given that opportunity, even though I fought for women's rights in the department.

So you can imagine how I felt when I heard about my appointment. I was overwhelmed. Not because I was the first woman in the country to make chief of a major city. But because in Portland, in my city, I had risen to the top. I could effect change and do innovative work within the department like never before.

Then the media arrived.

Frequently over the years, my promotions would generate press outside Portland. UPI or other national press would pick up the story and run a little article. Maybe I'd get a letter from someone in a different part of the country congratulating me. But truthfully, I had no concept of what my appointment as chief was going to mean. I admired women who were the first in their fields, women like Sally Ride and Geraldine Ferraro. I'd think, "Oh, my God! These women are so amazing; look at what they've done!" I certainly never put myself in that category. But other people did.

Nothing could have prepared me for the media frenzy. I knew it would be a big deal in Portland, but around the world? I did TV, newspaper, magazine, radio interviews. And not just for a day or two. It went on and on and on.

I was shocked.

In the beginning, all the attention was very heady. I was on *McNeil/Lehrer News Hour, NBC Nightly News, Merv Griffin, Good Morning America.* I was in *People, Ladies Home Journal,* the *New York Times, USA Today.* How exciting can life get? Yet after a while, when the media didn't let up, I was at a loss. I called the mayor and said, "I don't know what to do. This is going on and on, and with the media taking up so much of my time, I'm having a hard time doing my job."

"Keep doing the interviews," he said. "It's so important for Portland. It's the best publicity we can get. I want you to do all that you can possibly do."

So I kept going. And kept going. Eventually, I grew very, very tired of it. I had no privacy. Everything I said was examined and taken apart and second-guessed. Everything I did became significant. I'm a very laid-back person in a lot of ways. On the weekends, I love to just flop around in blue jeans and a T-shirt and sandals. Now I couldn't step out of my house without people watching me. I never knew when I was going to run into a camera. If I went downtown to a concert with friends, people would stop me on the street. I'd go to a restaurant, and people would come over to my table. It was a constant barrage. After a while, I simply stopped going out.

The focus of my work as chief was building bridges between the police and the community. The challenge was huge. I had inherited a city with a growing crime problem. Of 183 cities with more than one hundred thousand residents, we ranked eighth in violent crimes — murder, rape, robbery, and aggravated assault. We were sixth in property crimes — burglary, larceny, car theft, and arson. On the average, an officer handled more than seven hundred calls a year, compared to a national average of 480. Later, I would find out that the FBI had been monitoring Portland as a potential hot bed for riot.

My predecessor had been very autocratic. He didn't listen to the community. He was an "I know what's best" kind of guy. Under him, the police officers had become estranged from the neighborhoods they served. We had too many incidents of police violence against black people. We had too many scandals within the department, from the drug unit being corrupt to the infamous "possum incident." A few police officers had thrown a bunch of dead possums in front of a black-owned restaurant. What a horribly stupid thing to do. The restaurant owner called the press, and the press went out and took pictures. The community was outraged.

On my watch, one of my most urgent mandates was to heal the polarization between police officers on the street and the community, to find a way to get them working together. My entire career had been built on the belief that it was our job to listen to the community and do what they wanted us to do, to pay attention and be respectful of them. I wouldn't tolerate anything else from my officers. It's what caught the attention of Bud Clark when he was campaigning for mayor. Bud didn't know me from Adam, but he'd be out speaking to neighborhood groups and people would come up to him and say, "You know, you really should make Penny Harrington chief of police." The first time I met him, his opening comment to me was, "I think you've been running for chief longer than I've been running for mayor." In truth, I hadn't been campaigning at all; I simply had a reputation.

I ended up on the mayor's short list of potential candidates for chief. Our ideas meshed closely, and I think he felt very comfortable with what I wanted to do within the department. Undoubtedly, he was influenced by the fact that appointing a woman would bring Portland publicity. But I don't think he had any idea of the scope of that publicity.

As I started my new job, all eyes were on me. When I made changes, police departments in other parts of the country would pick up my ideas. When I started a new program, UPI would run a story, sending my idea out nationally. I instituted a nonsmoking policy on the force and got invited to speak to the AMA. It was exciting, it was rewarding, it was amazing how much impact I could have on a national level. I used to say that my mother never had to call me, because she'd know what I was doing through her local Lansing, Michigan, newspaper.

The incident that would unravel my appointment happened not long after I had taken the helm. Two officers accidentally killed an African American security guard using a carotid hold, which is pressure applied to the carotid artery in the neck. The carotid hold cuts off blood supply to the brain and is meant to subdue a suspect by causing him to pass out, leaving no ill effects when he regains consciousness. I immediately banned it and started investigating what had happened. It was tragic. The black community mourned the death of one of their members; in fact, the entire city festered. It was an accident, a lot of people understood that it was an accident, but the black community saw it as one more death at the hands of the police.

The day of the funeral, I got a call from a TV station asking for my comment on the officers who were going around town selling T-shirts that said, "Don't choke 'em. Smoke 'em," with a smoking gun on the front. It was the first I had heard about it. Some of my officers were out in the station parking lot selling these T-shirts on the very day the security guard was being buried. What blatant disrespect. What arrogance. It was outrageous.

Pandemonium broke out in the community. Signs went up on telephone poles and the sides of buildings in the black community saying, "Smoke 'em before they smoke you." Leaders in the black community said the police had a "hit-squad" mentality. I feared riots would break out over this incident. I had to hit it straight on.

I brought the officers before a hearing to determine how to reprimand them. After the hearing, the union president came into my office. "You're going to fire them, aren't you?"

"Yes, I am."

"Don't do it."

"How can I do anything else? This is outrageous."

He said I would "pay" for firing them.

I didn't back down.

At the same time that I was dealing with the T-shirt incident and the volatile atmosphere in the black community, I was greatly concerned for the two officers who had killed the security guard. They were falling apart. I relieved them of all duties and ordered them into counseling. I called every night to check on them and reassure them that I'd do what I could to help them, that I knew they had followed police procedure.

I don't think we fully understand what police officers go through when they kill someone in the line of duty. They suffer tremendously. As police chief, I had to be sensitive to and supportive of my officers as well as the community. It was a huge challenge to help both sides heal.

During the days that followed, my deputy chiefs and I went to every roll call of my officers to counter the union president's inflammatory accusations that I was jeopardizing their safety by banning the carotid hold. At the same time, I held meetings with leaders of the black community to explain what I was doing, wanting to keep everybody informed, to practice what I preached about community input. I went to meetings they organized within the community and was forthright about what had happened. The union president publicly called the leaders with whom I was working "vultures" and "opportunists."

I could never have anticipated something so disgraceful.

As I began my job as chief, I knew situations would arise that would test my skills. I don't mind being tested. But it was daunting to have something that intensely disrespectful and potentially explosive happen at the very beginning, before I had had time to establish myself.

If I hadn't been so politically naive, maybe things would have turned out differently. Maybe I would have seen that this was the beginning of the end. Maybe I could have done something about it. I believed the mayor when he said he wanted to clean up the police department. I thought he meant it. And I was set on accomplishing just that.

The union and I continued to be at loggerheads. Their ultraconservative "keep things the way they are" attitude meant disregarding what the public thought or felt. The union president became my nemesis. He epitomized everything that was wrong with the Portland police department. For example, he was being paid half-time by the city and half-time by the union, and yet he wasn't working a minute for the city. When I told him he either had to come in and work half-time for the City or I wasn't going to pay him, he told anybody who would listen that I was trying to break the union. He fought every reform I championed — like the cultural sensitivity training and diversity programs I initiated to turn the department toward a community policing philosophy and away from a rigid, law-enforcement model. He hated me, truly hated me. To newspaper reporters, to TV people off-camera, he called me a "stupid bitch."

Having worked around this man for years, I knew what he was like. I knew he was a bully. He pressured the mayor on several occasions, telling him I was doing terrible things. The mayor's response was, "As long as I'm the mayor around here, she's gonna be the chief of police."

Had I been more politically savvy, I would have seen that I was in danger. When the union president couldn't get me fired, he went after the mayor, accusing members of his staff of using drugs. He seemed obsessed now with getting rid of both of us. He accused me of being soft on drugs, because I reorganized the drug unit in a way he didn't like.

The drug unit had gone bad years earlier. Cops were dealing drugs. They stole drugs from dealers and used them to bribe informants on the street. They stole money from the department. They lied on search warrants, lied in court. Nearly the whole unit had gone corrupt. It was headline news.

At the time, I was in personnel and heavily involved in the firing of nearly the entire unit. How on earth could this have happened? I came to believe that the drug unit had become too isolated. They were like a rogue unit within the department, different from everyone else, withholding information, and basically out of control. They were located in a separated section of the building.

When I took over as chief, I moved them into the detective division, right in the middle of everything. The detectives who were working burglary and robbery were dealing with the same guys out there buying and selling drugs. It was all the same criminal element and, yet, they weren't even talking to the drug unit. Now they were in the same building and talking to one another. I also upgraded the unit from street officer to detective, making it a promotional position. As a result, the unit had people who were more highly qualified and already experts in investigation. They concentrated on high- and mid-level drug dealers, a very different breed from the street dealers. Officers on the beat, whose mandate was to work with the neighborhoods and do community policing, dealt with the street-level dealers causing the immediate neighborhood problems. This overhaul was so successful that the Houston chief of police picked it up and implemented it in his own department.

The union president hated it. He told the press that I was destroying the drug-enforcement capability of the department, that I was soft on drugs. And he started a drumbeat, saying to newspapers at any opportunity, "She's not doing a good job. She's soft on drugs." I ignored him, because he was so off base I thought no one would pay any attention to him. My reorganized drug unit was making some of the biggest drug busts in the history of the department. But he just kept it up and kept it up, continuing to accuse the mayor's staff of being involved in drugs and implying that I was covering up for them.

I had always been a cop. I hadn't built the kind of political networks I would need as chief. I had community support. I had support from a lot of people in the police department, but I had no political support. And so, as the attacks escalated, I had no one to call. I didn't know what to do. The hoorah started and just rolled on over me as the union president pressed on with his campaign to get rid of me, running nasty stories about me in the union newspaper. He kept that drumbeat going to turn people against me.

Before long, my husband, also a cop, was accused of leaking details of a federal drug investigation to a friend whose restaurant was under surveillance. It wasn't true. But the accusation put me in the position of having to investigate my own husband, an obvious conflict of interest. I went to the mayor and said, "Look, you need to investigate my husband because no one will believe I'm unbiased." I assigned investigators to the mayor's office.

Meanwhile, the union started pressuring the mayor to get an outside investigator, claiming I was too much in favor with the mayor and his office would be biased. It worked. The mayor put a retired federal attorney and a retired judge in charge of the investigation. I thought, "Whatever makes them happy." I knew they'd find nothing. I had work to do. I wasn't going to let this derail me.

While they were investigating my husband, the retired federal attorney suggested to the mayor that they also investigate my policies on drug enforcement. She's taking an unfair rap for being soft on drugs, he told the mayor. Why don't you have us look at that, too? We'll investigate her drug-enforcement policies. If she's doing the right thing, we'll say she's doing the right thing, and that'll put it to rest. The mayor agreed without consulting me. When I found out, I was aghast. I called the mayor, "You can't do that! You can't ask the men who are looking into the allegation against my husband to investigate my drug policies! You can't mix those issues in the minds of the public. Don't you see how that's going to look?"

"It's too late," he said. "I've already announced it. I've called a press conference."

Oh, God, this is all I need.

The ball kept rolling, and I think the men in charge of the investigation decided they wanted to go down in history as some big investigative panel. They convinced the mayor to hold public hearings. Televised public hearings. Which went on for two months. They uncovered no evidence that my husband knew anything about the federal drug investigation or that I was soft on drugs. The Houston chief of police testified that he had picked up my policies and implemented them in Houston. A chief of police from Salt Lake City testified that that my burglary programs were absolutely innovative. All the evidence underscored that I was doing a wonderful job. Drug arrests were up, crime was down, citizen complaints were down.

Most of the reporters who sat through the whole thing said to me, "This is gonna come to nothing. The people who thought you were doing a good job still think you're doing a good job. And the union still hates you. That's all there is to it."

Well, that's not what happened. The panel found that although my husband did not know about the investigation and therefore could not have leaked information, he had violated a superior's orders. I had told him not to talk to his friend, because I was worried about what was going on in the restaurant. I'd been tipped that the police were going to make a drug arrest there. I didn't know who their target was, but simply that the restaurant was the place for the bust. As it turned out, the guy himself was arrested.

Because my husband had asked him what was going on, he was in violation of a superior's orders. Mine! Oh, please. I told him this in the same way I'd tell him to take out the garbage. Had I wanted to give him an order, I would have told his captain, who would have told his lieutenant, who would have told his sergeant, who would have told him.

About me, they said that morale was very bad in the police department and that I needed to be replaced. Well, crap! I was firing people who needed to be fired, I was disciplining people, I was changing things. Of course, morale was bad. That was no secret.

From the beginning of the investigation, the mayor had said that if he didn't like the report, he'd throw it in the wastebasket. He knew I was doing a great job. He supported me all the way.

But "politics is politics." He had also said from day one that he would be in office for only one term. He wasn't going to run for re-election. That meant we had a lot of leeway to clean up things without dancing politically. A month on the job, I started hearing him talk about his re-election campaign. The whole dynamic changed. With the union president after him, with the investigation, with the threat of a recall campaign, he caved.

Next thing I knew, he was knocking at my front door, telling me I had to step down. There was nothing he could do. It was either him or me. A recall campaign against Bud Clark would never have been successful. Everybody loved what he was doing. But he was afraid. And he thought if he dumped me, he'd be okay.

I was stunned beyond belief. I had done nothing wrong. My husband had done nothing wrong. My drug policies were successful, as were all my other policies. Retire? I was forty-four. I couldn't retire. I was too young!

"Why don't you just become assistant chief?" the mayor offered.

"Are you nuts?" He wanted me to be there and watch my replacement dismantle everything I'd accomplished? He wanted me, after all the grief I'd taken, to accept a lesser position in the department? "No, that's not reasonable. I won't do it!"

"This is rotten," he said. "It's dirty. But there's nothing I can do."

I was at the peak of my career, and it was blowing up in my face. It didn't make any difference that I was doing a good job. All the stats in the world couldn't stop the force of a political decision. After eighteen months of stunning changes and successes but also horrific attacks, I was about to be fired. It was all my nightmares rolled into one. I was humiliated publicly, locally, nationally, even internationally.

Friends started dropping like flies. My closest friend in the police department, a woman I'd seen through agony for years, just vanished. I had saved her from an abusive boyfriend who broke her jaw. I had taken her into my home after she got out of the hospital. And now she just disappeared, not one call. She must have been terrified.

I started getting hateful phone calls from cops. One threatened to blow up my house. I'd get home and find thirty messages on the answering machine: "Bitch, you die!" My kids were harassed. The youngest was eleven. The other two were nineteen and twenty-one. And my sister, who was still in the police department, was harassed. I was vilified in the press. Whatever was wrong in the department, somehow it related back to me.

I cried for days. I couldn't stop. I felt like my whole life had ended. The dream was over. Not only had I lost my job, but my marriage was in deep trouble from all the stress we'd been through; my husband was literally ill from it. Now when I stepped out the front door, people were looking at me wondering if I was involved with drugs.

With no job and no income, I relied on the mayor's promise that if I resigned, he would get me a bridge pension, because I couldn't start drawing my actual pension until I was fifty. Instead of having him fire me, I agreed to resign. Within a week, he changed his mind. I had to sue to get my pension. It was beyond horrible. The lawsuit would take four years.

I was emotionally exhausted. I was broke. I didn't know what I was going to do. I started applying for police chief jobs in other cities. What a laugh. I was tainted. Something was terribly wrong with Penny Harrington. No one would hire me. I applied for more than two hundred jobs in policing.

That I survived, that I came out the other end, was a miracle.

After I left, the department undid all my changes. The drug unit went back to the way it was before my watch. It was like I had never been there. They wiped me off the face of their earth.

I learned much from my experience as police chief. Professionally, I learned the importance of political networks and a whole raft of practical things about playing that game. I grew up. But what I learned on a personal level was far more important. It still brings me to tears.

Lesson number one: There is nothing more important than your family and the love of the people who care about you. They can get you through anything.

Lesson number two: Stay true to what you know is right, even when it's damn painful. Not once during the hard times in Portland did I ever think of compromising what I believed. Had I backed down when the union president told me that if I fired those guys, I'd regret it, he would have owned me and the community would have lost respect for me. Because I didn't back down, I got axed. But in the long run, it was the only decision and the right decision. If you're honest and ethical and compassionate, it doesn't matter what people think of you. If you're doing the best that you know how to do, it will, in the long run, pay off. Today I make my living on my reputation. People believe in me, they trust me. They know if I tell them something, it's the truth. I'm not going to lie to them. I'm not going to give them some political gobbledygook.

Lesson number three: It's okay to be weak. Historically, I'd always had to be the strong one: "I'll take care of everything." For me to be totally down and have to ask people for help, especially for money, was huge. We had to borrow from my parents and my husband's parents. That hurt. Yet it taught me that people want to help, that, in a way, it's a gift when they can do something for you, especially when you're down.

Lesson number four: It's okay to admit that you lost.

Lesson number five: I can survive anything. Having been a single parent for eleven years before meeting my second husband, my biggest fear was losing my job. It was paramount that I had an income, that I had a home, that I could take care of me and my son. When I lost my job, I thought I lost everything important to me. Thank God I still had my family. A job is a job, and even though it's an important job, other things in life are more important.

These are huge life lessons. While some people learn their major lessons through health issues, I guess I wanted to learn mine on the national stage, getting horribly humiliated. Just in case I wasn't paying close attention, I gave myself something big enough that I couldn't miss it.

I thought my career in policing was over. I thought I would never top the pinnacle I had reached in Portland. I thought no one would ever listen to me again and that everything I had learned was gone, useless. No one would care. I was wrong. My experiences in Portland are what I draw on today to make my living and to make a difference nationally in policing. I've become a leading expert on issues of gender in policing and have just finished writing a book for the Department of Justice on the subject. I'm also an expert on issues of community policing and am highly sought out for my opinion, my advice, from people all around the country. How ironic.

I discovered that people in other parts of the country had a different perspective on what happened. They weren't in the middle of it and could see the truth and recognize the strength of my ethics. People in Washington, D.C., where I spend a lot of time now, said, "Everybody saw what was really going on. My God, you were the first woman, and they were just out to get you. Everybody knew that!" A man with whom I interviewed for a job said, "So you started your job as a reform chief. You went in to clean up the place. You started cleaning it up and alienated people because you were doing what you were hired to do. And then your boss couldn't take the heat and decided to dump you. It was the politically expedient thing to do. Happens all the time."

A few years ago, several of my programs in Portland were reimplemented under police chief Tom Potter. I heard that when he went out to the community with his plans, talking about everything he was going to do, folks in the neighborhoods said, "Well, that's what Penny Harrington did. That was her idea."

One of the fine rewards of being where I am today is that I can help other women who are going through similar situations. When I was living it, I had no one to turn to, because no other woman had been that high up in law enforcement. I had no one to call and ask, "Oh, my God, how did you survive this? What did you do?" Now I can be that person for other women. I often get calls from women who say, "I learned so much from what happened to you and how you handled it and how you survived it." Women come to me and say, "You're such an inspiration to me." That makes me feel so good.

My work today is focused on spousal abuse in the families of cops. I don't think I'll ever be in the soft issues business. Maybe that's my karma, to take on the really thorny issues in policing. And police family violence is a toughy; it's a big one. Forty percent of police officers surveyed in the United States say they use violence in their home. It's a more dangerous issue to uncover than anything I did in Portland. Because people pay attention to me, because I have a national reputation, because what I say carries a lot of weight, folks who want to keep policing the way it is and do things the old way hate my guts.

These days, I get new death threats. I have felt in peril several times in Los Angeles when I've taken on issues in the L.A.P.D. Now it's all over the news about how Los Angeles cops are corrupt, how they lie in court, plant evidence, abuse people. I'm working with CNN on a report about L.A.P.D. I'm working with *48 Hours* on police family violence. So I expect the threats to intensify. When I was on *60 Minutes,* I started getting hate mail again. In the beginning, it bothered me. When I was chief, it bothered my husband that I'd get death threats. My assistant, who was also my driver and bodyguard, would get upset and want to put all kinds of extra security around me. I wouldn't have it. "I'm not gonna live like that. I'm not gonna let these cowards who can't even sign their own names shut me up or terrify me so that I get to the point that I can't do my job." I'm not going to live in fear of these bullies.

The NAACP, the ACLU, or the community can stand up all they want and say, "The police are brutal. The police are bad. The police are corrupt."

But when a cop stands up and says it, when a cop with a national reputation stands up and says it, it makes a difference. People listen. And the police hate that.

We're put on earth to learn lessons and to work through issues. And, boy, have I worked through a lot and learned even more. Fifteen years ago, I didn't think I'd ever be happy again. I didn't think anything could ever replace what had been taken away from me. Not true. I'm so much stronger now and much happier than I've ever been.

Lesson number six: The end is not always the end.

In February 2000, Penny was featured on 60 Minutes, *talking about her work to expose spousal abuse within police families. Later that year, she was inducted into the Hall of Fame of the Michigan State School of Criminal Justice, the first woman to receive that honor. Author of* Triumph of Spirit, *she is currently director of the National Center for Women and Policing.*

Michèle Ohayon

"One of the dangers we face is staying in our safe little area, not wanting to shift anything, because if we shift, we have to invent something new, untested. And we don't want to, we want to stay the way we are, the way our parents were and our grandparents were.... And that's why we have to follow our hearts and do what we have to do, and damn the consequences."

Michèle Ohayon is an award-winning writer, director, and producer whose feature-length documentary, Colors Straight Up *— about a theater group for at-risk kids in Watts — won an Academy Award nomination as well as a dozen other awards. Her mission, as a filmmaker, is "to tell good, truthful stories about real people and to make films that open hearts and minds."*

Throughout my life, my mom would say to me, "You're very courageous." Why, I don't know.

I never thought of myself that way. My father, yes. In a way, I walked in his footsteps, because I put myself in dangerous and controversial situations. And yet our paths diverged when I became a filmmaker. Never in my wildest imagination would I have guessed that I'd end up with an Academy Award nomination. How I got there is best understood by the culture and the times in which I grew up.

I was born in Casablanca to Moroccan parents of the Jewish faith. My father was one of the organizers of the illegal immigration of the Jews from North Africa to Israel before the state of Israel was created, when it was still Palestine. Fearing a potential holocaust in North Africa, the Israeli government asked him to help them get Jews out of Morocco without the king's permission. My father traveled to remote mountain villages, going into the little synagogues, saying, "I can take you to the Promised Land. Do you want to come?" These people left behind everything — their property, their sheep, at times their parents — and followed their messianic dream. My father smuggled them over the border and clandestinely put them into boats to the Promised Land. I think he struggles with that today. What right did he have to take them from their homes? Are they happy in Israel? He's not sure. But he followed his mission and risked his life to get them there. He was a real-life hero.

Eventually, with a family of his own, he wanted to move to Israel. But the Israeli government said no, they needed him in Morocco. In 1965, a group of hostile Arabs found out that he was secretly selling Bibles and other Hebrew books in the basement of his stationary shop. As my entire family watched, they burned the shop to the ground. And then we fled. I was six years old.

At last, we were in Israel. But it wasn't what we expected. No longer needing my father's services, the government treated him like a second-class citizen. That must have broken his heart. I didn't learn the whole story until I was a teenager. Because he was always required to be very secretive, I had heard only bits and pieces. One day, I sat him down and said, "I want to hear it all." In a way, knowing about his underground work helped me understand who I was.

As North Africans, we were treated differently in Israel than the Eastern Europeans. We were looked down on, and I never felt that I belonged. Part of the strength of my family was that we hung onto our culture even in the midst of this discrimination. Imagine the American government saying to the Chinese, "If you want to be American, you've got to throw away your chopsticks, your rice, your teas, you've got to eat hamburger. Otherwise, you will never belong." That's how it was in Israel. My family clung to our customs, our music, our food, and it gave us strength and a unique spirit.

As a teenager, I was determined to overcome the attitude about me as a Moroccan, to excel in order to break down the prejudice. I was an excellent student in high school. I might have gone on to great academic success, but I had an awakening that put me on a different course: I realized that there was something very wrong with the Israeli-Arab conflict. At that time, like today, Israelis were very patriotic. Everybody served in the military. National security was paramount. All this conspired to create an environment in which Arabs were suppressed to keep them from being a threat to Israel. Morally, I felt this wasn't right. I had every reason to hate Arabs; they had burned my father's shop in Morocco and changed the future of my family. But I felt their treatment was wrong.

Because I adored my parents, because I came from a conservative family harassed by Arabs, this was a difficult conflict for me. Should I really stand up and say, publicly, "I support the Arab cause?" Or should I be the good girl, which I had always been, and follow anti-Arab sentiment? It was risky for me to stand up for Arabs in spite of the fact that my family held anger toward them and the Israelis suppressed them. It took courage to be my own person and to do what I felt was right — although, at the time, it didn't feel like courage.

Determined to have my parents look at Arabs differently, I argued that not all Arabs are the same. The Arabs in Morocco are different from the

Arabs in Israel, who are different from the Arabs in Lebanon, and so forth. However, it was such an emotional subject that logic was useless. To press the point, I started bringing my Arab friends home. In our culture, you always open your home and feed a guest, so my parents were forced to be in their company. I even brought an Arab friend home for a Shabbat dinner. There he was, sitting right next to me while Jewish prayers were being said. Occasions like this forced my parents to separate their past from the present, to look the "enemy" in the eye and appreciate that we are all human beings.

At seventeen, like others, I joined the army. Part of me wanted to be the good Israeli, to fight for my country, to be an officer. And I was on track to do just that. The temptation to belong, to excel, was great.

One day at target practice, an officer put the Arab headdress, the kafia, on the target. The message, of course, was, "Kill this Arab," rather than simply, "Shoot well, hit a mark."

"I'm not going to shoot that," I said. "Take it off, and I'll hit the bull's eye. I'm a good markswoman. But this isn't right. It's brainwashing."

People couldn't believe what I was saying. This is a country where security, nationality, and simply the word, "Israel," are sacred. Countering an officer is taboo. Because I continued to argue and stir things up, I became known as a rebel. As a result, I lost what would have been a prestigious assignment to the United Nations, where I was originally headed because I spoke several languages. Instead, they stuck me off in some obscure post. My parents were hurt, and my brother, who was headed for a high-security combat unit, was furious. Even I had doubts about my "bad behavior" and what I had lost as a result of it.

After my year in the military, I enrolled at Tel Aviv University. Filmmaking was like a calling. To pay for my film studies, I worked four nights a week in a bar. I made several short films and for my graduation thesis decided to make a movie about an Arab and a Jew who fall in love.

That, of course, was a shocking thing to do. It was the equivalent of making a love story about a black and a white in this country many years ago. I called my film *Pressure.*

As expected, my parents were alarmed. "Why do you have to do this kind of film?" my father asked. "Why does it have to be a love story between an Arab and a Jew? And why for your graduation thesis? You're shooting yourself in the foot. You'll never graduate with honors if you do this." All I could say was that I had to do it.

Smart people, my parents decided that, since they couldn't stop me, they'd help me. This is a great testament to them. Since they didn't have money to help fund the film, they gave me what they could: food. Every day they came to our location with big pots and pans of Moroccan food to feed my crew, who were working for nothing, since this was a labor of love. And of course the crew suddenly loved lunch breaks like never before. The couscous became legendary.

During the filming of *Pressure,* the police were on my tail because I was filming in the Arab side of Jerusalem. As an Israeli, you don't go there. It's dangerous. You may be shot, you may be kidnapped. But I wanted to use real people, even though the story was fictional. Later, the police said that I stirred people up, provoked the Arabs to rebel and revolt. Nonsense.

Pressure screened at the Montreal Film Festival, and the Jewish people there were outraged: "How dare an Israeli do that!" But in other places where I thought people would scream and throw tomatoes, the film got a lot of positive attention, I think in part because it put a very human face on a difficult issue. It won several awards, which kind of worried me. I wanted to shake up the system, and here the system was giving me awards. I thought, "Have I done something wrong?"

My next film was a documentary about the famous Bir Zeit University, located by a village under Israeli military occupation. The government was convinced that the school was a training ground for a core terrorist group. As a result, if the students demonstrated about anything, the school was closed down. I thought this was nonsense and decided to show that the students were innocent and that closing the school was wrong.

Once again, to put a personal face on a controversial issue, I decided to follow a Palestinian student, to document his life and show that he was just a normal person, not part of a terrorist group. To do this, I had to get into the refugee camp guarded by soldiers where the student lived in a shack. I found a brave cameraman and a soundman who would sneak into the camp with me. At that time, the government had closed the university, so the students weren't in classes. I interviewed professors at home and, yes, they were very vocal about their ideas, but they weren't terrorists. This predated the Intifida, which was when the Palestinians revolted openly against the Israelis.

When we first went into the refugee camp, I told my cameraman, "No matter what happens, keep shooting. I don't care if somebody points a rifle at you, keep filming." I wanted to capture the conflict. Sure enough, one day as we were following the Palestinian student, we saw Arab girls coming out of a high school singing and right behind them a big Israeli army vehicle heading straight at us.

"I'm stopping, I'm stopping!" the cameraman yelled.

"No, no, keep shooting, keep shooting!"

The soldiers stopped right next to us. We were arrested and taken to jail.

My cameraman was freaked out: "Oh, my God, what will my mom say, what will my dad say?" We were teenagers. I was nineteen. Sure, I was affected by what my parents would think, what my friends would say. I'd already been surprised by peers who on the surface agreed with me but who changed the moment I walked into their homes with an Arab. A lot of people were hypocritical. It was one thing to believe in something and another thing to live it.

But oddly, in front of that military vehicle and later in jail, I wasn't scared. When I'm around a camera, I have no fear whatsoever. My camera gives me a feeling of power, as if nothing can happen to me — it protects me. Kind of strange. Maybe it's because I'm on a mission and I'm not going to turn back just because some objective circumstances are more difficult then I thought they were going to be or because obstacles are in my way.

What were you doing there? asked the soldiers.

I pretended to be some stupid girl from Tel Aviv who didn't know what she was doing, just making some little student film. Of course they didn't believe me: "Okay, we'll call the college. Who's the head of the department?" I was hesitant to tell them, because the head was a very right-wing man who would most likely turn me in. When they called him, I tried to overhear the conversation but couldn't. They hung up. "Okay, you can go."

"What? What did he say? What happened?"

Later, I asked the professor why he hadn't snitched on me. "I had to put my feelings aside," he said, "because I believe in freedom of expression, and you shouldn't be arrested for making a film, even though you didn't have permission. Next time, ask for permission." He gave me hope. As filmmakers, we have to be able to show the truth, especially in documentary filmmaking.

The Bir Zeit documentary took me a year to make. When I was about to show it, I got a call from one of the professors featured in the film. "Look, if you want to show the movie, we'll support you all the way, but we're already getting threatening calls from the Secret Service." He was letting me know that I'd be putting them in danger.

I was torn. I had spent a lot of time and effort on a subject that I really wanted to expose. And yet people's safety was important. I made the very difficult decision to shelve the film and I never, ever showed it. I couldn't put them in danger. As ruthless as I am when I'm making a film — I don't care about anything — when it came to jeopardizing these people, I couldn't do it. They could have been jailed, and I don't mean for a week, but forever, for provoking against the State, because the film showed Israel as an offender and an oppressor. And the Israelis were afraid of that image. They still are.

Injustice bothers me, it really bothers me — maybe because I felt the injustice against my own skin. When I applied to study film at the university, the first thing I was asked was, "Why does a girl from Morocco want to be a filmmaker?" It was like asking a black person, "How come a black person wants to be a filmmaker?" I went on to prove myself, but the students at Bir Zeit were helpless because they were under political and social pressure. They had nowhere to go. I felt their struggle and identified with others in Israel who suffered more than I from the prejudices.

For the most part, I didn't tell my parents about my activities so as not to worry them. Of course, my mother always knew anyway. One time I went with a group of students to an occupied city in the West Bank to demonstrate about Bir Zeit. The army came and threw tear gas on us. I ran into the shop of an Arab, who immediately gave me an onion, because it makes you cry and washes out the tear gas. When I got home, I tried to act as if nothing had happened.

"Where have you been?" asked my mother. The demonstration was all over the TV news.

"Just out with some friends," I said as I walked by, looking away.

She stopped me. "You were there." She smelled the onion on me. She knew.

I held my breath.

She put her arms around me. As much as she opposed my views, she liked that I followed my heart.

One day I got a call from a director in Holland who wanted to make a film about a Palestinian artist returning to Israel after sixteen years in America. The director wanted to follow him on his journey from America back to Palestine but was afraid that he'd be arrested. Since I'd made movies in the West Bank and had contacts there, the director asked me to be the Israeli producer. I said sure.

Taking on this project meant that I had to vouch for the Palestinian artist, to guarantee that he wasn't a threat to Israeli security. He was my responsibility. I went to meet him and the Dutch director and crew at the Haifa harbor, where they had come by boat from Cyprus, having already shot footage there. Before disembarking, the Palestinian artist was separated from the crew and searched. We were all on edge.

On land, as we approached the border, filming, I saw that we, too, were going to be stopped. As the police came toward us, I turned to the cameraman, Theo, and said, "Shoot something else quick, kids running around, anything that has no political context." I had seconds, literally, for him to grasp what I was saying, that I needed something to give the police if they confiscated film. Theo got it instantly. I think that's when I fell in love with him. While I talked to the police, trying to keep things calm and buy a little time, he organized the crew and got fluff footage that I could hand over, instead of the Cyprus footage.

I was so impressed. This guy had understood me completely, with barely an exchange. I talked our way across the border without any incident, and we filmed that day in the West Bank. As the director interviewed the artist about the State of Israel, he became very vocal about his ideas, saying, "Israel is a fascist country." That was radical, even for me.

At the end of the day, on our way home, we were stopped by a whole convoy of military vehicles. A soldier in a watchtower had been surveilling us as we filmed and, suspicious of what we were doing, had radioed ahead.

I told the crew, "Stay in the van. Do not come out. I'm going to go talk to these guys. At least I speak their language. And hide the film."

I got out of the van and started toward the military vehicles. I was so scared. Not for myself, but for the Palestinian. *Israel is not a fascist state,* I thought. *They will not arrest him. He will go back home without any problems.* But I knew that the film we'd just shot put him in danger. And if he were jailed, there would be nobody to protect him.

The soldiers drew their rifles. I was the only one between them and the Palestinian. I think it was because I was so scared for him that I started yelling. I wasn't going to beg, I wasn't going to plead with these big, tough macho Israelis. Theo was watching from the van, and he said it was the moment when he fell in love with me, because he knew how scared I was.

"How dare you?" I screamed at them. "These are guests from Holland." I ranted on, inventing a story.

It worked. "Okay," said the officer in charge, "we'll let you go, but you have to give us your film." I stormed back to the van. Theo saw me coming and got the fluff piece he'd shot.

"Here's your footage!" I yelled at the officer. "And you haven't heard the end of this!"

As we drove away, cigarette between my fingers, I started to shake. That's when I realized how scared I had been.

Four years later, I married Theo. By then my parents were used to my "crazy" behavior and even embraced Theo, who was Catholic. The move to California was a little harder on them. My mom still asks me, "Why are you in Hollywood? You can make your movies about the unfortunate in the West Bank. You don't have to be there." But I feel this is part of my calling, to expose issues here, to show things that are unfair. Maybe because I grew up feeling like an outsider, I have a strong identification with blacks and Latinos in this country and feel an instinct to shed light at people on the margins of society. I never would have guessed that it would take me to an Academy Award nomination for a feature documentary about kids in Watts.

In *Colors Straight Up,* I followed at-risk kids who were part of a theater group run by a guy who definitely lived at the edge. He used theater as a way to get kids off the street and help them process what was going on in their lives as well as give them a sense of their own worth. I shot in some of the most dangerous areas of Los Angeles at night, going places where people thought I was nuts. But I had no fear. I'd become really ruthless. Not that things didn't cross my mind — yes, Grape Street is the worst street to be on at night — but I had to take risks to tell the story. My crew would be saying, "We should really get out of here," but if I needed to finish shooting a scene, I wasn't about to leave.

Later, when *Colors* was nominated for an Academy Award, people would say to me, "Oh, wow, you had a lot of guts to go there." But I never felt that. Maybe it's naive, but I believe that, if you're not afraid, nothing will happen to you. Plus, like I said, I get courage from my camera.

The times when I feel fear are before a shoot. *Okay, this is what I'm going to risk. This is what may happen.* Theo is usually my cameraman, and if we're filming in dangerous areas, I always leave instructions: This is my will, this is who is going to take care of the kids if something happens. I have fear, definitely. Yet somehow, once I'm in the field, it's gone.

To make *Colors* as authentic and truthful as possible, it was important for me to jump in all the way. The kids opened their homes to me, and I needed to open my home to them. So I'd bring them into my house even though I'd only met them a few weeks earlier and didn't know them that well. They'd stay overnight. I'd give them my kids' beds and tuck them in. The whole point of the film was that these kids are like everybody else. If I didn't trust them, why would they trust me? A lot of people said to me, "You're crazy. Now they know where you live and maybe they'll steal from you." I had to do it anyway. If I was proven wrong, then I'd be proven wrong. If they stole something, then they needed it, so let them have it.

As it turned out, the film was a great experience. Nobody stole from me.

Nobody harmed me. My daughter, who was two when I started and five when I finished, was exposed to a whole different culture. Especially in a white, isolated society, it's important that we expose, not only ourselves, but our kids to other cultures, even if it's risky. Words are not as important as our actions.

All that said, the older I get, the more difficult it is for me to take these risks, because more people are depending on me and I also put more people at risk. Maybe I make less courageous choices now, but I still try to follow my path. The great thing is that Theo is totally behind me. He's as crazy as I am, maybe more. He'll never say, "It's dangerous, don't do it." Never, ever. We're film animals, both of us. *I gotta get this shot, no matter what the cost.*

Working on a film together can be challenging for Theo and me. One night, I got a call from one of the *Colors* kids, Oscar. He was in jail. It was 3:00 in the morning. No way could I pull a crew together at that hour — especially since most of them worked for nothing. "Look," I said to Theo, "it's me and you and Danielle" — she was only two. "What do we do? If you shoot, who's going to stay with her? We can't leave her home alone." So we all went. I thought I'd go in first and set up the shot, and then Theo would go in and actually film while I stayed in the car with the baby. Well, it didn't happen that way. I had to be with Oscar the entire time and ended up filming him on video while Theo was in the jail parking lot with our two-year-old.

On particularly dangerous shoots, we always talk about whether I should go alone or take someone else. In a way, it's easier for me if Theo stays at home, because should something happen to me, I know he's there to take care of the kids. But so far we've ended up saying, "Well, that's ridiculous. We can't make choices out of fear. We have to make choices out of strength." Throughout my life, I've tried to make decisions out of strength, not out of fear, because I know the moment I make a decision out of fear, it will backfire.

I feel fortunate that Theo is as daring, or naive, as I am. He helps me when I waver. If I hesitate, he says, "You know what you have to do. It's maybe not convenient. It's maybe not the right time. You're pregnant. You're this. You're that. But you gotta do it." He's very good at that. Now that I have his support, it's easier. He keeps me on track.

In a way, I also keep Theo on track. Most of his work now is doing big studio films — if we both worked on documentaries, we'd be broke. When I was making *Colors,* he was shooting *Volcano.* Because I worked mostly on the weekends, he would shoot my no-budget film with me. Then, during the week, he would shoot a hundred-million-dollar film. How insane. The documentary work is good for his soul. And it keeps him on his feet. No assistants, no nothing. I travel with a very small crew. We all have to fit in one car, that's the rule — it's the only rule — everybody in one car. So he has to take the camera on his shoulder, and it keeps his hand-held camera-work flowing and sharp.

Making films the way I do is a way of life. It's the choices I make every day. From the beginning, I haven't played by the rules, as sacred as they might be. I don't want to be part of a big mass that's not thinking. Maybe that's one reason why people respond to the films I make, because I take them with me all the way — good, bad, whatever. I'll never be part of the subject, but I go in as far as I can, I get as close as possible.

It being a way of life also means creating bonds and friendships with the people I film, which can be very rewarding but isn't always convenient. Five years ago, I made a film about homeless women, and some of them became quite dependent on me, because I was their only link to the outside world. They'd call and say, "Can you help me with this? Can you help me with that?" As a filmmaker, once a project is finished, I have to move on to the next one, but I'm still in touch with these women. Same with the kids in South Central.

One of the dangers we face is staying in our safe little area, not wanting to shift anything, because if we shift, we have to invent something new, untested. And we don't want to, we want to stay the way we are, the way our parents were and our grandparents were. That, I think, is where we get into dogmas and conservatism. And that's why we have to follow our hearts and do what we have to do, and damn the consequences. If I think about the consequences, I do nothing, I get paralyzed, I don't even want to start a project. I have to go in blind. Have my own adventure.

When my kids are grown, I hope they have their own adventures. I know it will be hard for me to deal with their taking risks, but I hope that they find their own voices and do their own courageous things. Big leaders do big courageous things, but there are the everyday people who take the small courageous steps to change or shift or shake things a little... and then take another step and another and another. If we all did that, think how the world would change.

In 1992, Michèle directed her award-winning feature-length documentary, It Was a Wonderful Life, *about upper-middle-class women who become the "hidden homeless" and live out of their cars. Narrated by Jodie Foster, the film aired nationally on PBS and on Oxygen, as well as on worldwide TV, at international film festivals, in Los Angeles theaters, and throughout America. It won the Gold Award at the Houston Film Festival and continues to receive outstanding reviews and community accolades.*

Margaret Ensley

"Sometimes, this works gets overwhelming. I don't want to see another kid, I don't want to have to tell another story, I don't want to . . . my pain is so great sometimes, all I can do is cry. Every time another kid falls, I cry again."

Margaret Ensley is a mother who, seven years ago, started her day like she would any other day.

On February 22, 1993, my seventeen-year-old son, Micheal, came into the kitchen to tell me he was leaving for school.

"Okay, honey. I'll see you this evening. Bring hamburgers home." It was just a typical day. "Hurry up now, you're gonna miss your bus."

Micheal was going to a high school in Woodland Hills, because I lived in a neighborhood in South Central, Los Angeles, surrounded by Bloods and Crips. Not wanting him to get caught up in gang activity, I'd called the school board to find out if I could have him bussed to a school without gang problems. "Send him out to our valley school," the person on the other end had said. "We don't have that kind of issue there."

On his way to his second-period class, Micheal was walking down the hallway with his books on his back when a young man approached him. Apparently, this young man had seen him earlier in the morning and said that Micheal gave him a dirty look, like he wanted to fight. I'll never know if that's true, but Micheal must have anticipated a fight because he was removing his backpack when the young man pulled a .22 out of his pocket and shot him. Micheal spun and ran down the hallway before collapsing.

When that bullet hit my son, I was in a meeting at AT&T, where I was a supervisor. I was called out of that meeting by an emergency phone call, and I knew it was serious because I'd told my children, "Unless somebody's bleeding, never say 'emergency.'" I get panicked around that word. I hurried to the phone. My daughter was screaming, "Momma, Momma, sit down... are you sitting down, Momma?"

I sat down. "What is it?"

"It's Micheal..."

"What about Micheal? He's at school. I just sent him to school."

"Micheal's been shot!"

I dropped the phone and started screaming at the top of my lungs.

Some friends at work put me in a car and drove me out to the hospital at Northridge. It took us forty minutes to get there. When we pulled into the hospital parking lot, I saw cameramen outside. *What are they doing here?* I thought. I got out and the cameras starting flashing. *Why are they taking my picture? I'm just looking for Micheal. Where's my son?*

When I got inside, the doctor took me by the hands and sat me down. He said, "Mrs. Ensley, we did all we could do."

"What do you mean, you did all you could do? Where's Micheal? Where's my baby?"

He said, "Mrs. Ensley, your son is dead."

I couldn't cry.

I couldn't scream.

I couldn't do anything.

A few hours earlier, I had kissed my boy and told him I loved him, and now they were telling me that he was dead. *No no no, they're wrong. Where's Micheal? Where's my baby?* In shock, I went to the emergency room and saw Micheal lying on the operating table. He had the most beautiful brown eyes. They were half-closed. *Oh my God, Micheal. Who would want to hurt you? Why?*

Nothing around me was real. I couldn't connect. I was seeing without seeing, hearing without hearing. A detective arrived. He said they'd found the boy who had killed Micheal. He'd walked off campus and gone to a local donut shop and gotten himself a donut and a lemonade, with the gun in his pocket. That's where they found him. He showed no remorse, no nothing.

Later, at the trial, I thought this kid was going to say that Micheal had beaten him up, had threatened him in some way. "Did you know Micheal Ensley?" asked the judge.

"No, I didn't know him. I'd seen him around campus. He looked like he wanted to fight, and so I shot him."

I sat in that courtroom, and I honestly believe that I could have choked the life out of that kid with my bare hands.

I didn't know what to do. I felt like I had failed my son that his life should end at seventeen, just as we were making plans for graduation, for his future. I came home . . . I just . . . I just didn't know what to do.

The media started calling, CNN, talk shows. I wanted nothing to do with them. But then I realized that Micheal would always be just another South Central statistic unless I got out and talked about him as my son. Micheal was not a number. He was a brother to Necci, a young man that his family and friends loved. I went on a show in Los Angeles, and then Montel Williams called. They flew me to New York to talk about violence in schools with other mothers who had had similar tragedies. I'll never forget, as I was getting ready to leave, Montel walked over to me and said, "What are you going to do now, Margaret? When you go back home, what are you going to do?" I didn't know, I didn't know.

I came on home and thought, *I gotta do something. I'll always feel that I failed Micheal by not knowing that guns were carried on that school campus.* I assumed that the school he was attending was safe; they'd told me they didn't have gang problems out there. I thought that school and my home were the two safest places for my child. I didn't know the dangers. The school wasn't going to tell me, because they didn't want me or any other parent yanking their kid out, that's money. So I had been in a vacuum, thinking that everything was hunky-dory. Seven years ago, more than a hundred thousand guns were being carried on school campuses every day. I think it's gone up to about eight hundred thousand nationally. It was just mind-blowing to me when I found out. Why didn't I know this? Why didn't I know my son was in danger even though he was outside the 'hood.

I can't help Micheal, I thought, *but I can help other children.* It would be part of my healing.

Since Micheal's death, I've done everything I can to educate parents and teachers about the terrible problem of violence in schools. I organized a group called *Mothers Against Violence in Schools* in Los Angeles. I marched, I picketed, I testified in Congress, I lobbied — to remind myself that Micheal did not die in vain. He died as a catalyst for change. He's not here to be the drum major, but his mother is devoting the rest of her life to making children aware that violence is not the answer. We must learn how to live in our world of diversity, accepting people just as they are and not killing someone because they look at us funny or because they say something that hurts our feelings.

I've also become very involved with some of my state legislators, working on measures related to violence in schools. I can't even begin to count the number of times I've boarded a plane to Sacramento to lobby for tougher juvenile bills that, in the case of violent crimes, would try kids as young as fourteen as adults. I was bound and determined to help get that bill passed. Children are used by adults in violent crimes because they get lesser sentences. That isn't right. I've talked to a lot of parents who have lost children. "The shooter was fourteen," they'll say. "The shooter was twelve." Far too many kids are being used by gang members as shooters because they get their stripes when they kill somebody, and when they go to jail, it's only for ten years and then they're out.

The young man who killed Micheal was one month shy of sixteen. If it had been a month later, he would have been tried and punished as an adult. He could have been in jail for the rest of his life. Instead, he was tried in juvenile court, which meant he could only be kept in prison until he was twenty-five. What a tragedy. I was ready to take on the world because of that injustice. That meant knocking on a lot of doors up in Sacramento, that meant making some people very uncomfortable, calling people on the carpet for their attitudes about what was going on in Los Angeles. People didn't want to be bothered with violence in South Central. *It's not that urgent,* they'd say without using those words.

Once while in Sacramento, I was trying to talk to a legislator who wasn't the least bit interested in what I had to say. By the time I got back to Los Angeles, another kid had been shot at school. The next time I went up to Sacramento, I said, "Maybe you'll give me more than two minutes now that another kid has fallen victim on a school campus." I called him out. "Is it important enough now for you to give me some time?" That was my big obstacle — trying to wake people up. God, I must have beat on the issue, I can't tell you how many times. Trying to get people to see that it wasn't just a South Central problem, that Micheal was not just a statistic, that he was a living, breathing human being, a child not unlike their own children.

People in Sacramento used to hate to see me coming. They'd drop their heads. "There goes that crazy woman from South Central." I wouldn't care, because I felt like I had failed my son, and I wasn't going to fail now.

The passage of the juvenile bill was my biggest accomplishment. I lobbied until it passed. And then I became a member of the state attorney general's Violence Prevention Policy Council for a couple of years, as the only nonprofessional. It allowed me to work on a lot of issues related to violence in California, bringing people from all around the state to talk about the underlying issues. I also worked with the Youth Authority Boot Program, trying to reduce their recidivism rate.

Wherever I see the need, that's where you'll find me. It means I'm down at city hall, or fighting to get assault weapons banned and weapons off the street. It means flying to Sacramento and testifying on legislation. I do peace marches every year. I give workshops and do conferences, I go to schools, I do violence-prevention training, I do interventions with troubled youth. Whatever the need, I'm there. A few years ago, I retired to do this work full-time. Every year now, I give a scholarship in Micheal's name.

We need to listen to our children. We need to talk more openly with them. What are their concerns? What keeps them up at night? What causes them anxiety? And once they tell us, the onus is on us to secure their future, to make sure they're safe. If they don't feel safe in school, take them out until that school has demonstrated that they, too, are concerned about safety and you can see that they have a comprehensive safety program. We must give safety back to our children. We have to show them — not just talk about it. To do that, we've got to get guns off the street. We have way too many guns out there. Way too many. And especially in South Central. Gangs are prevalent. Micheal used to be terrified to even go to the library.

We have gone to sleep, as parents, as educators. We hit the snooze button. We had wake-up calls before Columbine. We had warning signs. But we went to sleep because it wasn't in our backyard, because we weren't faced with the tragedy up close. "It couldn't happen here, that's the kind of stuff they do in South Central." When we close our eyes to the realities of what's going on, we leave ourselves vulnerable. And that's exactly what happened. Parents went to sleep. Educators went to sleep. "No, no, no. Not here. Our kids aren't like that."

The day those kids started walking onto that Columbine campus in those trench coats should have been a wake-up call for everyone. No child should feel excluded on a school campus. At least find out why they're acting strangely. Question somebody. Talk to the parents. "Why is your child walking around our school in a trench coat? Is there an issue we need to deal with? Is it a self-esteem issue? Are kids picking on him? What's going on?" We allowed it to happen. The police had issues and run-ins with those kids without really finding out what made them tick. They weren't acting normal. And no one found out why.

Most people want to stay away from anything that's violence oriented, because they're afraid of getting too close to it. It's difficult to get people to have some ownership in it. Columbine. Oregon. Kentucky. We're all to blame, because we know that kids carry guns, we know that there's violence in schools, but until it becomes a catastrophic event, we don't pay attention. Look, we're parents — there's no way we should not know that someone's building a bomb in the basement. We're just as much to blame as the guy who pulled the trigger, because we saw it and we went back to sleep. It shouldn't have to take a Columbine or a Springfield, Oregon: one kid is one kid too many. The first child felled at a school campus, we should have been looking at what was going on. Somebody's gotta say, "Enough!"

They've been killing kids in South Central for years and, yet, it's a blurb on the last page of the newspaper. When Micheal was killed, he made the front page of the *Los Angeles Times.* Why? Because he was a black kid in a white neighborhood. They carried the story for a week. It became sensationalized because the violence was in the suburbs. The tragedy is that it could have been prevented.

The young man who killed Micheal had a history of battery and abusive behavior in school. He was a runaway, he was on probation, he was due to be removed from his home. A lot was going on. And yet supposedly nobody at school knew. He was a time bomb waiting to go off. At one of my lectures not long ago, I met a teacher who had had this kid in his class years earlier in a different school. He said that, even at a very early age, the kid was a time bomb. Rather than deal with the issue, they shuffled him from one school to another. And then it all caught up with him. Micheal became the target.

I was bitter, because if somebody had done something before that day in February when Micheal was walking down the hall, he would still be here. I'll be darned if I'm not going to do something to stop the violence... and keep doing and keep doing. It's a promise I made to Micheal. I stood in front of his crypt and said, "Never again, Micheal, will I allow children to be hurt or bullied or coerced at school and not get involved in some way, shape, form, or fashion. I won't." I'm committed. It's too late for my son, but not too late for the other kids if we, as conscientious citizens, make it a priority.

Sometimes this work gets overwhelming. I don't want to see another kid, I don't want to have to tell another story, I don't want to... my pain is so great sometimes, all I can do is cry. Every time another kid falls, I cry again.

The wound from Micheal's death is still with me. On the anniversary of his death this past year, I couldn't even speak. I had to go out by myself, just be to myself. The pain is ever present. A lot of parents have to shoulder this weight. When the incident happened in Columbine, I fell to my knees, because I knew that a parent was experiencing the same excruciating pain that I felt and there was nothing that I could do to bring that child back. It's something we all share. It's a common bond in our lives.

I take Micheal's picture with me everywhere. When I'm in the mall, somebody will walk up to me and hug me and say, "Keep up the fight. I know what you're trying to do, and I'm behind you." And then I'll hear a little kid say, "Mom, Mom! That's Micheal's mother, that's Micheal's mother." And that's when I'm reminded that somebody's heard our story. I've made an impact on somebody.

I was giving a speech at a youth center a while back, and a young man came up to me and said, "You don't know me, but it was because of you that I turned my life around. It's because of you that I joined the church and decided to dedicate my life to Christ, because I knew about that incident and I heard you speak." And I just stood there crying. If I don't do anything else in this world, I helped one person. And that's enough for me.

Margaret continues to advocate for safe schools and gun control through her organization, Mothers Against Violence in Schools (MAVIS).

Candice Slaughter Warmke

"The letter began, 'You are my last hope for freedom.' This time, I forced myself to read on."

When she walked out the door and down the driveway of her Ohio farm, her mind was riveted on a single thought: whether she would hear the bullet before it hit. Behind her, she felt the aim of her husband's rifle. Her feet seemed to move in slow motion, carrying her toward the Chevy truck and her five-year-old daughter. Not until she had backed out of the driveway and turned toward town did she start to shake.

Candice found refuge in a women's shelter, but when her husband tracked her there, she bought a one-way airplane ticket for Katie and sent her daughter to a safe place, not knowing when or if she would ever see her again. Then, she went into hiding.

I first began working with battered women in 1979.

When I started, I never imagined the journey on which I was embarking. I never imagined the amazing risks I would face personally, professionally, financially. I didn't know that men would throw themselves on my car, stalk me, threaten me, call me names. I didn't know that people would find out where I lived and come to my home to harass me, throw bricks through my window, and leave messages on my answering machine, the most frightening of which was from a man who said he knew where my daughter went to school. I didn't know that community leaders would try to sway sponsors of my work to cut me off financially. All this because I refused to be silent about the fact that I had been battered and I stood up for other women who had been abused. Painfully, a great part of the resentment came from women leading domestic violence movements in the early eighties who didn't want people in their ranks speaking out publicly about their own abuse.

After twelve years of this treatment, I finally stopped, tired of the politics of the domestic violence movement and the uncaring attitudes in the criminal justice system. I wanted to rest. I needed to heal my own problems. I took a part-time job consulting with Planned Parenthood and helped start the Florida Women's Foundation, the first woman's foundation in the state. Later, I was elected chairperson of the State Battered and Formerly Battered Women's Caucus. I guess I'll never completely stop helping battered women; it's in my blood. But at the time, I needed a break.

For six months, I watched our personal finances erode toward bankruptcy as a financial strategy my husband and I had planned went sour. I had a hard time sleeping at night, so much worry was rattling around inside my head. During this same time, I entered counseling to deal with memories of being sexually abused as a child. I began to think I was losing my mind. Even worse, I was trying to salvage the life of my angry, runaway fifteen-year-old daughter who wanted to quit school. She was on a self-destructive path, and it was clear to me why. Her father (my ex-husband) had been abusive, we had lived through our own war of domestic violence, and even though my daughter and I had escaped when she was five years old, it was affecting her teenage years. Out of desperation to keep her in school, I sent her a thousand miles away to live with relatives. My heart felt like it had been ripped out. I wanted to hide from the world.

Then one day, a letter came, addressed to me from Kimberly Bliss Soubielle, a woman who was in prison for murdering her abusive husband. She had gotten my name from a list of people who belonged to the state Coalition Against Domestic Violence. I guess she had picked me because I was known for my advocacy on behalf of battered women. From out of the blue came this cry for help, a battered woman pleading for her freedom with a woman who had also been battered. I had always had a soft place in my heart for battered women who ended up in prison. On several occasions, I had helped shelter good women who ended up in jail. I had also helped a woman who had later been killed. But I had never received a letter from a woman in prison before. I couldn't even read it all the way through. It was too painful. I had my own pain. My own problems were too overwhelming. I didn't answer.

A month later, I got another note from Kimberly Soubielle. This time, she sent a picture of herself sitting in a straight-backed chair holding Allison, her four-year-old daughter. Kimberly was dressed in her pink prison uniform. Both of them were smiling for the camera. Allison was so small. Somehow, they represented the hope I wanted to feel for my own relationship with my daughter. I wanted to believe that a bond exists between mother and daughter. I wanted to believe the bond is so strong that all the pain, all the unkind words and mean acts, cannot sever it. It is a cord of shared essence...primal. It can be twisted and stretched without breaking. I clung to the belief that, one day, my daughter and I would be together again.

Kimberly's picture haunted me. The letter began, "You are my last hope for freedom." This time, I forced myself to read on. I sobbed. My heart raged with the pain of my own past, the battering, all the ways my life had been forever changed by the violence. I allowed that rage to burn in my soul. I grieved the separation from my daughter. I mourned her absence.

Still, I didn't answer Kimberly's letter. As I worked in my home office, the photo of her and her daughter would surface in my piles of papers. No matter what I was doing, the picture seemed to suddenly reappear as a reminder. I wanted to throw it away, but I couldn't.

During that time, I would usually awaken around 3:00 and toss and turn until morning. One of these nights, rambling in the dark, I couldn't stop thinking about Kimberly and her daughter. It was distressing to think that this woman was in prison for defending her life, excruciating that she had been separated from her daughter. The unfairness of the system was overwhelming. I told myself I was ignoring her plea because I was powerless to do anything. I knew little about the judicial system. I knew nothing about the clemency process. I wasn't in a position of authority. There was nothing I could do to help.

But at 3:00 in the morning, reason doesn't always win out. I began thinking about how everything, in the final analysis, boils down to politics: It's all in who you know or don't know. By sunrise, I realized that the clemency law had nothing to do with the legal system. It was politics, and politics was something I knew about. I had volunteered on political campaigns, lobbied for legislation and money, been friends with politicians, and campaigned for political office myself in 1986, losing my run for Pasco County commissioner by only a few votes. I was a born organizer, and I was good at understanding people's political nature, who they are, what they think, what motivates them, how they operate.

I raced to my computer and typed out a plan to win clemency for Kimberly. I would unite other battered women around the state and country to lobby on her behalf. We would organize ourselves and play out our demands for clemency in the press. We would hold press conferences, talk to elected officials at the state level, and be consistently persistent. Our rallying cry would be: "Battered women have the right to self-defense."

I wrote to ask for Kimberly's permission to go ahead with my ideas. She wrote back immediately saying, "Yes! Yes! Yes! Whatever you want to do. You can't know how much this means to me." Little did I realize that this would be the birth of the battered women's clemency movement in Florida and that our efforts would have an impact on the rest of the world by establishing a process to review battered women's cases. I called it the Women in Prison Committee.

Every powerful person I came into contact with told me that Kimberly, and the other women like her, could never gain clemency. But dreams are a powerful force. The plan I had dreamt up early that morning brought women who had been abused together with the governor of Florida to try to convince him that battered women had a right to defend themselves.

Tenacity was our most important resource. We held press conferences in front of jails, in cemeteries, on the steps of the Capitol... any place that got us attention. We took reporters to prison with us to meet the women and report their stories (this was unheard of at the time). We faced the Florida cabinet members, one on one, and told them we wanted the women's cases reviewed, that we were formerly battered women, and we were not going to go away until they listened. Women wrote letters and held information get-togethers to recruit support. We traveled to law schools to train law students so they could assist us in putting together women's petitions for clemency.

In the beginning, the governor and his cabinet were unsympathetic. In their eyes, these women were murderers who had been judged fairly. So we used the media to tell the stories — *USA Today*, Florida newspapers, TV, radio. If a reporter was sympathetic, we fed them news constantly. I traveled around the state (and eventually other states as well) to hold workshops, organizing women and teaching them how to hold a press conference, how to coordinate a public action like a rally.

Leaders of the battered women's movement refused to support our campaign and tried to sabotage our efforts by publicly not supporting the clemency work. Prison officials made me jump through hoops again and again to visit the women in prison — I had to call one prison twenty times, long distance, to gain entry. I was ridiculed by the board of the foundation I had helped to start. At times, I doubted. Always, I was in pain from my daughter's absence.

Letters began to pour in from battered women in prison. There was no way to help so many without dragging the governor and his cabinet out of their ignorance into an understanding of why battered women deserved to be set free. Six months into the campaign, my husband, Jay, and I had a soul-searching talk, because to do what I needed to do would take a full-time commitment. With his support and encouragement, I quit my part-time job with Planned Parenthood and began to work as a full-time volunteer to free the women.

Everybody thought I was crazy when I said I was going to alter the clemency process. It was unheard of. Hardly anyone gained clemency, even under ordinary circumstances, which involved attorneys who had the legal knowledge to put on a good fight. I wasn't an attorney, but I believed we could win. And I had incredible women around me who volunteered because they believed me when I said we could change the process and gain the release of battered women. At one of the early organizing meetings, I showed up with fifteen handouts and faced a hundred people who were anxious to help. It was these women and the women in prison who gave me the courage and fortitude to keep going in the face of difficulty. It was the hugs and letters of the women behind bars and the looks they gave me that conveyed a new sense of hope where there had been none. It's difficult to explain, but I love these women unconditionally and I believe in their right to be home with their kids, living happy and safe lives.

Four and a half years after I began this fight, I attended a meeting of the original group of women who worked to gain clemency for battered women. Kimberly was there. Billie Jean Rains, who was released four months after Kimberly, talked about her letter-writing campaign on behalf of battered women still in prison. Being with these women was remarkable. I was never more aware of how powerful life can be when I dream big and take risks to help others. Each of the women we fought to free are still doing well and making a difference for others.

Many women have gained their freedom as a result of our efforts. Furthermore, great strides have been made in keeping some battered women who acted in self-defense out of prison. The Florida Bar Foundation granted more than a million dollars over three years to assist a new version of the Women in Prison Committee called the Battered Women's Clemency Project, which developed battered women's petitions for clemency. When that project ran out of money, the statewide battered women's coalition picked it up.

New law school graduates are better educated on family violence and clemency as the result of trainings conducted by our original Women in Prison Committee. Trainings for expert witnesses have made it possible to provide many competent experts for civil and criminal trials. Most important, Florida has led the way in forcing judges to let in expert witness testimony as admissible evidence in every battered woman's trial in Florida.

Other states now look to Florida as the leader of the battered women's clemency movement because of the work of a small group of volunteers who were formerly battered women. We created a revolution by saying that the system had to grant mercy to battered women, that women shouldn't be put in prison for defending their lives and the lives of their children. Movements were born in other states. Reporters told our story in Australia, France, Germany, Thailand, and Mexico, where clemency movements are afoot.

Of all that we gained, to me the most significant change on that meeting day was that my daughter drove me there on her way to her college class. And my new granddaughter smiled up at me from her car seat.

Candice is the CEO of Women's Peacepower Foundation, whose mission is to bring peace to the everyday lives of women and their families. The public foundation grants awards to people doing similar kinds of cutting-edge work as that done by the Women in Prison Committee under Candice's leadership. She's traveled around the world bringing together women from all walks of life to learn from one another about ways to end violence against women.

When the opening of the National Domestic Violence Hotline was announced, Candice was at the press conference and introduced then-President Clinton. "The president gave me a standing ovation, not bad for a farm woman from the hills of Ohio." She spends her summers with her husband and granddaughter building environmentally friendly structures on their forty-acre farm in southeast Ohio. "Catlyn loves it," she says. "She's learned to drive and pull nails, sling mud to make walls, and live without TV. Being connected to her every day is one of the best things in my life." Her daughter graduated from college and started her own business. From time to time, Candice hears from Kimberly, who earned a law degree after being released from prison, remarried, and is a new mother.

Heffa Schücking

"The times in my life when I felt I had to draw on courage concerned issues of a much more personal nature — things like honesty in relationships or raising a daughter on my own."

Best known for exposing the responsibility of northern industrialized countries for the destruction of tropical rainforests, Ildiko "Heffa" Schücking prepared the now-famous "Rainforest Memorandum," a documentation of the impact of Germany's consumption of minerals, oil, timber, and agricultural products on tropical forests. She went on to found Urgewald, a German environmental organization that supports forest people's struggles to defend their traditional lands against destructive development schemes.

A few years ago, my seventy-year-old mother saw a chilling TV report on the repression of the Kurdish minority in Turkey. The next day, she made some leaflets with the help of a friend, entered the Turkish embassy, and disrupted a reception honoring the seventy-third birthday of the Turkish republic. My mom had never heard about the problem before, but after seeing that TV program felt she had to take a stand — and the reception just happened to provide the right opportunity. Some people might think her response was courageous, but I doubt that she would consider it so. Knowing my mom, she wasn't afraid and didn't think twice about the possible consequences to her. She's just that kind of person.

I became an activist early in life. The events that politicized me were the Christmas bombings of Hanoi and Haiphong during the Vietnam War. At age twelve, I joined the peace movement, and, ever since, I've felt that issues like peace, human rights, and the environment cannot be left to politicians. At various times in my activist "career," I've been afraid — when taking part in illegal demonstrations against atomic energy plants in Germany, when the tear gas was going strong, when the police were liberally dispersing blows on people's heads with their sticks. Or when I was fourteen and taken to court for handing out leaflets criticizing police brutality. But I must say, I was never *really* afraid.

Somehow, in my measure of bravery, courage is associated with taking risks, doing something that you're afraid of. I'm not in danger of getting killed, tortured, or put in prison for criticizing the German government. If I get too rambunctious for their taste, the worst I have to fear is an occasional arrest or fine.

For some of the people I'm working with in Asia, Latin America, and Africa, it is a different matter. If they oppose the elite and the developers in their countries, they may end up without a job, in jail, or in an unmarked grave. They have to be courageous to do the work they do, and I admire them for it. And many of them are women — people like Medha Patkar in India or Wangari Maathai in Kenya, who are laying their lives on the line for social justice and the defense of nature.

Many of the destructive "development" projects in the Third World are being financed by agencies like the World Bank or the German Bank for Reconstruction (called KfW for short). The World Bank and the KfW are financing large mining, infrastructure, and energy projects that trash forests and destroy rivers, that lead to the eviction of tribal peoples from their homes, and that flood the fields of hundreds of thousands of small farmers in faraway countries like India or China. Urgewald, the organization I helped to found in 1992 in Germany, supports movements in the south that are opposing this path of development. We challenge German and international aid agencies and hold them accountable for the projects they're funding. Our work is about disempowering the "developers" and creating space for local communities in the Third World to shape their own future.

For our work in Germany, courage is not a requirement. Tenacity, on the other hand, is a must. Patience, spirit, and vision also come in handy. When you're taking on institutions like the World Bank, you've got to have the persistence to carry on, even when it seems like a losing battle. Changing or disempowering these institutions is a long-term goal, and the victories are few and far between.

I don't know about other places, but in Germany most of the people doing this work are women. I think there are two reasons for this. One, this work is not well paid and offers no major career opportunities, thus making it unattractive to the vast majority of men. Two, I think women are more capable of sticking with an issue, even if it doesn't make the headlines or get them into the evening news.

Some people tell me they consider it courageous that I embarked on this work with zero financial security and stayed at it doggedly for years without a salary. It doesn't seem that way to me, because it wasn't a hard choice to make. I felt it was my calling and followed it. Also, lots of people helped me and encouraged me along the way.

The times in my life when I felt I had to draw on courage concerned issues of a much more personal nature — things like honesty in relationships or raising a daughter on my own. My daughter's father skipped town a month before her arrival, at a time when I wasn't completely ready to take care of myself, let alone another human being. I was scared out of my mind.

During my pregnancy, I had campaigned for the Green Party, since it was the only political party in Germany with an environmental agenda. Around the time my daughter was born, I was voted into city council in the small town where I lived, a place where unwed mothers were expected to hide discreetly and spend their child-rearing years living on welfare and feeling ashamed — not something I felt like doing. So I became the speaker of the Green Party faction. There had never been a female party speaker in the history of this council, and it was time. For my fellow councilors, this took some getting used to. I'll never forget their shocked faces when I arrived at meetings with my daughter in tow and debated building ordinances and zoning while breast-feeding her.

Most male activists I know either don't have children or have a wife who takes care of the kids while they are off saving the planet. When my daughter was born, I had to develop a whole new way of doing things in order to be both an activist and a mother. Consequently, at the age of eleven, my daughter Lea is a very experienced person. As a baby, she attended press conferences and protests. Before starting school, she accompanied me to meetings with World Bank executive directors in Washington, D.C. She learned to read in Thailand when we visited destructive development projects on site. It wasn't always easy taking her along. Lea is and always has been a strong-willed person, but we both learned to make compromises to keep each other happy — no small feat in any relationship.

Kids don't come with a set of instructions on how to raise them. Lots of times, I was filled with doubt about whether I was making the right decisions. And plenty of times I made wrong ones. In spite of that, Lea has turned out to be a wonderful and caring person, and I'm proud of both of us.

Much of what I do isn't very spectacular, but it takes a day-to-day kind of courage to find the strength to create a happy life with a child and be an activist leader. It takes a lot of creativity to organize even simple things, like finding the space to read, write, and make phone calls (most of Lea's drawings depict me with a phone to my ear), and the climate isn't exactly sympathetic, even among fellow environmentalists.

I've been lucky, because at times when I most needed it to deal with life, courage came to me... from some hidden source that can be drawn on in moments of need. And thinking back, I realize that most of my lessons in courage have come from other women. People like my mom, who raised five kids largely by herself. And who is still making trouble at the age of seventy-two.

After three years of campaigning, Heffa and Urgewald were successful in driving three German companies and Germany's second largest private bank out of a dam project on the Narmada River in India. The dam would have flooded one of India's most productive agricultural areas and displaced more than forty thousand small farmers. In 1995, Germany's leading women's TV program, Mona Lisa, *declared Heffa Woman of the Year. She was also awarded a Goldman Environmental Award, given anually to six people around the world and known by some as the Nobel Prize of Environmentalism.*

Dai Qing

"I raised my hand to speak — it was the first time that I had followed my own conscience."

The daughter of a Chinese revolutionary martyr, Dai Qing was adopted by a man named Ye Jianying, a famous marshal in the People's Liberation Army. After training at an elite military academy, she was employed as a missile technician and then as a military intelligence agent. She eventually took up writing and became a columnist with a devoted following for one of China's largest dailies. One of China's premier investigative journalists, Dai Qing was incarcerated in Beijing's Qincheng prison following the 1989 Tiananmen crackdown. "When I was in prison," she says, "I prepared to be executed, and I have nothing to lose now. I will never, ever give up." No specific charges were brought against her, and she was released after ten months.

My parents and teachers will attest that I was a sensible child, always willing to follow orders.

During the Cultural Revolution of 1965 to 1976, I followed the call of Chairman Mao Zedong and engaged in rebellion. In 1979, I began my career as a writer, again in accordance with the orders and instructions of the Party. But in 1988, at the Sixth Congress of the All-China Women's Federation, I raised my hand to speak — it was the first time that I had followed my own conscience.

Earlier that year, my female colleagues at the *Enlightenment Daily,* a newspaper run by the Chinese Communist Party primarily for intellectuals, elected me to be their delegate to the Sixth Congress of the All-China Democratic Women's Federation. A mass organization of women workers, farmers, and intellectuals, the All-China Democratic Women's Federation is dedicated, in part, to the principle of women's liberation and education in patriotism and Communism.

When the news of my election spread, people couldn't help but laugh. It is well known that I loathe political meetings, and I knew literally nothing about this upcoming congress. At first, I thought my colleagues were playing a joke on me. As it turned out, the women from the newspaper weren't so much voting me in as they were voting out the officially appointed nominee of our work unit. In so doing, they demonstrated a degree of autonomous consciousness that has long been absent in the People's Republic of China. Such an act of solidarity was actually quite inspiring to witness, especially at a time when most Chinese had long forgotten about their rights and were sick and tired of political struggles. If all delegates for this Sixth Congress had been elected the way I had, the meeting itself would have taken a very different course.

I didn't know how to approach participating in the upcoming congress. When I started work as a journalist at the *Enlightenment Daily,* I had asked to be excused from conducting interviews at large-scale meetings and congresses. Such gatherings, where everything is "internally determined" by the government, were, I felt, a waste of time. My editor agreed to this condition without reservation and, so, for a number of years, I managed to avoid these meetings altogether.

This time, however, as the elected delegate from our unit, it seemed I had no choice but to pay more attention to what is known in China as "the women's circle." Over the next few months, I caught wind of rumors and discussions making the rounds of this group. One was that Madame Chen Muhua would soon become chairwoman of the Women's Federation, a decision preordained by the government, despite the fact that at the congress an election was to be held to *vote* on a new chairwoman. In addition, most people I talked to seemed to think her only qualification for the job was the fact that she is a woman.

I cannot recall how long it had been since I'd exercised my sacred right to vote. I had abstained from voting as a citizen of the People's Republic of China, as a member of various renowned mass organizations, and as a member of the Chinese Communist Party. My vote, or anyone else's, carries absolutely no weight in these bodies: Taking part in the charade of official elections is a waste of time and energy. But what about this vote for the chair of the Women's Federation? Could it be different?

I found myself at a loss at the congress: the fancy food, deluxe hotel, and recreational activities for the delegates were splendid, but the ridiculous speeches left me cold. With my hectic reporting schedule, I felt that spending time on this nonsense was too much of a sacrifice, so I took off for Inner Mongolia for three days to conduct some interviews. I didn't return until the meeting was into its fourth day, when my absence had been noted and I was immediately ordered to show up.

Sitting on a soft chair in the sparkling clean hotel reserved for the delegates, I quickly browsed through the notes from the previous sessions. At first, I was pleasantly surprised to learn that, over the course of the first three days, many educated women representing units affiliated with the central committee of the Chinese Communist Party had voiced concerns and criticisms, some of which ended up being adopted as official resolutions of the congress. Unfortunately, as I read further, I found that their ideas weren't all that revolutionary. For example: "[We] protest the lack of representation of women at the top levels of government." And, as a woman, I found it hard to listen to the delegates saying things such as "[We are] grateful to the central committee for paying so much attention to we women" and "we are moved to tears by our meetings with so many high-level leaders." It saddened me. Out of a total of 175 regular members of the top-level central committee in the Chinese Communist Party, women numbered only ten.

On the fifth morning of the congress, several delegates went to visit with Deng Yingchao, a former chairwoman of the Women's Federation and the widow of Zhou Enlai, China's second most important leader from 1949 to 1976 after Mao Zedong. During a subsequent photo session, I became acquainted with women who were delegates from organizations like the All-China Writer's Association, the *People's Daily,* the New China News Agency *(Xinhua),* the *Economic Daily,* the Children's Film Studio, and the Central Archive Research Institute. All were well-educated women of high status, and I suddenly regretted taking my three-day leave, because I had lost an opportunity to discuss with them issues involving gender relations in China. I also discovered that, from the outset of the meeting, the delegates to the Congress had tried but not been able to engage "nominee" Chen Muhua in a face-to-face discussion, a common experience perhaps unique to China, where decades of experience have proven the explosive nature of open congresses.

On the sixth morning, the day of the election, several delegates asked Lin Liyun, the presiding chairwoman of the congress, to forward a request for a meeting with nominee Chen Muhua, which was promptly denied. Those accustomed to having everything thoroughly arranged by the Communist Party didn't give much thought to our determination or to the seriousness of our request. They had forgotten that, while China may still be a backward country populated by millions of illiterates, it was, nevertheless, 1988. Party members, "young pioneers" from the past, and their offspring had acquired a modicum of modern consciousness. I was not going to vote for Chen Muhua, however, without knowing more about her. I hoped that, before the election, she would draw on her rich experience of working at the higher levels of leadership and explain away some of the rumors that surrounded her.

Later, we learned that on that very morning, as a small group of us were talking about how to make the congress more meaningful, Madame Chen Muhua was out playing golf. While we were discussing female employment and greater protection for women and children from all types of abuses — aware that child labor and teenage prostitution were staging a return and grade school classrooms were on the verge of collapse — the woman who was most likely to be our new leader had headed out in a hundred-thousand-dollar Mercedes limousine for a game whose daily cost is equal to a professor's salary for two months. And all the while claiming to be a leader of the poor working class.

The formal election began that afternoon. Following a routine explanation of the procedures by Lin Liyun, the representatives were scheduled to cast their votes. At that very moment, I raised my hand.

For someone to interrupt the assembly in such a way was totally unexpected, and Lin Liyun honestly did not know how to respond. She simply ignored me at first but was finally forced to recognize me when a member of the audience blurted out, "Someone is raising her hand." She told me to stand up. "What do you wish to say?"

"As a delegate, could I please ask a question before the ballots are cast?" I asked.

She indicated that I could.

"May I have a microphone?"

Because the organizers of the meeting never expected anyone to raise a question, the hall wasn't set up for people to ask questions from their seats. "Please come to the stage," said Chairwoman Lin Liyun.

I walked onto the stage. As I was offered a seat, a smattering of polite applause broke out. But it was only a smattering.

"Please sit down and state your question," said Lin Liyun.

"I prefer to stand," I said, holding onto the microphone.

"What question would you like to ask?"

I briefly reviewed the way in which the congress had been arranged and objected to the fact that delegates hadn't been given a chance to exchange ideas with the nominees.

Lin Liyun politely interrupted me, "Sorry, due to time constraints, it is impossible to get to know each delegate. What's your name?"

I told her my name and explained that I was a journalist.

Once again, there was applause from the audience and this time, though still thin, it came from all across the meeting hall. I felt a sense of warmth upon realizing that some of my readers were there.

I continued, "We have only simple descriptions of the nominees, and the delegates don't know for whom they should vote (there were three hundred various positions in the Federation out of three hundred and fifteen nominees.) I've conducted a small investigation and have discovered that some people plan to eliminate the first fifteen names on the ballot and others the last fifteen names. Some suggest that we simply cross out all those nominees with the surnames 'Wang' or 'Zhang' — roughly fifteen. I myself refuse to do this. I do not wish to abuse the expectations of my colleagues at the *Enlightenment Daily* and, thus, before the election, I would like to pose two questions to the nominee, Madame Chen Muhua."

The meeting hall went dead silent. Lin Liyun and Chen Muhua, who by this time had entered the room and was already seated at the center of the stage, discussed this matter briefly. Then Lin Liyun asked, "Is your question related to the election?"

"It is not related to the method of election, but it is related to content. In the absence of a reply from Chen Muhua to my two questions, I cannot decide whether to cast my ballot for her."

As members of the executive committee discussed the matter, someone in the audience shouted "Step down!" Then across the room came, "Don't answer her!" And another, "We have no questions to ask!" At the same time, the journalists who were standing behind me busily taking pictures whispered "Great!" and "Well done!"

A considerable commotion arose near the front of the stage. Lin Liyun got closer to the microphone and raised her voice, "Comrades, comrades, please be quiet." I can't remember exactly what she said next, but it was something like, "We didn't plan to have a dialogue during this congress. If everyone comes up to the stage to ask questions, it will be impossible for the meeting to go on." She hesitated only long enough for heads to nod, then continued, "Comrades, what do you think of this idea? The question from this delegate should not be answered here, but after the meeting. In this way, the congress can proceed smoothly!" Even before she finished her last word, earnest applause broke out among the audience.

After it died down, I turned to Lin Liyun. "If I am not mistaken, a congress that proceeds smoothly includes compliance with the democratic process for federation delegates." There was some applause, but nothing compared to the support shown the presiding chairwoman.

Lin Liyun once again explained that no questions would be allowed at the meeting, which received yet more warm applause. After this second round, I put down the microphone, walked across the stage, and returned to my seat. Journalists covering the congress immediately rushed toward me and inquired, "Delegate Dai Qing, what questions did you intend to ask?"

As the meeting continued on behind me, I replied to the journalists, "It has been quite some time since the nominee Chen Muhua has held a high-level position. I would like to ask her about the foreign trade deficit that China incurred when she was minister of MOFERT (Ministry of Foreign Economic Relations and Trade) and about the policy of abiding by a fixed interest rate, which caused prices to increase dramatically, creating potential social chaos. Due to the closed nature of policy making in our country, I am not sure how much she should be held personally accountable. I would like to ask Madame Chen how, once she is elected chairwoman, she would guarantee that similar mistakes wouldn't occur in her new position. Moreover, perhaps due to my limited reading, I have never read anything or heard any speeches by Madame Chen in which, as the nominee for chairwoman of the Women's Federation, she has laid out her views on matters involving women.

"If she replies to these questions, then I would like to ask another: Rumors indicate that a few years ago, during a refueling stop for her special aircraft, she refused to give a ride to a Chinese athlete who had taken ill suddenly and who later died due to delays in treatment. As chairwoman of the Women's Federation, apart from being efficient, clean, and upright, she should also be kind and benevolent, willing to help the weak and the poor. Perhaps that was merely a concocted story? Please clarify this to the public."

It is a great pity that none of the newspapers or journals, including the one where I used to work, reported these questions.

The voting began. While everyone was taking turns putting their ballots into the box, the experienced cadres of the Women's Federation organized delegates to sing revolutionary songs. The famous singer, Ma Yutao, stood up at her seat and sang, her voice still as brilliant as it had been in her youth. Inside the congress hall, delegates representing five hundred million Chinese women cheered and laughed. I felt a bit sentimental — had it been twenty or thirty years earlier, I would have been excited and enthusiastic. But it was no longer 1956 or 1966. China had experienced the Anti-Rightist movement that purged intellectuals from the Chinese Community Party, the three-year famine of 1960 to 1963 during which twenty million people died, the ten-year nightmare of the Cultural Revolution, and the ten-year economic reform. If we continued to be satisfied with simple shows of affection and confidence without criticism, then we left nothing to our children. They, like us, would forever follow others' principles and orders and remain in the long line of common people who, while purchasing winter cabbage, feel profound wrath and resentment toward all the swindling and corruption at high levels.

I felt like crying, not because I almost got kicked off the stage, but for all the Chinese women I've written about: political prisoners, victims of sexual abuse, women who know nothing about their rights, girls violated when they're young. The delegates could sing and celebrate and protect the authority of the Party all they wanted, but, what about the crimes against women?

The next day, it was announced that Chen Muhua was, as expected, elected chairwoman of the All-China Women's Federation. Only forty delegates failed to vote for her out of a total of three hundred. Two days later, the federation's new constitution and set of principles was passed. I was the only delegate to abstain from voting.

Dai Qing went on to crusade against the Three Gorges Dam, the largest hydroelectric project in the world, which China is building on the Yangtze River. Arguing that it will cause serious environmental damage and displace 1.5 million people, she compiled a series of essays by leading Chinese scientists and journalists denouncing China's plans. That book, Yangtze!

Yangtze! Debate Over the Three Gorges Project, *was banned in China following the Tiananmen crackdown. Offered political asylum by Germany and the United States following her release from prison, she chose instead to study abroad and became a Neiman Fellow at Harvard, a research fellow of the Freedom Forum at Columbia University, and a Humanities Research Fellow at the Australian National University. She is one of the voices of dissent in Ellen Perry's compelling documentary,* Great Wall Across the Yangtze.

In 1992, Dai Qing was awarded the Freedom Gold Pen Award and, in 1993, she received the Goldman Award from the Goldman Environmental Foundation in San Francisco as well as the Conde Nast Environmental Award.

Fadia Rafeedie

"When I finished, people rose to their feet, onstage and in the audience. The chancellor came up and told me I was courageous. But plenty of people were upset. Some thought, 'Oh my gosh, she embarrassed the university.' The opinions in the newspapers that week reflected the whole range, some defending me, some saying I was the most terrible person, that the university should be ashamed for awarding me the medal."

In the spring of 2000, Fadia Rafeedie prepared for the commencement convocation at the University of California, Berkeley, with unusual attention. She had just won the University Medal, given to the top graduating senior. A lover of books, she was a straight-A student who earned A-pluses in half her classes. A professor called her one of his finest students in twenty years, saying that, "she chose controversial topics and argued them persuasively against the grain of accepted 'expert' wisdom and the collective sentiment of the class." Another professor called her final essay a "tour de force." Some of her work had been published in a scholarly journal.

She had been accepted to Yale Law School. Now, as the winner of the prestigious University Medal, she would give a speech at the commencement convocation. And she would be sharing the stage with U.S. Secretary of State Madeleine Albright, whose foreign policies she bitterly opposed.

In the end, five of us were finalists for the University Medal. To win would be a great honor. I had no idea that to win would also put me in the thick of a political maelstrom.

The Committee on Prizes, which is composed of eight professors, conducted the interviews that would determine the winner. The last question they asked me was, "If given the opportunity to address your graduating class, what would you talk about?" I said that I would give my speech a global perspective, which, although not entirely sobering, would prick the conscience of my classmates. I would talk about the fact that while we were living in an age of exploding dot-coms, stock options, and outrageously high salaries straight out of college, at the same there was a great deal of human suffering in other parts of the world, exacerbated by the wealth of the United States and the power that its government often exercises, especially as this era's lone superpower. I would say, "Congratulations and do not sink into apathy."

In the spring of the new millennium, I knew that I couldn't give a speech without talking about the obliteration of the modern state of Iraq and the death of hundreds of thousands of Iraqi people from preventable illnesses, starvation, and bombing since the imposition of United States–backed economic sanctions after the Persian Gulf War. Indeed, Iraq illustrates a larger point about the arrogance of power. It's a terrible human tragedy. Was it appropriate to talk about this tragedy at the commencement convocation? I asked myself this and came to the conclusion that yes, a convocation is an event that challenges graduating seniors with issues that they'll likely face as this country's future leaders. It was appropriate.

The day before the Committee on Prizes conducted their interviews, the senior-class council chose the keynote speaker for the convocation. Madeleine Albright. A woman who was asked by Lesley Stahl of *60 Minutes* — who had just returned from Iraq — whether the price of continuing the sanctions was worth it. That price was half a million people dead, mostly children. To which, Madeleine Albright replied, "the price is worth it."

I don't know if the Committee on Prizes knew that Albright had been chosen as the keynote when they awarded the University Medal to me. I was full of emotion. It was the greatest honor. At the same time, now it would be the greatest challenge, because I would share the stage with a woman who I felt should be taken before a war crimes tribunal. What would I say in my speech? Should I turn to her and say in front of everyone, "You are personally responsible for genocide. How can you say that half a million lives is worth the cost of sanctions? Do you have a conscience? You, Madeleine Albright, have blood on your hands." Or should I keep my level of discourse lofty? Or should I insinuate rather than make direct confrontation and hope the audience would catch my drift? On the one hand, it was important not to put all the blame squarely on her shoulders. I'm not naive. I know she's part of a larger power structure. And yet there are moments when you need to strike out against symbols of power. I felt a great responsibility to use well my precious time on stage in front of six thousand people.

I learned that Albright's speechwriters contacted the university, asking to see my résumé, my essay, all the materials submitted to the Committee on Prizes, because she apparently was very interested that a Palestinian woman was going to be on stage with her and wanted to integrate me into her speech. Personally, I think she wanted to make me part of her legacy: here is an Arab woman we can understand, an intellectual daughter of immigrants, look at what we created, this is a legacy of Madeleine Albright, of the United States, the land of opportunity. I was offered a chance to meet with her beforehand, and I refused. This was the most important award I would probably ever receive in my life and to learn that I would share the moment with Madeleine Albright was chilling. It was like asking a Holocaust survivor to share the stage with a Nazi or a black woman to share the stage with a KKK member. That was the dynamic — and I don't flinch using those analogies. So either I boycotted the event or I stood up for what I believed destabilized the event for her.

I suspect she was surprised when she saw the materials I'd presented to the committee, because, in my résumé and in my essay, I talked about my beliefs. I'm against the United States sanctions in Iraq. I'm against the farce of the awful Israeli-Arab peace process, of which she was an architect. I'm pro-Palestinian and anti-Zionist.

The drama began to unfold. I was interviewed by a woman who was working on an ad campaign for Berkeley alumni. She wanted to print a photograph of Madeleine Albright and me. I told her that I wouldn't have a photo taken with Albright, because she's not someone I respect. I did not want to give Albright the opportunity to co-opt me as a symbol of an Arab who at all legitimized her. Besides, I had a different vision of what Berkeley stands for, and it was the antithesis of Madeleine Albright.

The *Oakland Tribune* ran a feature story about me, how I'm the daughter of refugees — which I'm not — and how I was going to be on stage with Madeleine Albright, "a kind of delicious irony that makes officialdom shudder." They quoted a law professor as saying that the irony was "a perfect expression of what Berkeley is all about. You couldn't plan a situation like this or get someone from central casting to do it... It is really fitting that we would have two points of view so absolutely opposed on an issue that is halfway around the world." He reduced me to the rabble-rousing, radical anti-American and her to the symbol of power, the good and kind authority figure.

Throughout the period before commencement, I dealt with disturbing issues of representation. It makes a significant difference to say, "Fadia is the daughter of Palestinian immigrants to this country" instead of the truth, which is that my parents immigrated to this country from Palestine. Perhaps the distinction is too subtle, but never for Palestinians, who know the implication of being treated as though we're a sect or tribe within a larger colonial state, Israel. To the contrary, Palestine was a country before 1948, and it remains a country in the hearts and minds of its people.

The university medalist is something of a big deal in the local papers, and I was taken aback by the way reporters dealt with me. "She's an Arab and she's a woman, but look how far she's come."

"Listen," I said to the *Oakland Tribune* reporter, "it's not accurate to posture me as an Arab woman who has achieved so much despite the fact that Arab women are so oppressed. That just reinforces the stereotype that the West uses to make the Eastern Arab Other exotic. Gender inequality is a crosscultural problem, though it might take a different form within an Arab context. But I didn't grow up with that kind of gender struggle in my family."

I was born in Ohio. My dad came over right after the 1967 war started. He studied political science and got his degree from Youngstown State University. And then he went back home and married my mom. They returned and lived in Youngstown until I was seven. Then, we moved to southern California, and that's where I grew up, in San Bernardino County. "Growing up, I didn't have double standards in the family," I continued with the *Oakland Tribune* reporter. "My parents supported me. The male influences in my life were highly supportive. It's inaccurate to assign a definition or category for all Arab women, as if they don't have agency." And yet that's the way they wrote about me.

To this day, a typical exchange starts, "Oh Fadia, where are you from?"

"Palestine." The person backs away, as though I've just made a controversial political statement.

"Oh, is that Jordan?" This happened to me even at Yale from a law student who majored in Middle Eastern studies. It's an assault on my identity.

"Palestine," I repeat.

"Oh, Israel…"

"No, Palestine."

"Oh, you're Muslim." Or "Why aren't you wearing a veil?" Or "What do you think about veiled women?"

First, I come from a Christian Arab background. Second, for women in the Arab world, a veil is often a sign of resistance to colonialism and to the Western standard of female beauty. And it's a religious choice that I respect. Frequently, people ask, "How did you break through and join our side as a Westerner?" It's such an attack on my agency and my integrity.

A week before commencement, about two hundred students, community members, and Berkeley residents representing some two dozen human rights organizations created a Madeleine Albright Unwelcoming Committee and put up a website. I didn't involve myself with it, because I was too distracted trying to write my speech and deal with interviews. I knew that other campuses had resisted her; the University of California, San Diego, was going to bring Albright in, and the students went crazy: "Don't you dare." They had fought it, because this woman stands for horrible crimes.

A coalition of Berkeley students who were concerned about Iraq, Colombia, the former Yugoslavia, and domestic issues within the United States came together to try to create a strategy for commencement day. From what I understand, they couldn't settle on one, so everybody came prepared to relay their message in the most effective way possible. To handle the dissent, the university set up a protest pit right outside the Greek Theater, a large outdoor theater near campus, hoping to contain the movement. It didn't work. The protestors ended up getting tickets to the event and sitting inside the amphitheater.

Traditionally, the university medalist sits next to the keynote speaker and delivers her speech right before the keynote. As we were downstairs getting ready to go onstage, I learned that the seating order had been changed. They'd put me on the opposite side of the stage from Albright. My parents, who were supposed to be sitting right in front of me in the audience, were now far away. I wasn't even sitting next to the other four finalists.

Once on stage, the chancellor announced that they had changed the speaking order. Madeleine Albright would be speaking first. I looked across at my family: *Can you believe this is happening?* Our senior class representative got up and began the introduction of Albright, referring to her as the greatest woman of our times, which was insulting not only to me but to many students.

When Albright stood up to take the podium, it was like firecrackers going off. From every corner of the Greek Theater, a different group chanted at her, "End the sanctions now! End the sanctions now!" or unfurled banners or threw flyers at her or yelled at her, calling her a war criminal, an imperialist. She didn't have the decency to address their concerns. One by one, many of the protestors were ejected, so that by the end of her speech, the audience was quieter. But still, the security people were dragging away people.

Although she was flustered, Albright didn't take even a moment to address what was going on. I imagine someone like Clinton would at least pause long enough to spew rhetoric about how we need to contain this evil man, Saddam Hussein, or throw out some other red herring. She didn't bother. Maybe because, a few years earlier, she had gone to Ohio State University for a CNN Town Hall Meeting and she was fielding questions when a man stood up and said, "Your policy in Iraq is abominable, how can you support this, how can you say that you're against a dictatorship when you've propped up equally illegal dictatorships in other parts of the world?" And, apparently, she was completely shocked. She didn't know how to answer, she was stuttering and bumbling, and they had to cut off his microphone. It was a humiliation for her. So I'm sure she was hoping she'd come to Berkeley and not have a dialogical exchange but simply a one-sided presentation — let me tell you what my legacy is — and then fly away back to D.C.

On she went with her speech, at one point saying, "We have also made progress in curbing violence against women. But despite these gains, around the world, terrible abuses persist. They include domestic violence, mutilation, dowry murders, honor crimes, and forced prostitution. Some say all this is cultural and there's nothing any of us can do about it. I say it's criminal, and we each have a responsibility to stop it."

How very ironic. It's criminal, and yet the death of half a million Iraqis was "worth it"? She assigned a value on human life in Iraq. Not only did she assign a value, she then dismissed that value. Listening to her, I squirmed in my seat. The hypocrisy was blatant.

At the end of her speech, she got a standing ovation. Everyone on stage rose to applaud her. I stayed in my chair and a photograph taken at that moment shows Secret Service agents hovering behind me. Did they think I was going to attack her? She turned and, one by one, shook hands with everyone on stage. Still I sat. When she got to me, our eyes locked. Maybe it was the first time that she realized that I was still sitting. She turned and continued on. Some people were upset that I didn't stand, that I refused to shake her hand. Since when should decorum be elevated over matters of life and death? I would never, for the sake of preserving image, even if I thought I was preserving the image of the university, lower myself to her level. Later, I learned that several professors felt the same way.

Albright didn't stay for the rest of the ceremony. She left, and the reporters left with her. I had been footnoted at the end of the ceremony, away from the attention of the press and their 6:00 deadlines. When the chancellor finally introduced me, I was flustered. My speech at that point was obsolete. The first two-thirds was to have been about benign things — what I learned from my classmates, thanking my family, my mother, my grandmother, all the niceties. And then, at the end, I was going to make a political statement. But after Albright leaving, after fifty-nine students being dragged out for exposing her policies, after the protest movement being squashed, I knew with clarity that my message needed to be direct.

As I began, people grew quiet, because they understood I was speaking not from a scripted speech but in an impromptu way, and they must have been curious about what I had to say. I knew that many of my classmates were irritated by the protesters, but the protestors' message was one that I supported and, whereas their voices had been stifled, I was in an "authorized" position to deliver it. The moment was very emotional. I spoke from my heart.

> I had a speech, and it's right here. It took me so long to draft it and I kept redrafting it, and this morning I changed it again, but I'm just going to put it to the side and I'm going to talk from my heart because what I witnessed here today, I have mixed feelings about... I was looking at my grandmothers who are in the audience — my grandmother who came from Palestine and her sister — who weren't really happy with all the protesters... that it wasn't respectful.... But I think what the protesters did was not embarrass our university. I think they dignified it.
>
> ... What I was going to tell Albright while she was sitting on the stage with me, I was going to remind her that, four years ago from this Friday when we were freshmen, I heard her on *60 Minutes* talking

to a reporter who had just returned from Iraq. The reporter was describing that a million children were dead due to the sanctions that this country was imposing on the people of Iraq.... "That's more children than have died in Hiroshima and Nagasaki. Do you think the price is worth it?" Albright looked into the camera and said, "The price is worth it."

Since that time, three times that number of people have died in Iraq. And I was going to ask her, "Do you really think the price is worth it?" We are about five thousand here today; next month, by the time we graduate, that's as many people who are going to die in Iraq because of the sanctions. This is what House Minority Whip David Boniors calls "infanticide masquerading as policy."

Now, I don't want to make the mood somber here because this is our commencement, but commencement means beginning, and I think it's important for us to begin where civilization itself began, and where it's now being destroyed. Let me talk to you a little bit more about the sanctions, because I think it's very important.... I see some people rolling their eyes right now, and other people nodding. These are controversial issues, but I need to speak about Iraq, because I think what's happening there is a genocide. It's another holocaust... 2.5 million people have died, and yet these sanctions continue.

For the last ten years, you wouldn't imagine the kinds of things that aren't being let into Iraq: heart machines, lung machines, needles.... In the hospitals, they clean the floors with gasoline, because detergent isn't even allowed in because of the sanctions.

These are all United States policies.

And Secretary Albright — I have no conflict with her, as an individual. I don't happen to respect her, but she belongs to a larger power structure.... She was introduced as the 'greatest woman of our times.' Now see, to me that's an insult. This woman is doing horrible things. She's allowing innocent people to suffer and to die.

Iraq used to be the country in the Arab World that had the best medical services and social services for its people, and now look at it. It's being obliterated. And a lot of times, you might hear it's because of Saddam Hussein.... He's a brutal dictator — I agree.... But again, I'm a history major, and history means origins. It means beginnings. We need to see who's responsible for how strong Saddam Hussein has gotten. When he was gassing the Kurds, he was gassing them using chemical weapons that were manufactured in Rochester, New York. And when he was fighting a long and protracted war with Iran, where a million people died, it was the CIA that was funding him. It was U.S. policy that built this dictator. When they didn't need him, they started imposing sanctions on his people. Sanctions — or any kind of policy — should be directed at people's governments, not at the people.

The cancer rate in Iraq has risen by over 70 percent since the Gulf War... every other day our country is still bombing Iraq... it releases a gas that the people breathe. It's making them ill, and they're dying and they don't have medicine.

... I'm speaking to a crowd that gave a standing ovation to the woman who typifies everything against which I stand, and I'm still telling you this because I think it's important to understand. And I think that, if I achieve nothing else, if this makes you think a little bit about Iraq, think a little bit about U.S. foreign policy, I've succeeded.

... I want to end my speech with a slogan that hangs over my bed in Arabic. It says, *"La tastaw-hishu tareeq el-haq, min qillit*

> *es-sa'ireen fihi,"* and that translates into, "Fear not the path of truth for the lack of people walking on it." I think our future is going to be the future of truth, and we're going to walk on that path, and we're going to fill it with many travelers.

When I finished, people rose to their feet, onstage and in the audience. The chancellor came up and told me I was courageous. But plenty of people were upset. Some thought, "Oh, my gosh, she embarrassed the university." The opinions in the newspapers that week reflected the whole range, some defending me, some saying I was the most terrible person, that the university should be ashamed for awarding me the medal. *The Oakland Tribune* said I gave a "rousing, militant speech." The alumni magazine article elicited the response that, if this is what comes out of Berkeley's history department, maybe we don't need the history department after all. I was chided by students who said I had been terribly inappropriate, that commencement wasn't the right forum for what I did. All I could say was, "When is there ever a right atmosphere to speak out against injustices? When is there ever a time when you don't disdain being in the presence of someone who represents everything against which you stand? There is never a *time* for that."

In the week after my commencement speech, more than a hundred people died in Iraq. In the face of these numbers, the American public has shown barbaric indifference, and I use that word *barbaric* in front of *indifference* as a way to give the term an ironic bent that I think is proper. I feel there is nothing worse than apathy.

Over the following summer, I received hundreds of letters from all over the world, from academicians at Harvard, Yale, MIT, and Stanford; from those writing in broken English from Germany, France, Bangladesh, El Salvador, Iceland, Iraq, and Palestine; from radio stations in South Africa and Canada. I got letters from bishops and sheiks and progressive Jews. I couldn't believe it. E-mails came in like wildfire. A French newspaper wrote a story about me. The ripple effect was amazing, and I was deeply moved to see the worldwide outrage.

Letters came from people who said, "I never thought about this. I'm glad you opened my eyes." Others wrote, "I've been working on the Iraq issue, too." Some people sent me documentaries that they'd done about Iraq or about people who had flown there to try to break the embargoes. "We're with you in solidarity," they wrote. One of my favorite journalists, Robert Fisk, wrote favorably about my speech in the *Independent* in London. *Ms.* magazine did a profile of me.

The opposition letters I received were more concerned with my style than the content. If I gave the speech again under less flustered conditions, I might not have lashed out at Madeleine Albright, saying I don't respect her. I blurted that out, and even though it's true, it gave some people an excuse not to hear my message. Did my style keep people from hearing what I had to say? What a shame. I wanted to get people thinking, asking, "What is our policy in Iraq? What's happening there? What's this oil-for-food program? Why do we still have the sanctions?" Instead they were offended that I didn't stand during the ovation. "How dare you say it's an insult that she was called the greatest woman of her time! Who are you to say that?" They were more concerned with the decorum, with what's proper, what's tactful.

I took my opposition letters seriously and spent a lot of time responding, suggesting websites to visit. The challenge was to get people to think and re-evaluate assumptions, to research and use their brains. Generally, I didn't get responses.

Later in the summer, I was in Palestine at a co-op of women workers when they asked me why I hadn't used my commencement speech to talk about Palestine. I think they were insulted. It wasn't the first time I'd been asked this. In my original speech, I was going to talk briefly about my uncle,

Wisam, an intellectual who had been a political prisoner in Israeli jails for six years when he heard I'd been accepted at Berkeley; the last time I saw him was between rifles as his house was being stormed and he was led away. Because of the way events changed on commencement day, I was flustered by the time I got up to speak. I tried to focus on one issue and make it very clear. And I tried to give voice to the students who were being marginalized, considered typical Berkeley rabble-rousers rather than instructional and inspiring people with a cause and a message. In the course of my speech, I said I am Palestinian and would like to talk about the liberation of my homeland, but even though the situation is terrible right now in Palestine, even though the United States is directly responsible for what's happening, even though Madeleine Albright does not help but exacerbates the situation and has no conscience, when I think that five thousand children are dying every month in Iraq, I feel I must talk about it. The situation is dire.

When I had finished my speech, I wondered if, in fifty years, I would look back and regret not talking about Palestine. To leftist intellectuals, defending the Somalians, Chechneyians, and Latin Americans is in vogue. Defending human rights and civil rights all around the world is in vogue, but Palestine is a hush-hush topic. The most progressive of all progressives will be conservative when it comes to the question of Palestinian independence and the right of Palestinian refugees to return to their homes. They don't want to step on the toes of a very powerful Zionist presence in the United States. They don't want to sound anti-Semitic, not understanding that Arabs are also Semites.

Will I regret losing this precious moment to shine a light on Palestine? No, I think not. By shining a light on Iraq, I also drew attention to what's happening in Palestine, because policies toward both countries are part of an overall design to recolonize the Arab World. In particular, I believe we're going to look back at what's happening in Iraq and we're going to be ashamed of ourselves as a civilization — much in the same way that we look at other human tragedies like dropping the atomic bomb or Vietnam or Rwanda. Regardless of what we feel about Saddam Hussein, no policy directed at a government should decimate a population. Innocent Iraqi civilians should not have to pay with their lives for the United States' sordid relationship with Hussein. We cannot demonize an entire people because of one dictator.

When I was giving my commencement speech, I wasn't considering all the ramifications, what might happen to me at Yale the following year when I went to law school, what might happen if one day I decide to work for the U.S. government. None of that entered my consciousness. I felt compelled to talk about the moral depravity of our foreign policy and, in particular, as it affects Iraq.

If I were to assign the label "courageous" to anything I did, it might be that I went out on a limb to be hated by sectors of my school community. Letters to the school newspaper said that I had no tact, that I had politicized the event. One letter to the alumni magazine said my speech was full of hate and was an empty vessel of rhetoric. I suffered from that. I suffered from people who had taken a position about the unbridled power of the United States, supporting it blindly. I was speaking to a patriotic audience who was insulted that Madeleine Albright was being heckled and that she was faced by a storm of protestors. Without listening to her message, they jumped to defend her, thinking it was an assault on the integrity of the United States. To the contrary, it was a protest with people trying to give an alternative vision of what democracy and freedom and human rights mean outside the imperial role that the United States plays.

While I was giving my speech, some people stood up and walked out. Others cried. Others went on to research and question. Those are the people I wanted to reach. Had I heard from only one person that I had opened his or her eyes, it would have been enough. One letter said it all for me, "Sometimes the smallest victories vindicate the larger injustices."

Fadia is currently studying law at Yale. She dreams of the day her uncle Wisam, with whom she corresponded throughout his imprisonment, is able to visit from the West Bank, a day when she can walk the Yale campus with him and bask together in libraries and bookstores. She dreams of having a daughter, whom she will name Amal, meaning "hope." She dreams of what the Turkish poet Nazim Hikmet once wrote, "The best of days are those which we have not yet lived."

Inspired to
PERSIST

Geraldine Ferraro

"I thought I could get something done if I went to Congress, have a greater impact on people's lives. So I ran, not knowing what a tough job it would be to run for office. Never anticipating that it would be so costly — emotionally, mentally, physically, and financially.... It was a horrendous personal campaign. Every time I'd read something awful directed at my husband or me, I'd be devastated. My kids would start crying. It was hard. It was very hard."

Geraldine Ferraro was the first woman from a major political party to be nominated for vice president of the United States. The year was 1984. Her running mate was Walter Mondale. She came to that prestigious honor following three terms in the U.S. House of Representatives from Queens, New York. She fought hard for women, spearheading efforts to pass the Equal Rights Amendment and sponsoring the Women's Economic Equity Act, which ended pension discrimination against women, provided job options for displaced homemakers, and enabled homemakers to open IRAs.

When I think about moments in my life that required courage, one of the first that comes to mind is the early death of my father, an event that colored the rest of my life and motivated me to excel.

My father, Dominick Ferraro, was an Italian immigrant from an affluent family of educated landowners and professionals. He owned a restaurant and store in Newburgh, New York. When I was eight, he died of a heart attack. My mother, who had grown up in the immigrant ghettoes of New York's Lower East Side and Italian Harlem, didn't even know that he had a heart condition. He never told her about his high blood pressure, because he didn't want to worry her. Meanwhile, he dropped dead at forty-four. Suddenly, all the safe things were gone.

Like other women who are suddenly left with financial responsibilities they know nothing about, my mother went through a very difficult time. She didn't know how to handle my father's business and sold it right away. In a very short period, we found ourselves in a terrible hole. We moved to the South Bronx. To amuse myself, I'd play stoopball off the steps with a Spalding ball, or hopscotch, or handball off the wall of a commercial garage. My brother played stickball in the street. This was a different life from the one I had experienced when my father was alive, and I was very aware that we no longer had money.

Before my father's death, my mother had had dreams for her children that seemed within reach. Now she and her dreams were suddenly vulnerable. Would she be able to make it without my father? What was I supposed to do to help her? How could I make good on her dreams for me?

To put us through school, Mother returned to crochet beading, a skill she'd learned at fourteen when she was sent to work in the garment district to help support her family. Once, while watching her work like a machine at her frame, I asked her to teach me. I sat down at the frame and started going in and out with the needle. It took me ten minutes to put on ten beads. She reached over, took the needle out of my hand, and said, "Gerry, get an education, or you'll starve to death."

Thus was my mother's devotion to education instilled in me. She didn't want me to have to make a living the way she did, bent over a crochet frame all hours of the day and night. If I wanted better, if I didn't want to be stuck in South Bronx, if I wanted more for my own children, then I would have to get an education. Education was everything. That's partly why my brother and I were shortly sent away to boarding school, made possible by scholarships.

My mother would take me on the bus and then the subway down to One-hundred and Twenty-fifth Street in Harlem. It was very safe at that time. She'd put me on a train and stay on the platform, waving while the train pulled out, and I'd wave back. Both of us would be crying. It was, I guess, courageous for a little girl. I was following the lead of my very courageous mother. I knew that I had to do my part — for me, for my mother — to realize the dream of a better life. It was as if mother and I had a deal, were in a partnership to better my life.

The first school that I was sent to was run by nuns and was very strict. At night, I'd hear the trains going up the Hudson River and cry myself to sleep. Being a brave little girl, I hid my loneliness. Subsequently, I transferred to a school closer to home. But I didn't go home every weekend. It was too expensive.

As high school graduation loomed, my mother struggled with how to put me through college. One day when she was talking with her family about it, my Uncle Tom said, "Oh, don't bother, Antonetta, she's pretty, she'll get married."

My wise mother must have bristled at that and said, "You're right, she is pretty, and she probably will get married. But if you educate a boy, you educate a boy alone. If you educate a girl, you educate a family. My Gerry's going to college. I just have to figure out how."

When I graduated from high school, I was at the top of my class. I got all kinds of scholarships and walked away with half the honors at graduation — not because I was the most brilliant person, but because I worked the hardest. College was a little easier. I kept a B average, which is what I needed to maintain the full tuition scholarship, but I worked part-time to help support myself and had a pretty good social life. And then I went to law school.

All the achievements of my youth came out of the drive sparked by my father's death. I have always thought that if he hadn't died, I probably would have been a very different person, perhaps with a softer life. Instead, I restlessly got involved and took on issues, even when I was a stay-at-home mom with three children. I don't sit still easily.

I married John Zaccaro two days after taking my New York State Bar exam. A year later, Donna was born, then John in 1964, and Laura in 1966. For thirteen years, I stayed home with our children and funneled my energy into activism as a parent and a community member. Periodically, I'd go into family court, pro bono, and help women with their complaints. Yet it wasn't enough. As much as I loved talking to our kids, I didn't want to start talking to myself when they weren't around. Or I'd be in deep trouble.

So in part for my sanity, in part because John and I had agreed that I'd return to work when all our kids were in school, and in part because I wanted to use my law degree, I began to think about returning to work. My cousin, Nick Ferraro, who was like a brother to me, had been elected district attorney of Queens. I had helped to get him elected, and I started to think about working for him as a prosecutor. He had a fascinating office, and I liked the criminal justice system. It would be a place where I could get a tremendous amount of experience really fast, which mattered to me since I was starting late. Had I started at twenty-four, I could have afforded to take ten, fifteen years to get experience and progress in my career. At thirty-eight, it was quite different.

When my youngest daughter entered the second grade, I became one of Nick's assistant prosecutors — but only after an intense committee scrutiny headed by Mario Cuomo. No one wanted it to look like nepotism, I most of all. I didn't want people thinking, "Oh, well, she doesn't know what she's doing. She's only here because her cousin is the D.A."

The other presumption I had to get over was that, because I was thirty-eight, I was supposed to know everything since I'd "been around." Which didn't follow, because I hadn't been practicing criminal law and, further, because the criminal law statues had changed since I'd gotten my "A" in criminal law. The truth was that the other prosecutors in the D.A.'s office knew much more than I did. And so the impressions were erroneous.

My first day in the office, I was very nervous and hit the ground running. During the next two months, I kept losing weight because of nerves. I was terrified I was going to make a horrible mistake — which I never did.

It was gutsy returning to work after thirteen years. I was working with twenty-four-year-old kids. I was afraid of not keeping up with them, of not being competitive, of not doing a good job. I was afraid that people would say, "Oh, my God! she's so old." Not only was I working with younger people, but my bosses were all younger than me. The bureau chief was thirty-four. The deputy bureau chiefs were twenty-eight and thirty. I was the "old lady."

To dispel the wrong assumptions about me, I worked harder than most. I made sure that what I did, I did right. I made sure that I carried not only my fair load of cases, but also more if asked. I made sure that I kept a discreet distance from my cousin. I was very careful.

As it turns out, I was fortunate to share my office with Tim Flaherty, also an assistant D.A. He was about my age and had worked for the prior D.A., so he wasn't a new political appointee; he had a tremendous amount of experience. If I needed any advice, I'd say, "Timmy, tell me what to do here." He was terrific. We became best friends, and when I ran for Congress, he quit the D.A's office and came to work for me as my chief of staff in the district.

During the time in the D.A.'s office, not only did I feel pressure to prove myself, but I also saw what I had lost being home for thirteen years. Having firsthand experience with how difficult it is for a displaced homemaker to re-enter the workplace, when I got to Congress, I wrote legislation to ease the transition. In the late seventies and early eighties, when I was pushing for this legislation, most of the women who had been out of the workforce were being dumped back in because they'd been widowed or divorced. It was a financial necessity. For me, it wasn't a necessity and so it was a bit easier.

My cousin went on to become a Supreme Court judge, and I worked under another D.A. for the majority of the time I was there. At the end, I had worked my way up to bureau chief, which is a supervising trial attorney. Normally one doesn't move that quickly in a law firm, especially as a woman at that time. So it was an opportune place for me to be. Plus, it was close to home. If my kids needed me, I could be there in a jiffy.

I started in the D.A.'s office in January of 1974 and worked there until April of 1978, when I quit to run for Congress. I had made that decision because I was frustrated dealing with problems on the surface and wanted to get down to the root causes of these problems. I thought I could get something done if I went to Congress, have a greater impact on people's lives. So I ran, not knowing what a tough job it would be to run for office. Never anticipating that it would be so costly — emotionally, mentally, physically, and financially. That took guts. I wasn't an elected official. I had never run for office. I used my own money. People said I was on an ego trip. It was a horrendous personal campaign. Every time I'd read something awful directed at me or my husband, I'd be devastated. My kids would start crying. It was hard. It was very hard.

Before my run, if people didn't agree with me, they'd usually say something like, "but she's nice." I'm not the kind of person who goes for the jugular. I don't make personal attacks. If somebody has a problem, I try to help. I had never in my entire life had people personally attack me. I became the target of such viciousness — and this was before personal attacks in political campaigns got really bad. I was absolutely stunned.

"You know, Gerry," said my husband, "your problem is that you want everybody to love you. And not everybody will even like you during a campaign." He was right. In fact, I would learn in the years to come that some people have a real hatred for others — in a way, I almost feel sorry for them, because it's all they have. Sixteen years after the 1984 campaign as Mondale's running mate, I still get anonymous letters from a guy who signs his name, "Conservative Willy." He writes the most vicious, terrible things — that poor, old, sick man. I can tell from the handwriting that he's old. I know he goes to my church. I know he's from my district. I almost feel sorry for a person like this who has to hide behind anonymity and spew his venom. I wonder what his life is like.

A few years ago, I wrote a book, *Framing a Life*, about my roots. I open the book by saying that "until I began my personal search, I never fully appreciated the tremendous courage and sacrifice of my Italian ancestors, who left behind the certainty of their homelands for a life of promise in America. Their dreams came true, not for themselves, but through me and others like me who reaped the rewards of their hard work and unflagging resolve." Had she been born a generation later, my mother would have reaped the great benefit of those rewards. Instead, she wasn't even able to go to high school, even though she was very smart. She had to work to help support her younger brothers and sisters, because her father had had a stroke. As I was writing the book, she told me how her principal had actually come to her house and spoken to her mother, saying, "Let her go to school. At least let her go at night if she has to work during the day."

"Absolutely not!" said my grandmother. "No daughter of mine goes out at night."

The principal pressed on, "Well, let her go to secretarial school then."

Now, my grandmother was an illiterate woman. She couldn't even write her own name. She'd sign with an "X."

"Please," begged the principal. "I'll pay for the secretarial school."

Up pipes my Uncle Tom, "Oh, you know secretaries, they all sit on the boss's lap."

That's all my grandmother needed to hear. As an Italian American mother, the virtue of her daughters was primary. Italian American girls were "good girls." They didn't go out at night. That meant no school for my mother. It was so sad.

When my mom was in her eighties, I had to take her to the emergency room because she was having trouble breathing; she'd been diagnosed with emphysema and was quite ill. The admissions nurse started asking me all the questions on the admitting form, to which I replied, "Why don't you get the information from her?"

"Does she understand?"

"Her body's falling apart, but her mind is perfectly clear."

So the nurse asked my mother her age, her social security number, her Medicare number. And then she queried, "Did you graduate from high school?" I found out later that they ask this because they want to be sure that older people know how to read the directions on prescription drugs.

My mother answered quickly, "No. But, I graduated from elementary school." Then she paused and looked down at her hands and said, "Big deal, huh?"

My heart ached. I went to her and put my arms around her. I was so stunned. I felt terrible for her. She'd gone through her entire life thinking that she was no big deal. "You better believe you're a big deal!" I said. "Do you know anybody else in this country who can say, 'My daughter ran for vice president of the United States'?"

With that, she smiled.

Geraldine's first book, Ferraro: My Story, *became a number-one* New York Times *best-seller. More recently, she's seen regularly on CNN and was cocommentator with Pat Buchanan on* Crossfire. *Today she's a partner at G & L Strategies, a New York–based corporate consulting firm that focuses on workplace and marketplace issues affecting women and minorities.*

Jean Griswold

"Some days have been filled with victories, others with struggle. I manage to get to work every day. In spite of my multiple sclerosis, I've been able to dream a dream and live it."

Despite a thirty-five-year battle with multiple sclerosis that left her dependent on a wheelchair, Jean Griswold founded and grew what is now a multimillion-dollar company providing health-care services for the elderly, the disabled, and children with special needs. She participates personally in training all new office directors and managers.

I live a ridiculously remarkable life.

I am physically capable of doing almost nothing. Yet I have managed to do a great deal. For thirty-five years, I've struggled with the increasingly frustrating ravages of multiple sclerosis, a progressive disease that attacks the central nervous system.

I'll never forget how surprised I was when dear old Dr. McClenahan, our family physician, came to our door, his little black medical bag in hand, and said, "Sit down." Instead of his stethoscope, out of his bag he pulled an orchid for me. It was his way of trying to soften the news that I had multiple sclerosis. He added, "Now, don't go to the library and look it up." But of course, I did.

I had just received a life sentence, or rather, a slow death sentence. I didn't say, "Why me?" I didn't want to waste precious time. I needed to get on with my life. I looked fine. I still had lots of energy and a mind that never stopped making plans for an exciting and productive life. My three sons were growing up, and it was time to stop delivering newspapers part-time and start work that would better utilize my degree in economics and business and my masters in counseling. I found an excellent job opening and gave my best friend as a reference. When called, she said, "Oh, she does very well for someone with multiple sclerosis." That was the kiss of death. Because of my condition, no one would hire me.

If I can't get a job, I said to myself, *I'll create one.* Or as *Forbes* would later report, "No one would hire her, so she hired herself."

I had always had a dream of starting my own business. Everything I read about entrepreneurs struck home for me. "Creator of new ideas and willing to give up everything to do something about it." "Never satisfied with the status quo." "Looking to fill a need before someone else does." "Late to bed and early to rise." "Workaholic." "Tireless, single-minded, and focused." I was highly organized and had an uncanny sense about people, sharpened by my life as the wife of Dr. Lincoln Griswold, the minister of our church up until a year earlier.

As I was pondering what to do, our church community suffered a tragic loss. An elderly widow in our congregation was unable to find anyone to stay with her at night. It wasn't a matter of money; she was very wealthy. Reliable, compassionate help was just hard to find. During the day while her maid was there, she managed fairly well. But after the maid went home, she became frightened and lonely. After 5:00 she got no water, so she eventually developed kidney problems. Too late, she went to the hospital, where she died.

Her death shocked me. How little it would have taken to help her. As I asked around, I realized that she wasn't alone in needing nonmedical home care. The aging population was exploding, the over-eighty-five population being one of the fastest growing groups, expected to triple in size between 1980 and 2030. Now it appears that the increase will be even greater: sevenfold between 1980 and 2050. The number of people needing help to stay safely and happily in their homes was increasing dramatically. It was a need no one seemed to be filling. If I could fill that need, I'd be helping people, something that had always been important to me.

When I discovered that people were willing to pay for in-home care, I realized it could become the business I'd dreamed of starting. So I jumped into what I later discovered was the fastest growing service industry on the horizon, the health-care field. The Overnight Sitting Service was born in my dining room.

Having been a minister's wife for twenty-five years, I had many church connections. It occurred to me that there were graduate students at the two local seminaries who cared about people, needed to earn money, and might be interested in working at night. I started recruiting.

News of my service spread by word of mouth, and requests for service began pouring in. It soon became clear that the need was for daytime as well as nighttime service. Overnight Sitting Service was no longer an adequate name. I prayed about it. And the answer came: Special Care.

I had hardly started Special Care when a knock came at the front door. It was a representative from the Pennsylvania Department of Labor in Harrisburg. "What are you doing here?" he asked.

His question shook me up, scared me, rattled my cool. "We're sending out nurses' aides to care for the elderly and disabled."

And just *who is we?"*

"My husband and I."

"There are regulations."

My spirits began to sink. On he went about my newborn business and, finally, he concluded that it was just a mom-and-pop operation. He agreed to show me how to restructure our pay setup so that we would be exempt from onerous regulations and not be in violation of the law.

Soon I needed help running Special Care. My dining room wasn't large enough to accommodate it. We spread into the living room and then enclosed a porch. The number of cars in the driveway grew to six, spilling onto the lawn and into the street in our lovely residential neighborhood.

Then came a crisis. A letter with a gold seal came from the township: "Cease and desist!" They were putting me out of business. My dream was shattered.

I argued with the township officials that people's lives were in our hands. We couldn't stop! Mrs. Stillwell could fall down the stairs trying to get to the kitchen to get her lunch if we didn't send someone. Mr. Brady would forget that he should no longer use the sharp woodworking tools in his workshop now that his Alzheimer's disease was getting worse. Mrs. Hollis couldn't get from her bed to the bathroom without help from Special Care.

They relented. I was given time to relocate.

The challenge was acute. My multiple sclerosis had gotten much worse. I could no longer drive. How would I be able to work if not in my own house? Could I find a place on or near a bus route so that aides without cars could come for the required interview? How would I find a place where I could work and live and carry on my dream?

Like any entrepreneur, I did what I had to do. Under pressure, I worked extra hard to find a solution. A half mile away, right on the bus route, was a commercially zoned building that could accommodate not only Special Care but also an apartment for me. Lincoln and I sold our home and, having put in a "stair-glide," moved into the apartment on the second floor. When the time came that I could no longer safely manage the stair-glide, the Commonwealth of Pennsylvania, through its Office of Vocational Rehabilitation, in recognition of the service I was providing, helped me install an elevator so that I could continue to get from my apartment to my office in my wheelchair.

My dream has thrived for more than eighteen years. Special Care has become the largest private company specializing in nonmedical home care in the state — and perhaps the country. We opened seventeen offices throughout Pennsylvania, from Philadelphia to Pittsburgh. Then as Special Care began to spread up and down the East Coast, we discovered how complex individual state laws could be; because of regulations in some states, we've had to use the name Griswold Special Care. Though we now have more than sixty offices, from Massachusetts to Florida, Special Care has been growing bigger *very carefully.* I'm determined to maintain control of quality.

What did I have to give up in order to start Special Care? Vacations were out. Hobbies were forgotten. Friends and family were shortchanged. Sleep time often gave way to brainstorming and wee-hours conferences with myself. Business was a part of every meal, every family gathering, every waking hour. If Special Care was going to succeed, I had to give it undivided attention.

Some days have been filled with victories, others with struggle. I manage to get to work every day. In spite of my multiple sclerosis, I've been able to dream a dream and live it. Special Care has become my arms and legs for reaching out with loving care to so many in need. And knowing that more than fifty thousand clients have been helped and that thousands of professional caregivers have found good work through Special Care has made all the effort and sacrifice worth it. As my husband says, "You manage to do the impossible. It just takes longer."

My "impossible dream" has survived and made a meaningful difference for so many — including me.

Jean describes her work as the convergence of two lifelong dreams: to be a businesswoman and to help others. What is truly courageous for her is to do something she doesn't have to do — accept awards and give speeches around the country, inspiring others to put their limitations in their place and to reach for their dreams.

Jean has received many awards, including Pennsylvania's Honor Roll of Women, Fifty Best Women in Business, Rutgers University's Hall of Distinguished Alumni, the City of Philadelphia's "Spirit of Philadelphia" Award, and others. Working Woman *bestowed the Entrepreneurial Excellence Award on Jean in the spring of 2000 for "inspiring legions of women entrepreneurs across the country with the story of your success." She has also been featured on* The Today Show *and in* Forbes *and* Entrepreneur.

Susan Vanderveen

"I was in an oxygen tent for seventeen days and, late one night at the hospital, my father was told I wouldn't make it to the morning."

When Susan Vanderveen was diagnosed with leukemia at age three, her family founded the National Leukemia Broadcast Council to raise money for leukemia research through radio and TV fundraisers. Susan was often a guest, and as she grew up she helped to produce the broadcasts.

At the age of three, I entered a world that was hard to understand unless you were inside it.

In this world, I gave myself up to mind- and body-altering drugs, medical opinions, and domineering equipment and machinery. I did not enter this world willingly. It was a terrible place for a child. The everyday challenges and struggles would overcome many adults.

Just before my fourth birthday, my mother took me to our pediatrician for my annual physical examination. It was the week before our summer vacation. I was cranky and tired during the trip to San Diego, California. My parents kept wondering why.

While we were gone, the pediatrician called. The blood test results had come back. When we returned, he finally reached us. I had leukemia. A bone marrow test at Children's Hospital of Los Angeles confirmed it: cancer of the blood-forming tissues. The odds of survival in 1972 were not very good. My family and I began a long and torturous ordeal.

The treatment was as brutal as the disease itself. It began with an intensive barrage of powerful chemotherapy drugs meant to put me into remission. Because the drugs couldn't distinguish between my good cells and my leukemia cells, they attacked both. I got sicker trying to get better.

Then, because leukemia cells hide in the spine and brain, I was given massive radiation treatments to those areas. I did go into remission but nearly lost my battle in the process. I developed an infection of the heart lining that put me on the critical list. And I contracted pneumocystis, a form of pneumonia for which there was no effective treatment, just an experimental drug permitted only as a last resort. I was in an oxygen tent for seventeen days, and, late one night at the hospital, my father was told I wouldn't make it to the morning. When I did recover, he was overwhelmed as he thanked the doctor. "We didn't do this one," said the doctor, acknowledging the hand of the divine.

The radiation shortened my spine and killed the roots of my teeth. It damaged my female hormone production, decreased my bone density, and left me with cataracts. The treatment so racked my lungs that, during the pneumonia, when the hospital radiologist looked at my X-ray, he said to his assistant, "This can't be her X-ray. This child is undoubtedly deceased."

My memories of this time dip into things like orange sherbet. I had nearly given up on eating, because it was difficult to work up the energy, especially when I had lost my appetite. But the sickly taste of medication lingered in my mouth, making me nauseated and causing me to vomit regularly. One night, a nurse came into my room with a cup of orange sherbet from the cafeteria; she was rather desperate to get something in me that didn't come back up. Orange sherbet. Such a simple thing. It became a touchstone, one thing I could look forward to without fear or dread.

Every four hours, someone would gently wake me for an injection or a blood draw or a handful of pills or whisk me away to somewhere I didn't want to go.

I lost all my hair. I hated going out in public, because people would stare at me. I was often mistaken for a boy. Children at school made fun. I wanted barrettes in my hair and a ponytail.

The bone marrow test was a recurring procedure and necessary to determine whether I was holding my remission. I never lost my fear of it. I'd struggle to free myself from the gurney as a large needle was pushed into my spine to draw a sample of marrow. My mother and father would help the nurses hold me down, talking to me, reassuring me it would be over soon, trying to comfort me. But nothing could comfort me. The pain was too great.

Ten years later, I was officially declared cured. Yet the aftereffects of the treatment became a new challenge. I lived between two worlds: the normal world most of us live in and the world of the outpatient. With my parents and sister, I worked radio and telethons to raise money for leukemia research. During the summers, I swam and swam to help my lungs. My weekly visits to Children's Hospital Outpatient Clinic for medication and testing became monthly and then yearly. Eventually, I was making those trips as an adult, on my own.

I enrolled at California State University at Northridge. Just after my twenty-fourth birthday, I began to experience short periods when I grew lightheaded and couldn't remember words. I'd be looking at a dollar bill, not able to draw up the word "dollar." When I told my doctor, he sent me to a neurologist at U.S.C. University Hospital.

The visit with the neurologist took me aback. It seemed that he had more on his mind than memory lapses. I grew nervous. When the testing began, I knew they were looking for something I would dread. During the three months of CAT scans and MRIs, I never told my family. But I knew it was a brain tumor.

The MRI revealed it, a small tumor. To determine whether it was malignant, the surgeon performed a brain biopsy to extract a piece of the tumor for the lab. The brain tumor was malignant, an astrocytoma. I would have to go through everything I'd gone through as a child. I had to prepare myself all over again.

The great irony was that this tumor was caused by the radiation given to me as a child. An astrocytoma is like an octopus. It shoots tentacles out from the center and weaves through the brain tissue, so it's very hard to remove. The doctors weren't sure they could get mine out. The night before surgery, the doctor came into my hospital room and told me that the operation could damage my short-term memory and speaking ability. Did I understand that?

The surgery took seven hours. The surgeons mapped my brain, as they call it. They got the tumor. My father had prayed that God would help them "do better than they think they can." The first thing the head neurologist said to him coming out of the operating room was, "We did better than we anticipated."

Living with cancer teaches many lessons. The importance of faith, the power of love, the need to believe in yourself, and the pure beauty of life. I make it a point to remember those lessons every God-given day.

When Susan was admitted to Children's Hospital, the National Leukemia Broadcast Council began funding the Hemotology/Oncology Clinic Therapeutic Playroom. In honor of her family, it was named the Susan Vanderveen Family Playroom. Today Susan works as a nanny and does volunteer work with animal organizations.

Maggie Spilner

"To realize that we are the creator of our life is liberating. Some people don't want to know that they create the bad stuff as well as the good. But once we see it, then we know where our power lies. And then we can change. Perhaps my greatest accomplishment in this process was coming to love myself even though I was agoraphobic."

Maggie Spilner is the walking editor of Prevention *magazine and the author of* Prevention's Complete Book of Walking: Everything You Need to Know to Walk Your Way to Better Health.

In my early twenties, I became agoraphobic.

Agoraphobia is a fear of open spaces and can escalate into a fear of leaving one's home. For me, it started with panic attacks. I didn't understand at first why it was happening to me. I felt betrayed by my body. The panic didn't seem to make any sense. From the gripping fear of walking around the block to my position as the walking editor of *Prevention* magazine has been a journey of great magnitude. And of equal magnitude has been my discovery that, in fact, my body did not betray me but perfectly reflected what I needed to face, that my mind and my body are intricately related. The journey of the past fifteen years has taken me into myself in ways I could not have anticipated.

It all started with a severe crisis in my marriage. My husband and I were high-school sweethearts and married young. But our relationship became severely dysfunctional and, when I was twenty-two, we hit a crisis that sent me into my first panic attack.

At the time, we were living in Allenstown, Pennsylvania, where I worked at a department store and a children's library, which is where I was when the call came from my husband. He was in deep trouble. (To honor the privacy of my children and my ex-husband, I've chosen not to detail this crisis.) When I heard what had happened, I was filled with a sensation of absolute dread. I wanted to run and hide. The emotions were so overpowering that I didn't know what to do.

A friend picked me up and took me to a doctor, who immediately prescribed Valium. That settled me down but did nothing for the trouble my husband was in and nothing for the confusion of our marriage. The drug kept me emotionally numb, which, having been raised in a gentle but emotionally repressed family, was a feeling that was all too familiar. Deep beneath the drug, deep inside, I was angry and too afraid to express it.

I knew that my mother had had what she called anxiety attacks. The first one that I remember happened when I was six years old. Regularly, she'd pile my sisters and me into the car and take the fairly long drive to her favorite antique shop. One day, halfway there, she simply turned around without explanation and went home. We never went back. Years later, I found out why.

As my panic attacks continued, like my mother, I looked for a variety of solutions. At the time, many types of emotional illness were viewed as nutritional or chemical imbalances in the body rather than as physical manifestations of emotional conflicts. When I was evaluated for anxiety and depression at a brain biology center in Princeton, New Jersey, no one asked about my marriage or my emotional life. Rather, they suggested a hypoglycemic diet with vitamin B_6 supplements. Following their recommendations, I adjusted my diet and cut out sugar, which helped a little. Yet so much more needed to be done.

Soon, I grew scared to go out for fear of having an attack in public. I felt so vulnerable, and that sense of vulnerability escalated each time I left my house until it became habitual. *I'm going out, oh, no, I'm vulnerable, I'm afraid.* I was afraid of fear itself. Any small challenge could trigger panic.

I told only my mother and sisters what was happening, leaving out many of the details. Unlike my mother, who eventually told everyone and got her problem out in the open, I kept it a secret, which exacerbated my feeling of isolation and insanity. I felt like I was going crazy, that any minute, I might metaphorically throw off all my clothes and run down the street naked, screaming, *This is the real me.* I read spiritual books and tried to apply principles that would help but often ended up denying my feelings rather than working through them.

I stayed in my marriage for another seven years, so out of touch with myself that I didn't know what to do, how to leave. Remarkably, during this time, I became the head teacher at a day care center. To this day, I don't know how I managed to do that. I could drive the kids in the school van, but when I got out, I often found it incredibly hard to walk across the parking lot. The fear of open space would descend on me, and I wanted to run and hide under the seat. "Okay, breathe deeply." I'd talk myself through it. "Go over, get involved, change your focus."

Eventually, my husband made the decision I was avoiding and left. I was completely on my own, with two infants and feeling abandoned. I had a house with no heat, a dog, and no car. Any time I left the house, I was scared.

The sensation of agoraphobia was like having a rubber band tied around my chest. As I walked toward the front door of my house, that band would start to tighten. When I opened the front door and stepped out, my legs would get wobbly. The farther I went, the tighter the rubber band stretched, until I felt like it was either going to snap, jettisoning me off into who knows what, or I was going to boomerang back to my house. I didn't know when I'd step beyond my point of tolerance and have to turn around and run home. And running home was scarier than waiting out the sensation, because I was giving in to the fear, which was an overwhelming feeling.

Because I didn't want anyone to know I was agoraphobic, I learned how to compensate for the fear. It might be as simple as turning down an invitation. If I did manage to go out with friends, I made sure they picked me up, because that way I felt safer. In an oddly similar way, if I needed to walk somewhere, which I did regularly after my husband left with the car, pushing a stroller or carrying an umbrella, anything I could hold onto gave me a greater sense that I would make it.

At the time, there were few effective treatments for agoraphobia. Doctors prescribed drugs, but they were much stronger back then and I was loath to take them. I had read the works of Edgar Cayce, the renowned psychic who introduced the modern world to the connection between mind, body, and spirit. He talked about people becoming dependent on tranquilizers and how this dependence stunts their spiritual growth because they never face their real issues. My only other choice was to undergo behavioral therapy that would give me techniques to deal with a panic attack. I tried that, but it didn't get rid of the panic, it only helped me manage it. I wanted more than that. I wanted real freedom.

I decided to experience whatever lay beneath my intense fear, to get to the bottom of it. I started investigating phobias and neuroses, researching and reading as much as I could get my hands on. It was all so depressing.

The message was basically, *Good luck.* The spiritual books at least gave me hope. I especially liked *The Seth Material* by Jane Roberts. A nonphysical entity channeled by the author, Seth said that our power is in the present and the past has no hold over us unless we believe it does. That was a very healing message for me. It carried me and gave me hope.

I never became housebound, but it got to the point that whenever I left my house, I suffered. Each time, I would tell myself, "Tomorrow I will find out what it is. Tomorrow will be the day." I felt like Scarlett in *Gone with the Wind: I'll think about it tomorrow. Tomorrow, it will be better. Tomorrow, I will find an answer.*

After my husband left, I knew that I had to move forward or I would die, not physically but in all ways that make life meaningful. I also needed a job that would support my children and me. One day, I opened the newspaper and saw a big ad that read, "Wanted, Energetic and Enthusiastic Person for Reader's Service." It struck me that, as demoralized as I was at the time, those were the only two words I could claim for myself. Energetic. Enthusiastic.

I decided to apply for the job, thinking it was mailbag editor for *Prevention* magazine, whose parent company is Rodale, a company I had interned at while in college. While driving one day, I was suddenly struck with a weird inspiration to write a cover letter as though I already had the job. "Dear *Prevention* readers," I wrote, "I'm your new reader's service correspondent." Which was pretty gutsy. I knew instantly that I would get an interview, and once in an interview, I'd be fine. Looking back, I don't know why I thought I'd be fine when everything about my life seemed so insecure.

That cover letter put my résumé at the top of the pile and strengthened my belief in my intuition. The person who hired me said she had gotten hundreds of applications and was looking for somebody with that extra bit of creativity. My cover letter tipped the scales in my favor.

Applying for the job at *Prevention* was part of my healing process. It was a huge step for me, because it involved all kinds of changes that took immense courage. I'd be going to a whole new place, farther from home. The day care center was only a mile away, and I could walk or ride my bike. Going to Rodale, I'd have to drive, and the thought of making the journey was frightening. It almost stopped me.

On the same day that I announced I'd be leaving the day care center, the dietician there, who was a good friend, also announced that she'd gotten a new job — at *Organic Gardening* magazine published by Rodale. The synchronicity was stunning and not only reaffirmed my choice but gave me a sense that I was being spiritually guided. I didn't tell her about my fears but I instantly had a bridge to my new workplace. Someone would be at Rodale who knew me, someone I could turn to if I panicked. She was the Valium in my pocket, my safety.

My first day at Rodale, I had the strangest feeling of coming home.

I was at Rodale for a few years, struggling to keep my life together as a single mom. Every day was like climbing Mt. Everest in my own backyard. Unless you've experienced a phobia, it's difficult to understand the terror in the face of what seems like nothing. I'd look out and think, "There's nothing to be afraid of here, and yet I feel so frightened. What the heck is going on?" Agoraphobia becomes pervasive.

When the *Prevention* editors decided to start a walking club, as ironic as it seems, I wanted to be a part of it. I was afraid I could become housebound if I wasn't diligent. The walking club was a way to push myself. I began a routine of walking, alone, downtown during my lunch break. With each block, I talked myself into going farther. "Okay, I'll go another block, just one more."

Maybe it was the rain one day that swept me off my feet as I walked during lunch. I love the rain, and my walk that day was bordering on the passionate. When I returned to work, I sat down at my desk and wrote a story about it. I ran up and put it on the executive editor's desk while he wasn't there. And then scurried off with no one seeing me. He didn't talk to me for about a week, and I thought that probably he had thrown my story in the trash. Then, one night when I was working late, he came down and said, "Congratulations, you're the new editor for *Walker's World* newsletter. You're going to be the Czarina of Walking." Obviously, he didn't know I was agoraphobic.

At that time, I had been promoted to editorial assistant. I had a knack for writing and a college degree in English. Intuitively, I knew that this opportunity was meant to be, that it was on my life path. It would take me places I needed to go, which eventually meant traveling to other countries and leading walking trips.

But first, I had much inner work to do. Again, synchronicity played a part in it. One day a psychotherapist from New York City came to *Prevention* on a whim. I met with her, fascinated that she used walking as a therapeutic technique, having clients walk on a treadmill in her office as a way to release negative energy and encouraging them to participate in weekly walking sessions in Central Park. She helped me see the emotional energy behind my condition. Apparently, agoraphobia can be related to a critical event around the age of two, just as a child is about to go out into the world and leave her mother's side. In my case, that event was the birth of my brother, who had cerebral palsy and would die when he was twelve. My most vivid memory of that time is standing between my mother's legs, saying "Don't worry, mommy, you've still got me" as she cried.

By finding some of the probable causes of my panic attacks, I thought I would have an "Aha!" experience, burst through the fear, and be done with it. However, for me, it wasn't one catalyzing event but the little increments of hidden emotion that I was constantly stuffing, avoiding, denying. My breakthrough came when I finally grasped that the anxiety was a friend, that it was telling me what I was avoiding. I had felt like my body was betraying me. I couldn't understand. I couldn't decode the messages. I finally understood that the anxiety, rather than a pure fear reaction, was an emotion telling me, "there are ten other feelings underneath here that you're trying to press down and we're going to bring them to the surface to show you."

As I searched for a way to overcome agoraphobia, I worked with therapists who helped me to see that there was a huge gap between my thinking processes and my emotions. My emotional life was hollow. I wasn't able to be real. The main thing that helped me heal was claiming my emotions, recognizing who I really was. Ironically, with a phobic person, this kind of counseling may at first make you feel worse, because you're bringing all your fears to the surface. I persisted, because I felt there was no other way. Yet I knew that I needed something else, something more than just talking and understanding.

In the midst of all this, I forced myself to keep moving forward with projects, traveling for my job, even doing public-speaking engagements. I could get up in front of seven hundred people at a walker's rally and give an animated talk. Sure, I was nervous; who wouldn't be? My friends thought I was gutsy, because to them, public speaking was scarier than just about anything else. When I told my closest friends that I was more frightened to walk around the block than to give a speech, they had a hard time understanding.

How on earth did I do all this? I still don't have an answer. Some days were better than others. I never knew why, and that was freaky. Some days, I had a hard time going down to the corner store to pick up milk. Other days, I'd be fine. Sometimes, to deal with the uncertainty, I think I may have pushed myself into an attack early in the day so I could get it over with. When I'd burst through the panic, I'd feel a huge sense of relief; maybe it was my endorphins kicking in like mad. Often, I could spend the rest of my day free of fear.

Then one day I was in the library at Rodale doing research for a story. I pulled out a folder, and the one next to it fell on the floor. I picked it up. It was marked, "Lehigh University Phobia Program." I opened the folder and read about what was one of the few phobia programs in the entire country at that time. It was fifteen miles from my home, and it was free.

Once again, synchronicity had a huge impact on my life. At this point, I was pretty worn down. I'd been trying hard to get over my phobia, but I still had it and I didn't know why. I signed up for the Lehigh program and entered their retraining program. With a "safe" person, I went downtown with a pad and pen. "Okay, walk and every block, rate your anxiety," she said. "Keep going until you get to the center of town and come back. I'll wait for you right here." I did that repeatedly, and then she took me to a bridge and said, "Okay, walk across the bridge, stop every once in a while and rate your anxiety. Go to the other side and come back." She took me to a mall, and said, "Walk through to the other side and come back. I'll wait in the parking lot." The basis of this program was to symbolically walk away from your mother, knowing that she was still waiting for you, and then come back — retracing those steps and retraining yourself, reassuring yourself. In my case, perhaps it was retracing the time when my mother was so preoccupied with a handicapped child that I didn't feel like anybody was waiting for me. I don't know for sure. I think my success — they said I was their most successful client — was the result of all the past emotional work I'd done, so that when I went through the retraining process, my phobia fell away quickly — and didn't return.

It had taken me fifteen years to feel "normal" again.

I didn't tell my children I was agoraphobic until they were seven and ten. I carried so much guilt about it. When I finally told my oldest, he said, "Oh, that's why you don't like going to the mall." It wasn't devastating to them to find out, but helpful. Later, my youngest son sent me a letter from college saying that he thought I should write a story about my life, that it was more interesting than many other stories he'd read and that people would want to hear it. My oldest son told me that I'd taught him about living passionately, that I was his "hero." Somehow, they were both able to comprehend the passage I'd made. These were the most important words ever said to me.

An odd twist to my recovery was that, when I finally felt safe, at the same time, I felt something was missing. *Where did it go?* When I went out, I'd think, *Hey, something's wrong. What is it?* The drama had become so much a part of my daily life that I felt its absence like a lingering doubt. Things that other people do every day without thinking had been huge mountains for me to overcome, things like going to the supermarket or the bank or taking my kids to the doctor. Once it was all over, I realized that something about the emotional drama was exciting. When a therapist first suggested that to me, I was furious. It made me cry. But later, I began to understand that part of me needed excitement, and the daily drama of the agoraphobia satisfied that need.

To realize that we are the creator of our life is liberating. Some people don't want to know they create the bad stuff as well as the good. But once we see it, then we know where our power lies. And then we can change. Perhaps my greatest accomplishment in this process was coming to love myself even though I was agoraphobic.

In all the years I was writing my walking columns, I never came forward publicly about being agoraphobic. When I wrote my second walking book, which came out this year, I decided that, even though I was scared to, I needed to write about it in the foreword. Was I tempting fate? Bringing it too close for comfort? I didn't want to lay myself at the feet of people who would be unkind and judgmental. That would be self-destructive. But I knew it was another step I needed to take. Hiding my phobia all those years was exhausting.

My first panic attack was a real eye-opener to my mother's courage. As a teenager, I'd get angry that she wouldn't come to my choir recitals. Only now do I realize that she was fighting her own fears. Only now do I see how strong she really was to simply keep on keeping on, with three daughters, a son with cerebral palsy, and a husband who suffered on and off from depression — all of them depending on her.

As I fought my own demons, I wondered what it was that makes some people succeed at overcoming agoraphobia and others not. It's a scary question. My mother is seventy-eight and has yet to find a way to heal. She still finds it very difficult to leave the house alone; she can go out with family or friends, but not too far. What is it that allowed me to persevere when my mother didn't? The only answer I've found is desire. In a way, my mother didn't have a strong enough desire to pursue her own healing. She seemed to accept her condition, whereas for some reason, I never could. I wanted to be free. I wanted to be free so much that I was willing to push myself, to face my fear.

During a recent *Prevention* Walker's Rally in Quebec, I was the host and gave a talk to about 150 people, a low-key, kitchen-table kind of talk about my real walking story. "So many of you have known me for so many years," I said, "and I want to share with you, before you read it, what's in the foreword to my book." And I told my story of being agoraphobic. Afterward, people came up and hugged me. No one had suspected. To them, I was the celebrity, the cheerleader, the inspiration — enthusiastic and energetic. To share the other side of myself felt like a final step in my story. A completion to a journey. A chapter closed.

Maggie became the walking columnist in Prevention *magazine and director of the National Walking Club. She coauthored her first book,* Prevention's Practical Encyclopedia of Walking for Health, *with Mark Bricklin who was then the executive editor of Prevention. She has been on walks in states from California to Vermont, and in England, Austria, Switzerland, Wales, among other countries.*

Gwendolyn Endicott

"On long nights, I would try to keep from remembering the woman who, just a few years earlier, at fifty-three, had everything: a successful teaching career, a beautiful house in the suburbs, a wardrobe of nice clothes, and a deep personal relationship. She was no more."

At age fifty-three, Gwendolyn Endicott sold her suburban home and left a thirty-year teaching career to preserve a rainforest.

On a late fall afternoon, I sit in circle with a college environmental class in the Forest House at Wanderland, the twenty-acre rainforest in which I live near the northern Oregon coast.

The students have come to spend the day with the forest and now gather to share their experiences of this place. I am suddenly startled by a woman in the circle who looks at me and says, "I don't think I have your courage." Her comment throws me back to my childhood when I was always afraid to speak. I can feel the constriction in my throat, the tightness of my breath. Looking back at what brought me to Wanderland seven years earlier, can I claim even a moment I would call "courageous"?

Was it when I walked into the rainforest that spring morning and saw such beauty, the day I fell in love? But no, that took no courage — only my heart. Or was it the day I signed the papers, making the down payment on a forest by telling the bank I was remodeling my kitchen? No, that was not courage but simple necessity. And the pain that gripped me low below my belly? That was fear. "Just keep breathing and let go," I would remind myself over and over.

Even when I sold my comfortable house to make another payment and moved into a nine-by-ten shed in the rainforest, leaving the soft carpeting, the gardens, and the hot tub, leaving the light switches and the water faucets, leaving hot water, sinks, and bathtubs, even then it was not courage but simply what I had to do. I loved the forest more, you see, than I loved those things.

No, it did not take much courage to live in the shed. "And all by yourself!" people would say to me. But my shed was cozy in winter. And the walk to the creek for water was usually pure pleasure. A propane lantern gave me light by which to read, and its steady golden hum lulled me easily to sleep.

Of course, the critters of the forest viewed the shed as a luxurious forest stump and paid me no mind as they regularly invaded my space. The mice were the worst. More than once, they drove me out entirely. One seemingly endless night, trying to sleep in the backseat of my car, I chased away memories of the luxurious waterbed in my old house and reassured myself, "It's a bit like spending a night on a bench in the San Francisco airport." On most nights, however, I only needed to step out the door of the shed and listen to the sound of water or watch the moon and starlight filter through the trees to remember why it was I lived in a shed.

"But the dream," people persist in asking me. "Wasn't there a time when you chose the dream? When you decided you wanted to create a rainforest healing and teaching center? Didn't the dream come first?"

Wanderland came into my life at a time when I was asking deeply in ritual and in prayer: *How can I help heal our violation of the earth?* I did not know that the answer would be my own healing. No, it was not a decision or even a dream that came first but rather a question, a desire. The dreaming, however, began soon after. Twice I dreamt that I was speeding down a freeway when I turned abruptly to the left and down a country road that dead-ended in a rainforest. I could go no farther. I got out of my car and walked a path through the forest, past my beautiful suburban home, past a shed that animals inhabited, down into an underground lecture hall where a woman spoke on "squaring the circle," bringing dreams into form. I had no idea what any of this meant at the time. Only now does the dream seem remarkable to me.

On the spring equinox of that year, I was driving around a small coastal village, Manzanita, because my motel room wasn't ready yet and it was raining. I had no thought of my dream that day. I wasn't looking for a forest, nor was I dissatisfied with my life. I was just driving. Took a left turn. Bumped along a country road. And into a forest. I got out of my car and walked into that forest with a vague sense of recognition. I felt like I was falling in love. Before the year was out, I would purchase twenty acres of the forest and move onto the land to begin the creation of a rainforest preserve.

I retired from my job teaching mythology at a community college to work in the forest on what would become a very large project: creating and building a center where people could come and learn about a rainforest — doing it with my own money and my own hands. Retiring from full-time work cut my income in half and increased my expenses by an amount I still cannot calculate.

In the beginning, having sold my house and moved into the shed in the forest, I would commute the two hours from the coast to Portland to continue part-time teaching at Portland Community College. A friend let me live in an unfinished attic, and it was the attic, not the shed, that most challenged my heart those first few years. I had a futon in the one "finished" corner (it had a floor) and an electric light bulb in the middle of the room. I had a bathtub and hot water, but there were no sinks. In fact, there were no sinks in my life for almost four years. It was in the attic that I sometimes felt crazy. "How did this happen to me?" I would ask myself. "An old woman living alone in a dusty attic." The sound of sirens from the busy street below shook the house until early morning hours. And on long nights, I would try to keep from remembering the woman who, just a few years earlier, at fifty-three, had everything: a successful teaching career, a beautiful house in the suburbs, a wardrobe of nice clothes, and a deep personal relationship. She was no more.

Out of her had been born a wild-haired woman in love with a rainforest — a woman with a dream, a woman who rarely kept clean fingernails or spot-free clothes from the sheer hard work of bringing that dream into form. Hard work to make a road. Hard work to clear a site for the Forest House. A summer spent building the foundation. The downpour on the day of the concrete pour. The concrete truck sliding off the road in the mud. Protective tarps filling with giant ponds of water, collapsing the walls of the house, flooding the floor. Time suspended on that day in the gray drizzling rain as I swept and mopped in a futile war against the water that threatened to ruin months of work. Cold and miserable, tears of frustration mixing with the rain that poured down my face, I tried to remember why I began this project four long years earlier.

Later that afternoon, I drove the five miles to a nearby town to keep my appointment with the artist who was working on the Wanderland

Rainforest sign. Standing in the warmth of his kitchen, cold clear through, my hands raw from mopping and deeply discouraged, I began telling my story to this man I barely knew.

"Let me make you a latte," he said. "I have this wonderful machine."

"No," I replied. "I'm not drinking coffee anymore."

"Sit down," he said. "Today you should have a latte."

I have never tasted anything more wonderful than that latte in his warm kitchen on that miserable day.

The Wanderland sign now stands at the entrance to the road that leads to the Forest House. The house is tall in the small forest clearing, roofed, and still not finished, but close. Friends have stopped asking when it will be done, but they come to help put in a window or staple insulation. They come to make gardens and ponds and trails that meander through the forest. We work to create a teaching place, a place where people can come to remember what a forest is — its plants and animals and ecosystems — for forests are disappearing and we are fast forgetting. All around us in this Pacific Coast watershed are clear-cuts. In the winter rains, the waters swell, the creeks and rivers run faster, flooding the pastures down below and the towns. Barren hillsides become moving mudslides, closing the highways. Two winters ago, the county was declared a Disaster Area.

I pay the county Forest Service to inform me of logging activities around me. I open, with dread, the yellow envelopes that come.

"CLEAR-CUT," says the form. "Scarification. High-risk area, 35- to 65-degree slope, streams, and underground water."

Hundreds of acres behind Wanderland are being clear-cut by a timber company whose forester used to live just across the valley but still within the watershed, in one of the towns where mudslides closed the main highway. The mudslides are the result of clear-cutting. The earth has nothing to hold onto to and lets go with ferocity. The Oregon State Forest Practices Act requires only that two trees and two logs be left per acre. The wildlife habitat is destroyed as it becomes more difficult for the animals to find food. Bear and elk and coyote and wolf have nowhere to go. Silt contaminates the streams so the fish cannot live. Coho salmon are becoming an endangered species in this watershed, as are other types of salmon. Smaller amphibious species like frogs are disappearing, and so are salamanders.

In a watershed like this, the boundary lines are only on paper. And even the paper lies. Next to "WATERSHED," the form says "NOT APPLICABLE." Not applicable?

"Why are we not saying what's happening?" I ask the state forester. "Why are we not saying that we're clear-cutting our watersheds?" Not saying allows people to be in denial. To say is to arouse people's fears, their reactions. I have asked twice before. When you love something, you care about what happens to it. I will keep on asking. Perhaps that is courage — not giving up. Years ago, I began to understand it as "beavering." The word came to me when, one day, I found a beautifully carved beaver stick left like an offering on the creek bank. Its message became my mantra and kept me going: "Take it gnaw by gnaw and don't get discouraged by looking at the big picture."

"Be sure to put a beaver on the Wanderland sign," I told the artist on the day of the latte. "Take it gnaw by gnaw," I reminded myself.

I have been working on the Wanderland project for nine years, with no end in sight. In the beginning, I felt a lot of fear and doubt. "You must be crazy!" rattled around in my head until it became a familiar litany over the years. Now I know it simply goes with the territory, as does discouragement. I cannot say when or if they will ever go away and leave me in peace.

The Wanderland experience has cast me back to a more primal relationship with the earth. I know what it is to live in a small earthen space shared with other creatures. I know what it is to be dirty beyond immediate repair and to be ousted repeatedly from my space. I have gone back far enough to know the gift of hot water and the magnificence of an electric light bulb, the luxury of a Crock-Pot™ and an electric teapot made possible by a seven-hundred-foot-long extension cord from a temporary electrical pole.

The first time I wintered in one room of the Forest House, secure with doors and windows to keep out my forest housemates, was not without a battle for right of occupancy with pack rats, birds, bats, mice, and skunks. My space felt luxuriously large, but the winter nights were very long, and I took to walking by flashlight in the forest, going nowhere in particular, simply following the glow of my light into worlds of wet and shimmering green.

On the eve of the New Year, I needed no flashlight. The forest was alit with moonlight, so bright it didn't seem like night at all. I left the house for just a short walk in the forest and then to town for a celebration with friends. Perhaps it was the moonlight, perhaps the drum that I carried instead of the flashlight. The night became the moon, the forest, and the waters, my drum singing, and me. At Frog Bog Pond, I floated two candles, one for my soul and one for my dreams. Holding a stone in my hands, I breathed out long and slow, imagining all my worry flowing out of me and into this dark stone. "May I give up worry in the New Year," I thought and gave the stone a toss into the pond. I watched as the splash put out my dream candle. "Just a small glitch in the magic," I thought, laughing into the forest night, playing my drum, playing my song, "May the forest live long, may the forest live long…"

Gwendolyn's book The Spinning Wheel: The Art of Mythmaking *contains stories of Wanderland rainforest gardens. Her second book,* Crone Trekking in Coyote Land: Stories and Mythical Musings, *was published in September of 2001. She has created and is program director of a not-for-profit corporation, Coal Creek Education Foundation, dedicated to showing the gifts of our native forests.*

Darcee O'Hearn

"I heard the charge of the waterfall and saw the horizon drop off as I was swept over, into the steam and the spray and the roaring water. Just like I'd done again and again and again. Only, this time it was different. This time, halfway down, I caught a ferocious rooster tail of water from a rock formation on the side that flipped me over."

Darcee O'Hearn was a white water kayaker in her early twenties, a member of the British Columbia Provincial Team. She competed in races at home and in the United States, always with her eye on the Canadian national team and ultimately the Olympics.

In the summer of 1996, at the age of twenty-six, I was training for the Olympic trials in white-water kayaking. It was a dream that would take me from my home in Cultus Lake to train in South America, and it would turn my life upside down.

Because we didn't have the funding in Canada for permanent coaches, I knew that to compete for the one spot that would be open on the Olympic team, I needed to find a better way to train competitively. At a race in Idaho, I met the people who would make it possible for me to train on the highly technical rivers of Chile, where big water, wild rapids, and steep waterfalls drew teams from many countries. I would go down a month ahead of the American squad and work as a cook for a kayaking company in exchange for free coaching with members of the U.S. team.

First, I had to make the money to get down there. For six months, I worked four jobs, starting with Sears in the morning, then the Y.M.C.A., then a gas station, and finally giving kayaking lessons. By December, I had a plane ticket to Chile and three hundred dollars in my pocket. I boarded a plane to South America, thinking the money would last me for four months. You might say I went on faith.

I was headed for the village that was captured on film in the movie *Alive*, the place a survivor of the crash of a plane carrying the Uruguay rugby team came upon when he walked out of the Andes for help. It was very primitive and secluded. Chickens wandered the pot-holed dirt roads and crept into our rooms, hunting the huge bugs that crawled over us as we slept. The village had maybe a dozen houses, one general store, a few restaurants, and one phone that never worked. Run-down, rickety buses carried livestock as well as people, with luggage strapped on top. I was the only Canadian in sight.

My first week, I made the awful mistake of drinking the water and got very sick. The second week, still unable to start my job as cook, I was replaced. As I lost time, I watched my money get eaten up on food and accommodations. With barely any left, I didn't know what to do. Usually, when I have trouble, I call my mum, but to phone internationally meant a trip to a larger city. You couldn't just pick up a pay phone here. I had no one to turn to, and I felt so lost that I broke down and cried.

By the time I started to feel better physically, I knew I couldn't sit around waiting for the American team. I had come to Chile to train on its big waters and I needed to get busy. Because of a drought, the rivers in the middle of the country were low. I decided to go south to find technical rivers with volume where I could train on my own.

Have you ever done something you can't believe you're doing but you just keep going? All of a sudden, I was on a bus even though I was scared to pieces and I didn't know whom I was going to run into or if I was going to get lost or where I'd end up. I just kind of went…and hoped for the best.

Lugging my big paddle, my backpack, and my kayak, I boarded the bus south. Getting a thirteen-foot kayak on the top of a bus haphazardly loaded with luggage was pretty hilarious. Packed in with people whose language I didn't understand, I jostled along for eight hours to the small town of Pucon, where adventure tourism flourished and rafting companies ran thrill rides down the Trancuro, the "infamous" Futaleufu and the Bio Bio with its "savage rapids."

I took a room at a hostel, where I was relieved to meet an American, some Germans who spoke English, and a girl from Quebec named Isabelle, who spoke several languages, including Spanish. We became friends, and she went with me to a rafting company to interpret. They hired me as a safety kayaker, which meant running along with the pleasure rafts to pull them off the rocks if they got stuck and to pick up anyone who got tossed out going over rapids or waterfalls.

As excited as I was to have a job and to get on the water, I was equally nervous, because I'd never run an extremely technical river with huge waterfalls and boiling rapids. To paddle technical water, you first walk the river and pick a line you want to follow, the safest route. Then, when you put on, you have to remember what that line looks like from the shore and stay on it or you can get badly hurt. Going off line on technical rivers can have serious consequences.

The first time I went down the Alto Trancuro, I was so nervous.

Kayakers use a thing called a spit test. If you can't spit, you shouldn't run the river, because you're too scared and you'll make a mistake. Walking the bank to find my line, seeing the rapids and waterfalls, especially the Salto Feo, "ugly waterfall" in Spanish, I tried to spit. Nothing.

The Salto Feo was the steepest drop, about seventeen feet. It was gnarly. "There's no way in the living world that I'll go over that waterfall in my kayak," I said to my friend, who had already run the Salto and went down ahead of me. Seeing him safely negotiate it, I thought, *Okay, Darcee, you're capable of paddling this water. You're capable of staying on line. Let's go.* So I got in my boat and held my breath and shwoo!...over I went. The sound was thunderous, intense, and I was just a little kayak with a little paddle challenging the water as it hurled me over the falls to the bottom, where the volume and pressure of water on my boat swept me out like a pea shot between your fingertips, launching me into the air.

I was hooked.

The Alto Trancuro sharpened my skills quickly. The water would explode against itself and throw me twenty feet off a wave. I'd get stuck in a hole and recirculate, turning and turning and turning, with massive water exploding all around me. I felt so insignificant to what was around me. The experience was powerful.

For a few weeks, I paddled these extreme waters, reveling in the challenge of the runs and also the warmth of the water. Up in Canada, they were having ice storms, and I knew what that meant: a sheet of ice over my jacket, icicles on my helmet, the shaft of my paddle iced over. Being on the warm waters of Chile's rivers was a great relief. I'd never paddled so well in my life. I started having ultimate runs, besting my time on a specific line. The way I was paddling, I was sure I would return home and make the Canadian national team, compete in Worlds, and earn a spot on the Olympic squad. I was at the peak of my potential. It was unbelievable. My confidence soared.

My life was going to take off. I was sure of it.

In Canada, people had told me it was impossible that I'd ever earn a spot on the Olympic team. That had lit a fire in me. If someone tells me I can't do something, it usually triggers an adventure. I wanted to be the best female kayaker in the world, and that's what kept me going. It was a dream. And when I have dreams, usually nothing stops me. Usually.

One day, I woke up, had my favorite breakfast sandwich just like every other day, hopped on the bus to the river with the tourists, got my kayak together, and put onto the river. I worked the first run alone. The water level had been dropping, which caused the pleasure raft to more easily broach, getting stuck on rocks. Getting it off was hard work, and I was grateful that a safety kayaker from Africa joined me for the second run.

Going over the waterfalls, the raft easily did an ender, which means the force of the water makes it stands up on end. The back part of the raft gets crushed into the front part, squishing the people together, and, when it lands at the bottom, the raft goes poing! and the tourists get tossed out into the river. When the water level is normal, people float along harmlessly, but because the river was bony, people got scratched and bruised on the rocks exposed by the low water level. We worked quickly to pick them up and get them back into the raft.

At the bottom of that run, I was exhausted. The African kayaker and I started to leave, talking about how we couldn't wait to get back to the hostel to have something to eat and relax. "No, no," I heard at my back, "you have to do one more run."

I turned. "No, that's it. No more." I knew it would be dangerous to run the Trancuro when I was tired.

"You want to keep your job," said the rafter, "you go again."

I had an awful feeling about it.

At the side of the road with a camera around his neck was Ivo, a member of the Chilean national team, a great kayaker. He was drinking a cup of coffee. Using sign language, I asked him if he would do the run for me. I hoped he had understood me when he said yes. As the tourists were boarding the bus to go up river for another run, I told the rafter that the Chilean would make the run for me. He said, "You go. You want job, you go."

Now, he didn't make me do it, because nobody can make me do anything. But I felt compelled. Why he wanted me, I don't know. Why the African kayaker didn't go too, I don't know. Why Ivo ended up driving the bus, I don't know. Much about what followed I can only guess, can only figure that it was somehow meant to be.

No kidding, the clouds literally rolled in, the skies became cloudy, and a storm was brewing. I had such an ominous feeling. I hadn't been worried about the safety of the tourists before, but this time, I tightened all their life jackets, even though it wasn't my job. I had a horrible feeling that something bad was going to happen. I tightened their helmet straps and said, "You hang on," and I showed them how to stick their feet into the slots so they wouldn't fall out of the boat. I don't know if they understood me, because they didn't speak English and I was gesturing to try to get them to comprehend what I was saying.

We put on the river. Before the Salto Feo is a flat section where the raft slows and people can jump in and swim around for a while. The rafter and I had hand signals, and I gave him the sign that I'd meet them at the bottom of the waterfall. I was tired. I wanted to get off the river. I pulled out ahead of them.

At the head of the Salto Feo, I noticed Ivo on the bank. He waved to me, and I waved back. He swung up his camera to take a picture, and I gave him a thumbs-up. I heard the charge of the waterfall and saw the horizon drop off as I was swept over, into the steam and the spray and the roaring water. Just like I'd done again and again and again. Only, this time it was different. This time, halfway down, I caught a ferocious rooster tail of water from a rock formation on the side that flipped me over. Flipping wasn't unusual; I'd done it many times and tucked forward to protect myself. What was unusual, however, was that I was hurling, upside down, toward an exposed rock formation below. When I landed, I heard a thunderous crack like a baseball bat on a line drive at the back of my neck. *Oh, shit.* I knew right away I was in trouble.

The velocity of water pounding down on me was deafening. I slid off the rock and, still upside down, churned in the water heading downstream. I saw my arm in front of me; it was out of its socket and distorted. The pain was so intense that I started blacking out. Everything was becoming darker and darker, and I was getting weaker and weaker. *I'm going to die.* Slowly, I faded out.

I was about to go completely black when I screamed inside, No! And I kept yelling *Nonononononononono* in my head. I didn't have a lot of time. I was headed toward a class-five waterfall about seventy meters away. I wouldn't survive it. My neck was broken, my arm was dislocated, and I was trapped upside down in my kayak.

Suddenly, a horrible vision came, a demonic vision, starkly vivid: a claw, metallic, shiny, a pearly color. The size of a large man's hand, it was about half a millimeter thick at the base and then narrowed into a razor edge. It had an extremely smooth surface on the top and was thick and heavy. Underneath were gouge marks, serrated lines that ran the length of the claw. It was right in my face. I heard awful heckling. The claw receded for a second and then lunged at me and stopped a centimeter from my face, quickly jerked back, and then dove into my chest. This vision kept cutting me open, splitting me in two. I begged for mercy, for it to stop. The heckling intensified as the claw turned to the side and flipped me over — this is what I was seeing under the water — and the back of claw hammered against my spine, stuffing me between two rocks.

"No!" I shot back to reality, screaming inside, "You will not take me! I am not ready to go!" I was only twenty-six and I had too much living to do. I wasn't going to die that day. I gasped for air with my mouth closed. I could see light coming through the top of the water and I knew that I had to roll up. How, I had no idea. But I knew I had one shot and no more air. I reached toward the surface and flipped my hips. Unbelievably, I righted myself.

Air surged into my lungs. Heaving, I saw Ivo running down the bank toward me. I was forty meters from the next waterfall, a class six. Willing myself to the shore, I forced every fiber of my body to ferry me there. Ivo reached down and grabbed the bow of my boat. And saved my life.

Yet it still wasn't over. We had to get up the cliff. That's when the light came. I'm not kidding; light surrounded me, my boat, and Ivo. I don't know how, but we were gently carried up the cliff. I can't describe to you how gentle it was and how it felt to be placed on the earth. The light stayed around us, and I could hear a voice saying, "Keep your neck straight, don't move it."

Ivo was trying to pull me out of the kayak, and every time he touched me, I screamed because I knew I couldn't be moved. "¡Atrás! ¡Atrás!" I'd learned the word, because I'd had to say "paddle back" in Spanish. Finally he understood and knew that I needed to be supported and kept conscious. He sat on the back of my kayak and leaned up against me to keep me from falling back.

The rain had started, and it tickled my face. I tried to reach up to wipe it off and saw my right arm jerking in spasms. With my left arm, I held myself up, trying not to lose consciousness. I was blacking out and coming to and thinking, *I have to stay awake. If I let my head drop, I'll be dead.* Have you ever been hit so hard that you have a funny taste in your mouth? Such intense pain that acid flows in your stomach and you feel like throwing up and it keeps getting black and you can hear *shwoo, shwooo, shwooo,* like the rushing of blood through your veins?

Finally, the raft came down the river, and one of the tourists ran up to the road, to the bus that had a radio and they called for help. Sylvia, a lady from Holland who spoke English and had befriended me, came running through the forest and down the bank. Before I could get anything out, she said, "I know what happened. I know everything." Two nights earlier, she had had a dream about it.

"Please, Sylvia, they can't touch me, they can't move my neck. My neck is broken."

"I know, I know."

Later, she told me that, as she was running toward me, she saw the light circling me. She felt a force that kept the four paramedics running behind her from reaching me before she did, so that she could get to me before anyone touched me. She held me for a moment, and then she took control of the chaos from all the tourists around me. In Spanish, she quickly told the paramedics what to do. And she said it was as though the force lifted so they could come forward and put the neck brace on me. As soon as I was in the brace, the light around me vanished. Whether it was God or angels or the light, they knew I was going to be all right now.

When I got to the local clinic about a half hour away, word had spread about the accident, and people crowded around me. The only thing I remember is staring up at the ceiling inside, which was marked with water stains, and thinking, *This place is too dirty to be a hospital.* Every now and then, someone's head would appear over me while I waited to be X-rayed. And waited. And waited. The doctor wouldn't do anything until he could verify my medical insurance. I had hidden my papers in the hostel, because so many people were coming and going that anyone could have taken them. For fifty minutes, I lay in the clinic, the pain indescribable, waiting for someone to get my papers. Finally, Isabelle rushed in with them.

When the X-ray came back, the doctor said what I already knew, "You've broken your neck." I was put in an ambulance and sent over bumpy roads to an intensive-care hospital an hour and a half away in Temuco.

The man peering over me now was Dr. Lopez. With his beard, mustache, and chubby face, he looked like an angel. "We have to do a CAT scan," he said. I kept thinking, *It's okay, it's just a sprain, my neck isn't really broken, they were wrong.* I was stubborn; I didn't want to believe that anything so bad could happen to me. I told Dr. Lopez he had to get me better, because I had to go to the Olympic trials in four months. He pulled a hair from my head and said to me, "You this close to dead." Reality began to wash over me. Someone brought a phone, and I called my parents. When I heard their voices, I started to cry, then I sobbed and sobbed.

The CAT scan showed that I'd ruptured vertebrae five and six and fractured number two. Dr. Lopez said that if it weren't for the strength of my neck muscles and shoulders, I wouldn't have been able to hold my head up when I righted my kayak. The intensity of my muscle spasms had saved my life. I was in surgery for seven hours as the doctors fused my vertebrae, using bone from my hip.

When I regained consciousness, not remembering exactly where I was or how I'd gotten there, I saw surgeons standing all around me. Dr. Lopez leaned over and said, "Wiggle your toes."

Oh my God, my neck, am I paralyzed?

I held my breath.

And wiggled my toes.

The surgeons broke into smiles and started clapping with relief. "You're going to be okay," said Dr. Lopez, as the other surgeons left. "It was the first time we've done that operation." Dr. Lopez had come to this hospital only six months earlier.

A week after my accident, a seventeen-year-old boy from Santiago was rushed to the same hospital in Temuco. He'd had an identical accident in the same place on the river and broken his neck. He didn't recover the way I did. He was paralyzed, a quadriplegic, on a respirator for the rest of his life. I, on the other hand, slowly regained full mobility. Why? Why did I recover and he didn't? I felt guilty. Lying in my hospital bed, depressed for this boy who had had his whole life ahead of him, I decided to do something to raise awareness about spinal cord injuries. I would bicycle across Canada.

When I returned to Canada, I went home to my parents and stayed for four months, recovering. In the beginning, I kept thinking, *I'll still make the trials, I can still go.* But slowly I realized I wasn't going to the Olympic trials. When I was fully recovered, I went out with my kayak to put in on the Chilliwack River. I was so scared that my legs were shaking. I never went out on that river. I haven't been in a kayak since then. I sold all my equipment.

In 1999, I turned my focus to my Cycle Canada trip to raise awareness about spinal cord injuries. I spent four months trying to find sponsors, trying to get a motor home or road support. I needed someone in Chilliwack, where I was living, who would take calls for me to let people know I was coming through their town. Most of all, I needed a tour coordinator. So I advertised the job to all the service clubs. Nobody answered. A few weeks before I was scheduled to take off, I got a call from a woman who said she was interested in the job. It was my mum.

I began the tour by dipping the tires of my bike in the Pacific Ocean, hoping that three months later, I'd dip them in the Atlantic. The terrain in British Columbia is mountainous, and that first day was so hard that I thought, *I can't do this.* Day two was equally grueling and I thought, *Man, I really can't to this.* Each day I was sure I'd have to stop. Finally, I made a promise to myself that I'd go as far as my hometown of Trail, and then I'd stop.

In Trail, I had a big welcome and saw my mum and dad. Everyone was so excited for Cycle Canada that I thought, I can't let them down. So I kept going.

The rain was relentless, swept sideways by ferocious winds.

Lightning scared me so much that I hid in a shed, waiting out the storm in the cold.

Winds were so severe that I thought I'd be blown over.

Every time a truck roared by, I felt like I was about to be thrown.

I was afraid, tired, and lonely at times. However, I was also taken in and cared for, fed and housed and encouraged. All along the route, I did newspaper, radio, and TV interviews talking about spinal cord injuries. By the time I hit the Atlantic Provinces, I was so proud to be Canadian. People came out for me all along the roadsides, urging me on, welcoming me. I was so moved.

Along the coast of the Irish Loop, I finally saw the ocean. Waves were crashing and the sun was setting, throwing orange against the rocks. The sky was ablaze with red. I laid down my bike. I heard this music in my mind and had something like an out-of-body experience, watching my legs carry me to the water so I could dip my feet in. My sore, scratched, bruised, strong legs carrying me to the water. In my heart, that's when I completed my tour. Several days later, I officially ended it at St. John's Harbor, where volunteers from the Canadian Paraplegic Association met me and the police escorted me to the finish line.

People ask me if I wasn't scared biking alone across Canada. Sometimes. But the people of Canada are my friends and kept me company. I felt cared for and safe.

Perhaps my most rewarding moment was at the very end when I visited a young boy named Chris at the Halifax Hospital. He'd had a diving accident and was confined to a wheelchair. I spoke with him and encouraged him. I told him that I believed he had the courage and strength to recover.

Someone asked him later if he had a hero. He said me. He said that I had made the difference. With that simple comment, my trip was worthwhile.

I have a new dream now. To be the best I can be and to reach my potential at all times, to never settle. I want to encourage others to be the best that they can be, to tap into their talents and believe they can do anything. Even if someone has had a tough time growing up — and I sure did — that doesn't mean that the rest of life has to be tough. An abusive childhood can turn people toward drugs and alcohol, toward saying "I didn't have a choice, I was dealt bad cards." Or we can take what we've been given and use it as a tool to shape our lives in a positive way.

Everything that's given to us is given because God knows that we can handle it. He's not going to give us something we can't handle. Sometimes it just takes will or courage to go forward. We create our own lives. I wouldn't trade my experience for anything. It made me realize the strength of my will, that I can do anything. It was an intensely spiritual experience, full of divine coincidences. It showed me that the power of the human spirit is unfathomable.

Darcee recently graduated from the British Columbia Institute of Technology, where she earned a degree in forestry. Wanting to further understanding among environmentalists, lumber companies, and the government, she made a documentary showing their different perspectives on forest management. "It's too chaotic here right now," she said last winter, "with people pointing fingers at each other and beating each other up over the forests. We need to cool things down and be able to hear each other."

Directory

Rayla Allison
E-mail: raylaallison@msn.com

Regina Ballinger
E-mail: rjballinger@worldnet.att.net

Dr. Marcy Basel
E-mail: Mjbasel1@aol.com

Sonya Bell
c/o Rhonda Bowen
South Carolina School for the Deaf and Blind
355 Cedar Springs Road
Spartanburg, SC 29302
(864) 577-7627
(864) 577-7805 (fax)

Joan Borysenko
Mind, Body, Health Sciences, Inc.
393 Dixon Road
Boulder, CO 80302
E-mail: luziemas@aol.com
Website: www.joanborysenko.com

Paula Brisker
Outdoor Records
P.O. Box 3319
Half Moon Bay, CA 94019
E-mail: musemail@otherdoor.com
Websites: www.otherdoor.com;
www.paulabrisker.com

Kathy Buckley
Website: www.kathybuckley.com

Julia Butterfly Hill
Website: www.circleoflifefoundation.org

Cherie Carter-Scott
The MMS Institute
Websites: www.themms.com;
www.drcherie.com

Judy Collins
Website: www.judycollins.com

Dai Qing
c/o Professor Lawrence Sullivan
Department of Political Studies
Adelphi University
Long Island, NY 11530

Carrie Barefoot Dickerson
P.O. Box 2584
Claremore, OK 74018-2584

Gwendolyn Endicott
E-mail: endicotg@teleport.com
Website: www.wanderlandrainforest.org

Margaret Ensley
MAVIS
P.O. Box 197
Los Angeles, CA 90044-0197

Lynne Franks
E-mail: lynne@seedfusion.com
Website: www.seedfusion.com

Jean Griswold
Special Care
705 Bethlehem Pike
Erdenheim, PA 19038
(215) 233-5385
(215) 836-7169 (fax)

Penny Harrington
National Center for Women and Policing
8105 West Third Street
Los Angeles, CA 90048
(323) 651-2532

Judith Light
1888 Century Park East
Fifth Floor
Los Angeles, CA 90067
Website: www.judithlight.com

Reverend Mary Manin Morrissey
Living Enrichment Center
29500 SW Graham's Ferry Road
Wilsonville, OR 97070-9516
1-800-893-1000
(503) 582-4213 (fax)
E-mail: marym@lecworld.org
Website: www.lecworld.org

Anne Firth Murray
E-mail: afmurray@igc.org;
afmurray@stanford.edu
Michèle Ohayon
(323) 871-2119 (fax)
E-mail: michoula@pacbell.net

Darcee O'Hearn
E-mail: darceeo@hotmail.com

Susan Point
3917 West 51st Avenue
Vancouver, B.C. V6N 3V9
(604) 266-7374
E-mail: s.point@home.com

Fadia Rafeedie
Yale Station
P.O. Box 207292
New Haven, CT 06520-7292
E-mail: fadia.rafeedie@yale.edu

Debbie Rosas
E-mail: debbie@nia-nia.com
Website: www.nia-nia.com

SARK
Website: www.campsark.com

Heffa Schücking
E-mail: urgewald@koeln.netsurf.de
Website: www.urgewald.de

Joanne Spencer
701 Sixteenth Avenue
Seattle, WA 98122
E-mail: jomespencer@aol.com

Maggie Spilner
Walking Editor, Prevention Magazine
E-mail:MaggieSpilner@rodale.com
Please write People Who Dare in the subject line

Gabrielle Strong
Ain Dah Yung
1089 Portland Avenue
St. Paul, MN 55104
(651) 227-4184

Julie Su
Civil Rights Attorney
Asian Pacific American Legal Center
1145 Wilshire Boulevard, Second Floor
Los Angeles, CA 90017
(213) 977-7500
(213) 977-7595 (fax)
E-mail: jsu@apalc.org

Elaine Suranie
E-mail: outgirlint@aol.com

Susan Sweetser
E-mail: ssweetser@nationallife.com

Iyanla Vanzant
Website: www.innervisionsworldwide.com

Candice Slaughter Warmke
Women's Peacepower Foundation
cwarmke@earthlink.net
Website: www.peacepower.org

My Story of Courage

You are a part of this book. Your courage, your story. Think about a defining moment in your life, when you were required to do something you thought you could not do or to be someone you never imagined you could be. Something that moved you beyond where you would ordinarily go.

> *Courage is doing that which we think we cannot do but know we must. Courage is being true to who we are. Courage is being willing to be wrong, to fail, to make mistakes, in the pursuit of what's right. Courage is living a life that does not compromise who we are and what we believe.*

Give yourself permission to tell the truth about who you are, to acknowledge your courage. Take time with this, come back to it to embellish, to refine, to deepen. This is your story.

New World Library is dedicated to
publishing books and cassettes that inspire
and challenge us to improve the quality
of our lives and our world.
Our books and cassettes are available
at bookstores everywhere.
For a complete catalog, contact:

New World Library
14 Pamaron Way
Novato, California 94949
Phone: (415) 884-2100
Fax: (415) 884-2199
Or call toll free: (800) 972-6657
Catalog requests: Ext. 50
Ordering: Ext. 52
E-mail: escort@nwlib.com
www.newworldlibrary.com